THE LAST GUARDIANS

THE LAST GUARDIANS

The Crisis in the RCMP – and in Canada

PAUL PALANGO

M&S

Canadian Cataloguing in Publication Data

Palango, Paul, 1950-
  The last guardians: the crisis in the RCMP – and in Canada

Includes index.
ISBN 0-7710-6906-5

1. Royal Canadian Mounted Police.   I. Title.

HV8157.P35 1998   363.2'0971   C98-931701-3

We acknowledge the financial support of the Government of Canada through
the Book Publishing Industry Development Program for our publishing
activities. We further acknowledge the support of the Canada Council
for the Arts and the Ontario Arts Council for our publishing program.

Typeset in Minion by M&S, Toronto

Printed and bound in Canada

McClelland & Stewart Inc.
The Canadian Publishers
481 University Avenue
Toronto, Ontario
M5G 2E9

1 2 3 4 5   02 01 00 99 98

For Lindsay

Almost from the moment of your first breath, your wonderful green eyes have spoken for you; about your intelligence, strength, and promise. May you employ your abundant talents well, and often, in pursuit of the greater good.

Love, Dad

CONTENTS

ACKNOWLEDGEMENTS

I
Kathleen McGuire Hubbard

After my first book, *Above the Law: The Crooks, the Politicians, the Mounties and Rod Stamler*, was published in 1994, I thought I could never become interested in writing about policing again, especially about the RCMP. But, as they say, never say never. One day I was having a conversation with my good friend Kathleen McGuire Hubbard. Kate's background in political economy seemed always to lead us into debates about rather esoteric subjects. She was always suspicious of Pierre Trudeau's intentions and felt that he had undermined Canadian federalism. I was a Trudeau fan and argued that there was abundant evidence of Trudeau's "nationalism." But then, one day, as these things happen, I began to see some validity to her argument. That set me off on a course of thinking and consideration about the nature of federalism in Canada and about this book. Kate was a great help in the planning stages, in both helping to conceptualize the story and digging out and bringing to my attention valuable research, which gave me the confidence to attack this difficult and controversial subject. She also spent endless hours on the phone, listening to and critiquing my ideas. Her insights were invaluable. I can't thank her enough, nor her children, Daniel and Ashleigh Hubbard.

II

My literary agent, Karen O'Reilly, took my first rough ideas and helped me hone them into a marketable proposal. Her brilliance and enthusiasm kick-started the project, and she caught the attention of Avie Bennett and Doug Gibson at McClelland & Stewart, who made me a second-time M&S author.

The next woman in the birth of this book is my soft-spoken editor, Pat Kennedy. Her timely suggestions were welcomed and always appreciated. Whatever this book might be, it would be nothing without Pat, Karen, Kate. And, of course, thanks to copy editor, Peter Buck, for his careful and perceptive comments.

Then there is Jane Jacobs, whose ideas and philosophy helped define many of my views. I thank her for her graciousness and time.

For my first book, Geoffrey Stevens played a key role, helping me with my proposal. This time around, as managing editor of *Maclean's* magazine, Geoff commissioned me to do a story on the RCMP. This gave me the opportunity to open doors within the RCMP, and the needed financial support to help me travel to conduct some research. The RCMP co-operated fully with the research and writing of this book. Commissioner Philip Murray opened the doors of the force to me, and allowed me to roam around almost at will. All Mounties encouraged me to tell their story, warts and all. If there was one thing that they demanded of me, it was this: that I be fair and that everything I write about be placed in the context of the times.

So many Mounties and RCMP employees helped me that I can't possibly name them all. Foremost among them, however, was Sergeant Mike Gaudet, a media-relations officer at headquarters, who always did his best to get me what I needed. He never once let me down. In Ottawa, there were also, among others, assistant commissioners John L'Abbé, Joop Plomp, and D. C. (Cleve) Cooper, Chief Superintendent Dawson Hovey, superintendents Tim Quigley, Tim Killam, and Jean Phillion, inspectors Al Misener, Kevin M. Mole, and Bill Anderson; Staff Sergeant J. W. (Jack) Briscoe, Derek Johnston, Sergeant Greg Johnson, R. J. (Bob) Kennedy, historian Glenn Wright, Dr. Harold Peel, forensic chemist Joe Buckle, chemist A. Brian Yamashita, Dr. Della Wilkinson, Todd P. McDermott, Sergeant Sheldon Dickie, Corporal John Bureaux, Dennis Rich, Michael Foran, and Peter Fraser.

In Manitoba, Sergeant Reg Trowell in Winnipeg provided useful insights, while in Dauphin, Superintendent Gary MacPherson, Sergeant Gerry Jennings, and Staff Sergeant Ron Marlin were extremely helpful, as were the citizens of Dauphin, including Al Crippen, Gloria Yaworski, Jack Hrehirchuk, Vicky Yakemishin, Jim Puffalt, Barb St. Goddard, Gloria Racette, Connie Tanasichuck, Susan Nurse, Sherry Perri, and Kimberly Pascal. In Duck Bay, I'll never forget the evening I spent with Constable Ken Aspen.

In Regina, I thank Sergeant Mike Seliske for his time, hospitality, and the library privileges he granted me at Depot. Then there was the time and effort of so many, but especially Corporal Pat Webb, Sergeant Jim Lechner, corporals Bart Wood, J. J. Gaéten Roussel, Jacques Maillet (in the skid car), Della Flood, Gary Morin, Peter Kirchberger, Mike Harvey, Norm Gaumont, and the cadets of Troop 22. Special thanks to Damien Brown and the staff at Orleans, one of the best restaurants on the prairies, who made my stay in Regina all the more enjoyable.

In Burnaby and the Lower Mainland: inspectors Dennis Schlecker and Ron Dick proved invaluable, and I thank staff sergeants Dave Woods, Paul Willms, Elton Deans, Barry Hickman, and Jim Westman, corporals Rod Booth and Greg Stevenson, and constables Vas Kassam and Ken Cornell; in Langley, constables Mike Funicelli and Stephen Thatcher. Also helpful were Burnaby mayor Doug Drummond, councillors Doug Evans and Jim Young, Abby Anderson, Dennis Hong, and Brian Sarginson, and forensic accountant Ron Parks in Vancouver. Special thanks to Barbara Schlecker and Melanie Funicelli for their time and hospitality.

In Sparwood, B.C., there was Sergeant Jake Bouwman, Constable Dave Wilks, and lawyer Glen Purdy.

Closer to home, in southern Ontario, I received tremendous co-operation from a number of Mounties, including inspectors Gary Nichols and Rod Knecht, and Sergeant J. G. S. (Gabe) Marion in Newmarket, and the entire staff at the Bowmanville detachment, including Inspector Al Roney, staff sergeants Ross Kossatz, Jim Vickery, and John Bothwell, sergeants Vern Secord and Gil Carlson, Corporal Christopher Barrett, and constables Susan Riddell and Ian MacNeill.

I owe a special debt to the former Mounties who contributed much to my understanding of the issues addressed in this book. These especially include former commissioner Norman Inkster, former deputy commissioner Henry Jensen, former assistant commissioners Michel Thivierge and Rod Stamler, and former commercial-crime investigators John Beer and Glen Harloff. Other ex-law-enforcement officers who contributed to this book were Dick Dewhirst (sergeant, Metro Toronto Police); Sandy Boucher (superintendent, Royal Hong Kong Constabulary); and Howard Williams (chief superintendent, Ontario Provincial Police).

Forensic accountants Tedd Avey and Brian Crockatt agreed to allow me to write about the events in Chapter One. I also owe a debt of gratitude to forensic accountant Al Langley of Toronto and my colleagues in the Toronto chapter of the Association of Certified Fraud Examiners. And, of course, there were the many lawyers who in some way played a part in this project. They include Bryan Finlay, Q.C., Barnet Kussner, David Wingfield, and Ken Prehogan, all of Weir & Foulds in Toronto, and Peter Jacobsen.

Among private investigators, Kevin Bousquet of the Corpa Group in Mississauga, Ian Robinson in Hamilton, and former CIA agent John Quirk in Boca Raton, Florida, were very helpful. Among "public investigators," there were Harvey Cashore and Declan Hill of CBC-TV's *the fifth estate*.

A number of municipal police officers contributed to this book, but foremost among them were Dave Carnell and Tim Kavanagh of the York Regional Police, whose own experiences were in many ways the genesis of this book. Unfortunately, their story didn't make the final cut, mainly because what happened to them is a book of its own.

Then there are the people of Hamilton, especially my anonymous friends on the Hamilton Wentworth Regional Police, MPP Toni Skarica, Michael Waxman, Rose Lax, Malcolm Elliott, and all the "crackpots" and members of the John Kay Memorial Society, especially "the keeper of the flame," the irrepressible bailiff Lorne Park, and Michael Hilson, Terry and Joe LaCorte, Terry Ott, George Watson, John Gallagher, Ann Varangu, Richard Leitner, John Munro, all the Daves, and Rico the Moonman. I owe a special thanks to Donna Crockett and Frank Martin for the use of the "hideout," to Dr. Tony Asaro, the official chiropractor of this project, to Wayne Narciso, publisher of *Hamilton Magazine*, to my friends from 29 South Street West, Dundas, Eric Findlay, Ryan Findlay, and their dad, Rob Findlay, as well as John Findlay, Priscilla Low, and Danielle DiFrancesco.

Finally, my sister, Carol Palango Hoard, helped me enormously with this book, as did her late husband, Roy, whose sudden death stunned us all. Of course, there are wonderful parents, Arnold and Lea Palango, who have always stood behind me, even as they continue to wonder about some of the things I do. As my mother often puts it: "Where did you come from?" Even though she was there, she still doesn't believe it was her.

All of which brings me to my immediate family. This was a gruelling and difficult project, the kind that can sometimes tear relationships apart, but Cheryl, as usual, was always there to provide the comfort and assurance that I could eventually see it through. After twenty-six years of marriage, I continue to be amazed by her resilience, relationship management skills, and the depth of her love for me. She deserves better! When I wrote my first book, my daughter, Lindsay, was my reader. This time around, she had grown up and moved away. I missed her input deeply. Finally, and last as usual, is the irrepressible Virginia, who through all her trials and tribulations rarely fails to put a smile on my face. I love you dearly and thank all three of you for your patience and understanding.

Introduction

.... ● ....

THE REPORTER'S PERSPECTIVE

IT IS A CONFUSING world out there, filled with contradiction and disappointment. Wade through the blizzard of advertising and marketing materials and it doesn't take long to realize that hardly anything is what it really seems to be. Hollywood spends tens of millions of dollars making one bad movie after another, but seems to recoup its investment time and time again with slick marketing campaigns. Fast-food chains have made billions of dollars for their shareholders, as a critic once put it, "selling the suggestion of food with the promise of flavour." In the constant barrage of information, it appears to be virtually impossible to separate the real deal from the poseur. In fact, there may be left only a few constants upon which one can truly rely, one of them being that the Royal Canadian Mounted Police will always be the best-looking police force in the world, dressed to kill in breeches, red serge, and felt hats.

There has never been a police force that has benefited so much from Hollywood and marketing as has the Mounties. The U.S. Postal Inspection Service is an older police force by a year, but didn't get much modern-day ink for chasing Butch Cassidy and the Sundance Kid all the way to Bolivia. The best thing that ever happened to the FBI was, perhaps, the spooky 1990s television show, *The X-Files*. But almost from the moment the Mounties were formed in 1873, they caught the public imagination, oddly enough, primarily in the United States, where they were seen to be professional and daring. In 1877, for example, a squad of Mounties crossed the border, which wasn't quite as rigid a concept then

1

as it is today, and tracked down and arrested a band of ruthless whisky traders. The editor of the *Fort Benton Record*, a Montana newspaper, wrote: "They fetch their men every time."

In 1919, Hollywood made its first Mountie movie, starring Tom Mix. Dozens of features and shorts would follow over the next four decades, and the Mounties would soon be transformed into romantic, swashbuckling heroes, who did indeed always get their man. The 1928 operetta *Rose Marie*, a story of a triangle involving a fugitive, his sister, and the Mountie who is pursuing him, was remade into a major 1936 Hollywood talkie, starring Nelson Eddy, as the Mountie, and Jeanette MacDonald, who fall in love singing "Indian Love Call." Then there was Gary Cooper in the 1940 adventure *The Northwest Mounted Police* and Alan Ladd, as the Mountie hero, in 1954's *Saskatchewan*.

As fodder for movies, the Mounties peaked in the 1950s, as nobility subsequently went out of fashion. Since then there have been three notable RCMP characters. The first was cartoon character Dudley Doright, a star of *The Rocky and Bullwinkle Show*. Then came Sergeant Holt Renfrew of the Mounties, the bumbling sleuth created by Canadian comedian Dave Broadfoot. Renfrew worked out of a log cabin on the fourteenth floor of Mountie headquarters ("because there was no thirteenth floor"). Finally, there is Benton Fraser, the Mountie character played by Paul Gross in the popular television series *Due South*. The storyline places Fraser in an unlikely partnership with a streetwise Chicago cop, where Fraser's boring, steadfast – though sexy – Canadianness always manages to win the day. Benton Fraser is dedicated, professional, perhaps a little unspectacular, but as singleminded and powerful as a slow-moving and ultimately unstoppable train.

There has always been something universally appealing about the Mounties. As a symbol of old-fashioned values and positive influences, there are perhaps few more wholesome and untarnished images. This is no doubt one of the reasons the Disney Corporation was so eager in 1995 to buy up the world rights to the force's image. Quebec artist Marc Tétro has made a fortune selling, for fifty dollars or more each, T-shirts on which stylized Mounties are depicted as a symbol of Canada, the only country in the world that markets its national police force as its most attractive icon. But that is the reputation of the Mounties, good men and women who reflect a good and decent law-abiding country, a place the United Nations has ranked as being the best in the world in which to live. Few institutions anywhere in the world have generated as much public goodwill as have the Royal Canadian Mounted Police. But is it all deserved? Are the Mounties all that they seem to be?

In my attempt to answer that question, this project began. The RCMP is the one Canadian police force primarily empowered to conduct investigations into complex, multi-jurisdictional economic crime as part of its federal policing mandate. However, it became apparent to me and others that, throughout the late eighties and nineties, the Mounties seemed largely incapable or unwilling to investigate such cases. Even if they were, the justice system seemed just as uninterested in prosecuting suspects. I was particularly attracted to this area because the rate of fraud and economic crime had begun to soar across the country. It wasn't just that the criminals were getting smarter and had better access to new technologies; law-enforcement standards clearly had slipped.

My original intention was to use a series of notable economic-crime cases from across the country, including the Alan Eagleson, Nanaimo Commonwealth, and Bre-X cases, to prove once and for all that the Mounties were not doing their job as a federal police force. "I'm the Mountie Who Never Got His Man," the show-stopping song sung by Bert Lahr in the 1954 remake of *Rose Marie*, had been transformed from a comic moment in a movie to an apt commentary on what was happening within the force. More and more, the Mounties were not getting their man.

In January 1997, *Maclean's* magazine assigned me to find out why that was so. For my first book, *Above the Law*, the RCMP refused to co-operate officially with me. This time around, I expected no different response. On behalf of *Maclean's* and myself, I first approached the RCMP in February 1997 about a possible interview with Commissioner Philip Murray. The request was rejected. "We don't think you will be balanced in your report," I was told by a spokesperson.

Undeterred, I faxed back a second request. As I had come to see it, the RCMP's myriad problems seemed to be the result of the force trying to absorb more than three decades of social, political, and economic imperatives. In my second fax, I laid out areas that I intended to explore for my *Maclean's* piece. These included:

1) The RCMP's successful attempts over the years to stave off the setting up of rival law-enforcement agencies;
2) The perception that the RCMP had become not so much a police force as a police-service business;
3) The effects of "demilitarization" on the RCMP;
4) The impact of promotion policies that placed more weight on general abilities than on specialized ones, the argument that the RCMP's approach to promotion is anachronistic and ultimately works against the national interest;
5) The suggestion that the RCMP continued to be top-heavy with administration;
6) The stated belief of at least twenty former high-ranking members of the force that the RCMP had largely lost its ability to investigate complex, multi-jurisdictional crimes;
7) The fact that the RCMP was technologically behind the times;
8) The fact that other police forces find the RCMP difficult to work with;
9) The RCMP's pay structure, which lags far behind those of other police forces;
10) The force's popular philosophy, adopted over the years, of personal empowerment as a guiding principle with regard to operations ("Is there a perceived potential downside to personal empowerment of police officers?");
11) The effectiveness and efficacy of proceeds-of-crime units ("Are there downsides to the use of proceeds-of-crime legislation *vis-à-vis* policing and the rule of law?");
12) The implementation and effects of decentralization policy, especially in the Toronto area.

The commissioner must have thought I was on the right track. He invited me to spend a week in Ottawa, where he promised to open every door in the force to me.

Almost two months later, the trip was finalized. In Ottawa, the force eagerly showed me almost anything I wanted to see. I was the first non-employee to visit the force's state-of-the-art wiretapping facility. During the week I met or interviewed dozens of Mounties and civilians from all ranks, concluding with a fifty-minute interview with Commissioner Murray.

My RCMP story, "Why the Mounties Can't Get Their Man: Giving Up on White-Collar Crime," graced the cover of the Maclean's issue of July 28, 1997. In that story, I quoted Murray describing how the country was headed towards a two-tier system of policing, particularly in the area of economic-crime investigation, part of the force's federal jurisdiction. This was seen by some as a bombshell. For the first time an RCMP commissioner had legitimized the notion of private investigation of criminal activities. Forensic-accounting firms, the great beneficiaries of such a policy, were ecstatic. The president of one security company told me afterwards: "Commissioner Murray's statement in Maclean's added a million dollars of annual billings to my company's business."

For me, the Maclean's story changed the direction of the book I was planning to write. No longer would I have to mount a case-by-case study to prove that the Mounties weren't doing their job in investigating economic crime. Commissioner Murray had conceded that point. Now, I would try to show how and why the RCMP had come to this fork in the road and what the implications might be for Canada as a whole.

As I re-adjusted my focus, I found myself wrestling with a larger, not smaller, story. This new story demanded that I go beyond the simple dynamics of white-collar-crime investigation. Every time I asked myself the questions how or why, I ended up travelling historical trails that had long been erased from public-policy maps. But I didn't spend all my time lost in books and newspaper morgues.

During my week in Ottawa, Commissioner Murray suggested that I travel across the country and see for myself what was going on. So I hit the road, visiting Mounties from St. John's to Victoria. I was surprised by both their candour and their concerns about the direction(s) in which the force seemed to be heading.

For most of them, the world had changed, and not for the better. Shifts in Canadian society had begun to be reflected in the RCMP's own culture. Meanwhile, new government initiatives had created a treacherous environment for the everyday police officer in Canada. The police seemed to be just as confused and disoriented as most ordinary citizens, perhaps even more so.

My experiences on the road with the police and ordinary citizens forced me to look not only at them, but at the workings of Canada itself. I began to see this country in a much different light. To a man and woman, all the Mounties I met seemed to me to be good and decent people, not perfect, but dedicated men and women who loved Canada more than anything else. I came to see the Mounties as a reflection of the soul of the country. I soon realized that, through this single, great national institution, I could for once see and articulate what has gone wrong with Canada. Cutting through the myths, the self-promotion, and the hyperbole of everyday life, I became convinced that the RCMP was one of the few institutions left guarding a disintegrating society. This led me into areas that I hadn't contemplated visiting, territories of thought that I found both disturbing and intriguing.

No matter where I went, I could find conflict within the force. From personnel problems to budgeting to law-enforcement techniques, the one thread linking all the problems was the pervasiveness of business-like thinking within the force. Some would say this a good thing, others would not, but the very existence of business-like thinking within a guardian institution raises questions and concerns.

Seymour Melman, a professor of industrial engineering at Columbia University, has been one of the most astute observers of the potentially destructive relationships between government and business. In his wonderfully researched and argued 1983 book, *Profits Without Production*, Melman showed the consequences of investing power in the hands of the "ideal" type of corporate manager, who is willing to put the money entrusted to him wherever its rate of return is highest, regardless of the effects on industry, working people, or the community. Melman faulted sociologists and business educators who, after the Second World War, declared that America had become a "post-industrial society" and instructed the nation's MBAs to concentrate on profits, downplaying the need for efficient production.

Today, this thirst for profits has been applied to policing, which has resulted in "efficiencies" that many police argue are, in the larger scheme of things, not efficient at all but dangerous and a threat to the rule of law. This raises a more fundamental question: Is there too much government in business or too much business in government?

A number of modern philosophers address this issue, among them Jane Jacobs in her book *Systems of Survival: A Dialogue on the Moral Foundations of Commerce and Politics* (1992). Jacobs explores the notion that there really are only two basic ways of thinking in modern society: the commercial syndrome and the guardian syndrome, as she calls them. According to her thesis, those involved in commerce have and should have certain recognizable attributes, such as risk-taking, invention, efficiency, and the desire to make a profit. On the other hand, guardians – government, bureaucrats, police, and investigative journalists, for example – are expected to defend the "greater good." Among other qualities, they honour traditions, have a sense of public duty, and do not or should never take risks.

Since the end of the Second World War, North Americans have been bombarded with the notion that government has grown too large and cumbersome, and that government meddling has harmed the interests of business. What intrigued me about Jacobs's hypothesis – with which some other philosophers and most politicians don't entirely agree – is the suggestion that modern society may well be making a big mistake in its rush to adopt the mindset of business. She warns of the danger of "monstrous hybrids," which attempt to subscribe to both syndromes. As a result, they lack purity of vision or purpose and, therefore, are incapable of serving adequately either the public interest or their shareholders' interest, depending upon the nature of the enterprise.

Has the RCMP become a monstrous hybrid, a vivid example of what faces all police forces? If so, is it capable of serving as a true and effective guardian of the public interest?

Society's first four guardians – family, church, school, and work – have seen their power and influence erode with time. The justice system, best exemplified by the police, is the last guardian. In the past, when the first four were functioning better, each used its various coercive powers to induce order and compliance. The power of the family resided in genetics, tradition, and love; the school used learning, discipline, and peer pressure; the church, faith and guilt; and work kept people in line with the promise of sustenance and financial security. All their powers were only as strong as the bond an individual had with the guardian institution.

The police are empowered by society to enforce the rule of law. That is, everyone is protected by and treated equally under the law. The law is more than just another social program or division of power, it is the circulatory system of a democracy. It would seem to me that, for the law to work properly, the police must have purity of vision and purpose. Their power is blatant; disobey the law, and the police can and will bring you before the justice system, where you can be disciplined in a real fashion and, perhaps, even stripped of your liberty.

In the long slide away from the notions of sacrifice for the public good, civic duty, and guardianship, the police have found themselves caught in a whirlwind, buffeted from all sides. The police are deemed to be out of control, insensitive, incompetent, poorly trained, and unaccountable one day, indispensable the next. The message from the media, driven by mostly meaningless and often self-serving statistics from police agencies themselves, is totally confusing. Violent crime is up, then violent crime is down; but the relationship between the number of police officers and the number of crimes reported is usually ignored. That is, more cops generally translate into higher crime rates, and vice versa. It's anyone's guess what's really going on and what the real issues might be.

Academia has provided little help. Virtually every major study by criminology experts around the world looks at one area of policing: the number, role, and attitude of the uniformed constable, the lowliest but most visible representative of the police in a given, usually urban, area. There is little in libraries about the impact on society of detective work, crime analysis, and police administration. These are areas that are nearly impossible to qualify or quantify. To the modern business-minded planner these are therefore the easiest targets for budget and program cuts. Take away the cop on the beat and everyone notices, but no one easily misses the detectives, crime analysts, and administrators, who are responsible for truly important police work – until it's too late.

At a time when we are being deluged by talk about the need for law and order and for "getting back to the basics," John Ralston Saul has articulated the dangers confronting us as a society. In works such as *Voltaire's Bastards: The Dictatorship of Reason in the West* (1992) and *The Unconscious Civilization* (1995), Saul consistently points to what he sees as the evils of the technocratic dictatorship that is determined to dismantle democracy.

The very public debate over policing in Canada has been carried out according to surprisingly narrow and predictable ground rules. Over the past thirty-five years, Canada has claimed to be a leader in the field of modernizing policing, but the guiding principles of successive governments have been applied with varying degrees of success to the administration of police forces. Provincialism, decentralization, bilingualism, multiculturalism, civilianization, business-oriented strategies, and downsizing, to name some, are trends that have generally been accepted to be implicitly good for the country, and for the justice system as a whole. However, what has become lost are fundamentally more serious issues, which speak to concerns about the current and future role of the public police in Canada. What happens when a guardian organization, like a police force, becomes the captive of ideologies that are antithetical to its stated purpose – and what are the long-term implications, if any, for society in general?

As Canada's best-known national symbol, the RCMP is one of the oldest and most respected public institutions in the country. On the surface, at least, it embodies Jane Jacobs's definition of a classic guardian. Among some members there remains a purity of vision that is both gratifying and compelling. The Mounties also are clearly a touchstone for the larger political and economic picture in Canada. At a time when the issue of national unity is once again on the public agenda, the importance of the role of the RCMP as a federal police force cannot be overlooked. It is the last national institution – other than the federal government – linking the country together.

No democratic country in the world seems to love and revere its police force as much as Canadians do the RCMP. For some, especially outside the larger cities, the force may well be the last shining symbol of all that is good and right about Canada from sea to sea to sea. In an age where it is virtually impossible to believe in anything – governments, the justice system, religion, schools, and the media – the Mounties appear to be the only pure-hearted, independent guardians left, an indomitable public institution with a pristine image.

The truth seems to lie somewhere within the boundaries of all these paradoxes, the truth not only about the state of the RCMP and its future, but about the state of Canada. The RCMP is Canada and, like Canada, the RCMP is not entirely what it seems. To fully understand what bedevils the RCMP, one must appreciate what bedevils Canada, and ironically one way to do that is to see Canada through the eyes of its greatest police force. To that end, we are headed on a meandering road through the present and the past. What has Canada become? How did it get that way? And, perhaps most importantly, why has this happened?

In this book my self-assigned mission was to conduct a one-man commission into the Royal Canadian Mounted Police, its current state and what the future may hold. To accomplish this, I've turned the telescope around. The RCMP is the one institution where all the public-policy issues in Canada seem to coalesce in one way or another. By focusing almost entirely on the RCMP, I will attempt to show by inference what has happened to Canada and other national institutions. The thesis this time might be best described in a question: How have social, political, and economic imperatives been used to usurp the rule of law in Canada and what are the implications for ordinary Canadians?

I have not intended to write a polemic or academic treatise, but an engaging and thought-provoking discussion of a series of important public-policy issues about which ordinary citizens might otherwise be unaware. However, I remain confident that Hollywood or Pierre Berton would never tell the story quite this way.

My report follows. I welcome your comments, criticisms, and insights. Now, let's hit the road.

Chapter One

······················ ● ··················

INTRODUCING ANTON PILLER, THE RCMP, AND CANADA

TWO RENTED MINIVANS pull out of the financial district of Toronto on an autumn afternoon; there are four people in one, three in the other. In a few minutes they are in the eastbound lanes of the Gardiner Expressway, then they head north on the Don Valley Parkway. At the top of the parkway, both vans move into the right lane and exit onto Highway 401, which cuts 850 kilometres across southern Ontario, linking Michigan with Quebec. Heading east, the two vans pass through Scarborough, Pickering, Ajax, Whitby, and Oshawa. At Bowmanville, almost seventy kilometres into their trip, the vans pass the Toronto East offices of the Royal Canadian Mounted Police, who, a few short years ago, might have been interested in their mission. This is no longer the case.

The vans head into open countryside. Near Newcastle, they head up highways 35 and 115. Finally, after about eighty minutes of driving, they arrive in Peterborough, an old, conservative city of 67,000 people, located on the Trent Canal system. Marketers like to test new products in Peterborough. If Peterborough likes it, the thinking goes, so will the rest of Canada – that is, the rest of Canada outside Quebec, for, in French Canada, taste buds and sensibilities are entirely different.

During the ride the people in each van exchange a few war stories about similar missions. Executing a search usually isn't that problematic. Each member of the team has his or her job to do. One conducts the search. Another catalogues the items found, and so on.

The plan in Peterborough is for the raiding party to visit the residences of three suspects. For weeks they have been building their case, conducting surveillance, analysing the suspects' garbage, and combing public databases for information about their history, relationships, and possible assets. The alleged crime they are investigating is a cross-border fraud, the total take estimated at $1.4 million, a substantial matter. The complainant is one of the largest U.S.-based multinational companies in the world. The suspects are a group of people who might loosely be described as businessmen, but in this case they are suspected of having used a series of more than a dozen shell companies to pull off an intricate scam.

At each of the houses the team will visit, a City of Peterborough police officer will be present, but will not participate. He is there only to make sure that nothing untoward happens.

This raid is not what one might think. The people in the van aren't police officers, though three – Sandy Boucher, Howard Williams, and Dick Dewhirst – have been. Boucher, born in London, England, was once a superintendent in the drug squad of the Royal Hong Kong Police. Williams was a top investigator in the Ontario Provincial Police before going into the private sector. Dewhirst, an illegal-gambling specialist, finished his career with the Metro Toronto Police working on organized crime. He loved the job so much that his personalized automobile licence plate is OL DICK. Two of the others are lawyers and one is an accountant, all three in the service of the final member of the party, Brian Crockatt, a forensic accountant from the firm of Lindquist, Avey, Macdonald, Baskerville, and this isn't their first big job for the multinational company. The ex-police officers, all now private detectives, are also employees of Lindquist, Avey, modern-day mercenaries in the war against crime.

To get through the front door of the three residences they plan to visit that day, they have armed themselves with an Anton Piller order. Drafted by lawyer John Olah and endorsed by a Toronto judge, the wide-ranging order allows them to enter the various residences to search for documents and other materials. It commands each defendant to allow the raiders to take files and gain access to their computers, including security codes and e-mail passwords. In other words any information potentially of use to the plaintiff is fair game.

When the legal profession discusses an Anton Piller order, it prefers to use technical terms such as "relief" or "injunction," or euphemisms such as "the civilian acquisition of information." But by any description it is a search warrant. It is designed for use primarily by any corporation able to make the case that it has suffered losses from thieves, pirates, or spies.

The legal precedent is a 1976 British Court of Appeal decision – *Anton Piller KG v. Manufacturing Processes Ltd.*[1] – delivered by the esteemed Lord Denning. In that case Piller's lawyers were able to show that the defendant, Manufacturing Processes Ltd., was involved in a scheme to obtain confidential drawings and designs from Anton Piller KG. Piller had argued that "unless they were given immediate relief from the court without prior notice to the defendants, there was a substantial risk that the drawings and information would be sent to Germany and used by a rival manufacturer." Piller convinced the court to give it a restraining order against the defendant in the case. The court further ordered the defendants "to permit one or two of the plaintiffs and one or two of their solicitors to enter the defendants' premises for the purpose of inspecting documents, files or things, and removing those which belong to the plaintiff."

In Peterborough that's what the raiding team intends to do: use an Anton Piller order to search for proof of the alleged scam.

There is one major difference between a police search warrant and an Anton Piller order. In a criminal case, the police can break down a door, but the private investigators in Peterborough were required to show each defendant the court order and ask for permission to enter each residence. Although the Peterborough raiders didn't find much that day, the prospect of continued surveillance and return visits put so much pressure on the defendants that they surrendered some of the sought-after materials a few days later. To the surprise of the investigators, the defendants faxed in their confessions to the company, and handed over the evidence. The bill for the day of the raid was about $20,000. The multinational company apparently didn't even blink; the fee was just one more entry on the forensic accountants' ever-expanding tab.

When it was all over, both Boucher and Dewhirst were astounded by the breadth of the search the judge had allowed. In the hundreds of search warrants they had executed as police officers in their respective jurisdictions, criminal law dictated that they had to state specifically what they were trying to find. "For the police to get a search warrant," Dewhirst said, "they have to swear that what they're looking for has been seen there. With an Anton Piller, all you have to say is that you think it might be there or that it ought to be there. I guess it's a nice thing to have if you're defending the rights of those who lose money."

The use of the Anton Piller order has become one of the foremost weapons of civil litigation and private prosecutions in Canada, an absolute necessity for corporations in a fly-by-night world. Critics have argued that it seems to be little more than a licence to rummage in another person's private affairs, one of the most draconian measures to be found in modern society.[2] Toronto lawyer Kenneth Prehogan, who specializes in Anton Piller orders, refers to them as, at best, "judicial breakaway[s] on an open net" and, at worst, "civil nuclear weapons." Others say they are being employed to turn the adversarial process into an inquisitorial one, in which Anton Piller orders are used as a means of finding out what sort of charges a potential plaintiff might make. The pressure that an Anton Piller order puts on a defendant cannot be minimized.

In defending their use, the courts have argued that innocent people have nothing to fear from an Anton Piller order, while the guilty deserve no protection. This is a departure from the usual respect afforded procedural safeguards. As University of Toronto law professor Robert J. Sharpe put it in 1983: "Such arguments could justify the invasion of many fundamental rights. A broad power to grant injunctions is not a mandate to the judiciary to right all wrongs at the expense of other basic values."[3]

The entire incident in Peterborough intrigued and disturbed former Hong Kong policeman Boucher, who had left the colony for Canada just before the 1997 transition to Chinese rule. "In Hong Kong the police would have treated this as a criminal case, and conducted the entire investigation. In Hong Kong the police were the police and the private investigators were always lowlifes doing divorce work and other trashy stuff. I don't understand how it got to be this way in Canada."[4]

Many Canadians don't, either.

•   •   •

In the late sixties and seventies, the RCMP Commercial Crime Branch was the foremost policing operation in the country, one of the first whose work was based solely on function, not territory. That function was the investigation of fraud in its most serious forms. Created in response to growing evidence of the presence of organized crime in the business and political world, the Commercial Crime Branch took on everything thrown at it: corporate fraud, stock-market manipulation, and political corruption – so-called white-collar crime. Throughout the seventies, CCB investigators created a new vision of policing and justice in Canada.

In those days, the Commercial Crime Branch would have eagerly conducted the Peterborough investigation, but today the RCMP says it does not have the personnel or resources to do such white-collar-crime investigations. Such a claim seems incredible in light of the fact that the RCMP has more than 20,000 employees – 14,700 of them police officers – spread out across a relatively peaceful country, and that it spends $1.9 billion in federal tax dollars every year.

Although the RCMP appears to be a formidable federal police operation, however, it is not. Current commissioner Philip Murray says the force is having difficulty performing its federal functions, because there is no political will to fight white-collar crime, and because the Economic Crime Unit, as the Commercial Crime Branch is now known, has seen its personnel and resources depleted across the country.

Joseph Philip Robert Murray is the eighteenth commissioner of the RCMP.[5] Born and raised in Ottawa, now in his mid-fifties, he has been a Mountie since leaving high school. With his impeccable manners and thin, barely perceptible moustache, Murray is to all appearances a throwback to the old-fashioned Mounties of moviedom. But his appearance belies his grasp of modern problems confronting the force and the high-technology solutions often required to address them. Perhaps there is no greater dilemma facing the police than the reality that there is more work for them than there are available jobs. Governments, dedicated to driving down deficits, cutting costs, and privatizing services, have demanded that the public police give up their monopoly on policing. One of the primary areas for reductions is in the investigation of criminal fraud.

"The long-term implications are that we're going to end up with two-tier policing," says Murray in his fifth-floor office at RCMP headquarters, a converted monastery on Vanier Parkway in Ottawa's east end. "What we're going to end up with is forensic-accounting firms dealing with those kinds of crimes over the long term because the public purse simply will not be able to accommodate it. To me, that's very unfortunate if we end up there." He adds that it's not government policy that has caused this, "just a reality that we're facing. The general public is simply not willing to spend more, to invest more in taxes. Governments are trying to get their budgets down to zero base and start attacking the debt, so anything that isn't high-profile has a tendency to fall off the table."

When he says that, you can instantly tell how much each word hurts as it rolls off his tongue. His anguish is palpable, as is his apparent sense of helplessness.

Canada promotes itself as a country governed by the rule of law; that is, all people are both equally protected by the law and equal under the law. But how can the rule of law work when the public police and the criminal-justice system are ceding jurisdiction to corporations and individuals, who are being allowed and even encouraged to use extraordinary civil powers to enforce the criminal law in their own interests?

Thirty years ago, Prime Minister Pierre Trudeau resisted various efforts within the bureaucracy, which, if realized, might have weakened the role of the RCMP as a federal police force. Trudeau insisted that the police be free to conduct their work without interference, and that the RCMP have sole jurisdiction in the investigation of commercial crime, the only full-fledged federal law-enforcement agency in the country. Canada would be governed by the rule of law, Trudeau said, and the Mounties would be the country's prime guardians. But since Trudeau left politics in 1984, this ideal has been eroded. Enormous areas of crime are ceasing to be attended to by the public police, and this is all being done outside the realm of public debate, evolving without direction or consideration of any long-term implications.

The disturbing fact is that the RCMP is handing over important economic-crime investigations to the private sector at a time when Canada is being recognized around the world as a platform for economic crime. In recent years, criminals have been flocking to Canada, and Toronto has earned the reputation as a hub of economic crime.[6] The entire country is seen to be a safe haven from which to dupe victims, a place where the police, the courts, and the government don't seem to care all that much about such activities. At the same time, fraud of all kinds is estimated to be as much as a 1.5- to 6-per-cent drag on the country's $800-billion gross domestic product. That's a bill of between $12 billion and $48 billion in misappropriation and theft every year – and it's growing at a near-exponential rate.[7]

Social scientists and demographers alike believe that violent crime is on the wane and fraudulent activity on the increase among aging baby boomers.[8] Under normal circumstances, it would be logical to assume that the real and predicted growth of fraud would dictate that the police be strong and willing to fight such crime. That would seem to be in the country's best interests, but the government appears to have other priorities.

Why have Canadian governments, the justice system, and police become so blasé about serious fraud and corruption? That's not the case in many other democratic societies.

In the United States, presidents have been subjected to the rigours of the justice system, and governors and other senior politicians have regularly been investigated, arrested, and jailed. U.S. corporations have been fined hundreds of millions of dollars and seen top executives, officers, and employees jailed or the corporations reduced to bankruptcy after being found liable to society in either criminal or civil courts. Great Britain has its Serious Fraud Office and France its own investigative apparatus to investigate *every* complaint promptly. In France, high-ranking politicians and businessmen, such as the wealthy and powerful Bernard Tapie, have been brought to justice for corrupt practices. In Japan, police in recent years have cracked down on most forms of white-collar crime. Throughout the eighties and early nineties in Italy, of all places, more than one thousand senior politicians, judges, generals, police, and businessmen went to jail over the fallout from the P2 Masonic scandal. In Mexico, one of the most corrupt locales in the world, investigations into widespread corruption among the country's elite has rocked the country with tales of hundreds of millions of dollars being looted from the public treasury by the former president and his family. Yet in Canada few similar investigations or prosecutions seem to occur – and we can assume that Canadians are not necessarily more ethical than anyone else. Why? What usually happens in Canada is that apparently solid cases inevitably seem to fail or, if they do get to court, are more likely than not to fail spectacularly, sullying the police and justice system in the process.

So when the RCMP commissioner says that the force is retreating from the investigation and prosecution of white-collar crime, one might have thought there would be a political outcry from the highest levels and from the public. But that's not what has happened. Even when the commissioner said such was the case in *Maclean's* magazine in July 1997, the country just seemed to yawn. The entire country seems willing to accept the argument that is constantly being driven home: that *all* government departments must pitch in equally to help reduce public debt – without looking at the relative costs to society. While the intention of cost-cutting might be considered noble, the effects of its indiscriminate application are far-reaching and largely ignored. The duty of the police, after all, is to enforce all the laws of the country. By deciding to abandon certain investigations as too expensive, the RCMP, with the tacit consent of government, seems to have somehow acquired the right to unilaterally redefine the scope of the justice system in Canada without political debate, the sole justification being that such action will provide real savings for the federal taxpayer.

It therefore seems obvious that more is going on behind the scenes than first meets the eye. But what? The RCMP's stated inability to deal with much white-collar crime means there is a gaping hole in the force, like the one in the ozone layer over the North Pole. This hole is the growing inability of the RCMP to carry out its policing duties, especially at the federal level, to its fullest extent and in the purest possible way. Based on the evidence, it could reasonably be argued that the hole is growing and dangerous.

Chapter Two

•

THE LEGACY OF NORMAN INKSTER

"THE RCMP MAY NEVER recover from the Inkster years," says RCMP Inspector Dennis Schlecker as he sips on some fruit juice in his North Delta, B.C., backyard one summer Saturday afternoon. Although he is an officer, one of the white-shirted elite within the RCMP, Schlecker is not, and has never been, afraid to speak his mind. His wife, Barbara, believes that's one of the reasons he has not yet reached an even higher rank. But Schlecker doesn't seem all that concerned about rank. What he worries about is the RCMP. Like most Mounties, he bleeds scarlet. Like most Mounties, he is a fan of current commissioner Philip Murray. Like most Mounties, Schlecker doesn't think much of former commissioner Norman Inkster, who ran the force from September 1987 to June 1994. Schlecker believes that Inkster should have been held responsible somehow for all that hobbles the RCMP today. "Sometimes you wonder what Inkster was thinking," Schlecker says.

Sergeant Jake Bouwman might agree. Bouwman is one of the heroes of the RCMP these days. He runs a six-man detachment in Sparwood, B.C., in the Crowsnest Pass, just west of the Alberta border. Along with a local lawyer, Glen Purdy, Bouwman has helped develop a system whereby many juveniles facing criminal charges are diverted from the court system (the details of the system will be discussed in Chapter Eleven). Commissioner Philip Murray holds Bouwman up as an example of the kind of innovative and dedicated police officer under his command. Bouwman returns the favour. He's been a Mountie for twenty-eight years and, like Schlecker, thinks the world of Murray, but not much of his predecessor. "I think that in the annals of history Norman Inkster will not go down as being one of the great commissioners of the RCMP," says Bouwman as he ploughs through a slice of pie one Sunday evening at the Black Nugget Motor Inn restaurant in Sparwood.

The majority of Mounties abide by the paramilitary code of conduct which dictates that one never speak ill publicly of their own members because to do so might bring the entire organization into disrepute. But the Inkster thing just won't go away within the RCMP. The popular perception is that, while he was commissioner, Inkster sold the force down the river. Mounties think that he gave in too easily to government, that he didn't have the spine to stand up for the best interests of the RCMP, which to all Mounties mirror the best interests of Canada. "He just rolled over on everything," says Bouwman. "If the government said there were going to be across-the-board cutbacks, Inkster said, 'We can do it.' If the government said it needed peacekeepers somewhere in the Third World, Inkster said, 'We can do it.' Inkster became synonymous with the notion, we can do more for less. But everything the Mounties did for the government was never enough. They always came back for more, and Inkster didn't know how to say no. Maybe he did fight for us behind closed doors, but I don't think so. I have no respect for the man."

As harsh and unforgiving as Bouwman might sound, there is no question that under Inkster's command, for whatever reason, things went very badly for the RCMP. And, between 1980 and the present, Inkster seems to have had more control over the direction the force has taken, and a freer hand, than any of his predecessors or his successor.

Prior to being named commissioner, Inkster had served as the force's personnel director. He knew the inner workings of the force like the back of his hand. He decided who would be a Mountie and what a Mountie would be. He set the bar for promotions and decided who got over it. Then he became deputy commissioner of operations from 1985 to 1987, in charge of police investigations, even though he had virtually no experience as a police investigator. Finally, he caught the eye of James Kelleher, solicitor general of the day, who liked Inkster's technocratic style. Kelleher recommended Inkster to Prime Minister Brian Mulroney, who, as was his prerogative, named him commissioner. In the six months before Inkster moved into the commissioner's chair, he kept an office beside Kelleher's in the House of Commons, where the two men shared their vision for a modern RCMP. Each of them wanted to transform it from the paramilitary organization that it had always been into something more modern and business-like. The task was a monumental one, and some would say it was career suicide to even attempt it.

Commissioner Inkster received a salary of $125,000 a year. Some might think being commissioner of the RCMP is at least equivalent in pay and influence to being the chief of police in a major metropolis such as Toronto, New York, or London. In fact, the RCMP commissioner is paid much less money than any one of them – and most other Canadian police chiefs – despite having a much more complicated job. The chief of the Hamilton–Wentworth Regional Police, overseeing a city of 307,000, is paid more than the RCMP commissioner. A good international comparison is with the U.S. Federal Bureau of Investigation, which has the relatively one-dimensional task of enforcing federal statutes only. FBI street investigators make about $140,000 (Canadian) per year. The director of the FBI makes more than three times what the RCMP commissioner is paid. Even if the difference in salary levels between Canada and United States is acknowledged, this points to a problem.

Yet, only in some unknown totalitarian state might there be a job with the potential responsibilities and power that the RCMP commissioner seems to have in Canada. The RCMP can be found handing out traffic tickets and manning laser radar guns on both coasts. Mounties investigate everything from the tiniest allegations of mischief to the most heinous murders. The Mounties run a national police intelligence unit and provide the technical support for all police departments in the country through their National Police Services branch. They are in charge of Canada's crime-record databases, and conduct fingerprint and DNA analysis, among myriad other country-wide forensic duties. The force is a world leader in the development of security and other operational equipment and, among numerous other innovations, has developed its own anti-bomb suits and its own blast-proof vehicles. In Ottawa and around the country, Mounties protect federal politicians, visiting dignitaries, and VIPs. Abroad they serve as intelligence and security officers in Canada's embassies and consulates. The RCMP has its own air force, with twenty-eight planes and helicopters, including a Westwind jet, which is used by the commissioner on weekends – if it is not being used to ferry police officers, prisoners, or protected witnesses around the country. The RCMP Musical Ride entertains paying customers around the world, and, every day at noon, Mounties in full-dress red serge and stetsons parade on Parliament Hill for the tourists. Even all that fails to describe adequately the reach and scope of the Royal Canadian Mounted Police on a given day. Over the course of 125 years, the Mounties have gone from being just a federal police force to the Everypolice of Canada.

With all these duties, the RCMP might be assumed already to be spread thin, but during Inkster's tenure it seemed to members like Jake Bouwman that the commissioner was attempting to implement every social, political, and economic imperative of the government, without questioning the potential impact on the force.

Most members agree with such social and political objectives as the recruitment of more women, French Canadians and visible minorities to the RCMP. White males with a paramilitaristic attitude had served the country well for years, but everyone recognizes that times have changed. Even some of the most redneck conservatives and unrealistic traditionalists admit that the force needed to better reflect the society it was trying to police, even if it meant occasionally altering recruitment policies and the marginal lowering of suitability and physical standards. Nevertheless, some Mounties think Inkster, in the actions he took, lessened the effectiveness of the force. To them he seemed erratic and somewhat out of control, a little too hungry for easy headlines, always trying to please the politicians, the pressure groups, and the editorial writers, at the expense of real policing needs.

When new Sikh members fought to wear turbans while on duty, Inkster supported their potentially divisive campaign against the traditionalists. In doing so, the commissioner won editorial plaudits across the country, in spite of the anomaly that regular members weren't

allowed to wear a visible crucifix while in uniform. Inkster treated that
as a different issue. The Sikh members won their case, then, soon afterwards, they stopped wearing turbans while on duty, though they retain
them on ceremonial occasions. Nobody ever put out a press release about
the change of attitude. Inkster also seemed to spend more time and effort
on appearances than on the real and potential negative effects that his
policies would have on the ability of the force to perform its primary
function – policing.

In the field of economic priorities, when the government imposed a
five-year pay freeze on the civil service, Inkster went along with it for the
RCMP. Adhering to government wishes may have been one thing, but it
was the determination of Inkster to apply a business model to the force
that wreaked the most havoc. He not only went along with the government cutbacks, as he was required to do, but he even went as far as
rewarding divisional commanders who managed to cut additional money
from their budgets. The savings were considerable, but the cost has been
steep and incalculable. The lack of pay and the reduction in overtime virtually turned the force into a nine-to-five operation. Many demoralized
Mounties have essentially been working to rule ever since, in spite of the
fact that a successful criminal investigation usually requires something
more than routine attention from the police.

As the force came to run itself more like a business in the eighties,
civilians were hired to take over administrative and other "menial" work
being done by police officers. The intention was to free up more police
officers for work on the street, but that is not what happened. The projected salary savings were soon lost, because civilians ended up being paid
almost much as the regular police officers. Meanwhile, hiring of police
officers was frozen or reduced to the point where, today, virtually every
RCMP policing unit is operating shorthanded.

A variation of the civilianization plan was the hiring of more than one
thousand special constables over the years. The special-constable status
was implemented in the old Security Service – the Watcher Service – after
the Second World War to help fight the Cold War against Russian spies in
Canada. These Mounties were surveillance specialists selected for their

ability to blend in with a crowd – the old, the short, the fat, and the bland. Most couldn't meet police entrance requirements, didn't look anything like regular police officers, and were paid significantly less than regular members of the RCMP.

With the rise of international terrorism in the early seventies, more special constables were hired to guard airports. They were in uniform, but didn't require the training that a police officer did. By the mid-eighties, a threat by Armenian terrorists in Canada and the Air India bombing led to the hiring of even more special constables to act as guards at embassies, consulates, and government buildings around the country. The special constables created all sorts of administrative problems for the force.

Shortly after becoming commissioner, Inkster, the consummate administrator, along with one of his deputies, decided to solve the problem by giving the special constables a "career path." With the waving of a bureaucratic wand, he immediately transformed the special constables into regular members of the force, allowing their seniority as special constables to count for promotion purposes. When they had been hired, few, if any, were required to meet the standards of a regular RCMP constable. Therefore, standards were then lowered significantly to make room for them in the force. "None of these people even wanted to be police officers, and many others normally wouldn't qualify, but many of them are investigators today. Some are heading up investigative units. Is it any wonder we have problems?" asked Staff Sergeant Jim Vickery, of the Bowmanville, Ontario, drug squad. Almost overnight, it seemed to individual Mounties, the force had gone from being one of the world's great police forces to being just another government bureaucracy. Morale sank to an all-time low, and experienced, quality officers began to leave in droves, disappointed and disillusioned.

The real problem, his critics within the force believed, was that Inkster was just too inexperienced as a regular police officer and didn't really understand the police culture. Most of all, Inkster was seen to be too political to be an effective commissioner. He was seen to be too ready to toe the government line. Inkster never put up a real fight – and his subservient attitude extended to the way the RCMP conducted high-profile criminal investigations. Inkster insisted that the force report weekly to the political level about such investigations.

In some respects, this was due to Inkster's place in history. He had risen to the top of the RCMP under Commissioner Robert Simmonds in the aftermath of the 1981 McDonald Royal Commission, set up to investigate the Security Service, the counter-intelligence wing of the RCMP (about which more later). One of the McDonald Commission recommendations was that all high-profile investigations undertaken by the RCMP be reported to the government on a regular basis. The reason for this was to avoid some of the controversies in which the Security Service had become entangled – such as the burning down of a barn – in the fight against Quebec separatists during the sixties and early seventies. The McDonald Commission intended that checks and balances be put in place so that the government of the day could be held accountable for the activities of the Security Service. It is important to note that, while some Mounties drifted back and forth between policing and the Security Service, members attached to the Security Service were not peace officers. They were counter-intelligence specialists. Such arrangements exist in most federal police forces around the world.

Canada became a notable exception in 1984, when the Security Service split off from the RCMP to become the Canadian Security Intelligence Service, a civilian organization responsible for counter-intelligence. After the separation, however, Commissioner Simmonds felt compelled to continue reporting to the new Mulroney government what the RCMP was doing in some high-profile *criminal* investigations, even though the McDonald recommendation clearly did not intend that politicians should have oversight of police investigations. Quite the contrary.

In 1985, Inkster was appointed deputy commissioner of operations, where he "learned the system." After Inkster replaced Simmonds in 1987, most Mounties feel he showed little discretion in what he allowed the political level to know about ongoing high-profile criminal investigations (not just counter-intelligence). He decided that the force's policy would be to keep the government informed of all such investigations, a highly unusual practice in any democracy, and a critical lapse in judgement during the Mulroney regime, since, as it turned out, virtually every one of those high-profile federal investigations throughout the eighties involved the Mulroney government – from numerous petty schemes to the infamous allegations that millions of dollars of kickbacks had been paid to Mulroney in the $1.8-billion purchase of Airbus jets by Air Canada in 1988. No matter which case they were investigating, throughout the nine-year Mulroney reign the RCMP was mired in controversy and ultimately derailed. RCMP investigators often found themselves on treacherous ground, having to play a cat-and-mouse game with their own commissioner to prevent the government from learning what they were doing. This was not the way police work was supposed to be done.[1] In a democracy the police are agents of the law and responsible only to the law. But under Inkster the Mounties had in effect been converted into a *de facto* government agency.

Inevitably, Inkster was perceived to have become too much a part of government, overly involved in the Ottawa whirl to the point at which some Mounties began to fear that he had forgotten that he was heading a "guardian" agency. To his internal critics, Inkster seemed more engrossed and interested in being a bureaucrat than a police officer – or perhaps more an entrepreneur than a servant of the law. Mounties complained, even to Inkster himself, that he didn't really know what police officers did, how they did it, or, perhaps most importantly, why they did what they did. In 1989, for example, he told a House of Commons committee the number of RCMP investigations being conducted against politicians, causing the force to let out a collective gasp. Inkster seemed to have not a clue that what he had done might not be considered the appropriate course of action for a police officer to take in such a situation. Friendly and open was not an option for a guardian.

Members of the force didn't like their commissioner being chummy with a man they distrusted, Mulroney. Every time Inkster was seen with Mulroney, such as at a New Year's Eve party at Mulroney's Harrington Lake retreat, the collective RCMP would just shake its head.

That kind of behaviour led to the darkest criticism of Inkster, that, in his eagerness to please, he had allowed the RCMP to fall under the effective political control of what was perceived by many to be a blatantly corrupt government. Mulroney made it clear that he didn't like the police investigating him and his friends. At one point, as reported in my previous book, he even kicked an RCMP car in disgust, after learning about an investigation into his friend, Senator Michel Cogger. At every level, Inkster appeared to go along with government initiatives, the intention of which seemed to be the weakening of the force in general, but especially in the area of federal investigations. Many within the force believed that was Mulroney's long-term agenda.

The prevailing feeling was that, with his acceptance of political oversight of criminal investigations and his willingness to please the government by slashing the budget of the RCMP, Inkster let down the history and traditions of the Mounties. In doing so, he opened the door to the growth of private investigation and private policing in Canada – among other things.

That, in essence, is the blame-it-on-one-man theory of what happened to the Mounties.

•   •   •

Norman Inkster says that, over the years, he's heard the complaints about his stewardship of the force, but it doesn't seem to bother him that much. "I'm proud of my accomplishments," he said in an interview in August 1997. Inkster defended himself, saying that, during his seven years as commissioner, he had not had as much power as some might imagine, and no real choice in most of the decisions he made. Inkster painted a picture of the commissioner as a bureaucrat, hemmed in by legislation, precedent, and politics, always fighting for survival. In Inkster's view, the problems facing any commissioner are legion, not the least being that, both within and without the force, expectations of the RCMP seem unrealistic.

Under Inkster, the force's own surveys documented sinking morale, largely due to the prolonged pay freeze, as a key problem. Inkster blamed RCMP members themselves. He said the morale problem began more than twenty years ago, when RCMP members in the mid-seventies demanded and eventually won the right to be paid overtime. Prior to that,

RCMP members just did the job until the job was done. Back then, Inkster argued, Mounties had a sense of public duty and readily accepted that part of their pay was, philosophically speaking, the satisfaction gained from serving the public well. When the force began to pay overtime, job satisfaction came to be determined by one measure only – money. Inkster says: "The biggest significant change was overtime. Having lived in both those regimes, I can tell you that, among some people, there was an immediate change in attitude. When the availability of overtime became controlled by budgets, so that you had $30 million or $31 million in the pot, and that money was gone, I recall people saying, 'If I'm not getting paid for it, I'm not working.'"

But the real problem facing the RCMP may well be those unrealistic expectations, that ordinary Canadians do not seem to know what the Mounties are supposed to be doing. As Inkster puts it: "Canada demands that the RCMP be all things to all people all the time, but the country doesn't allocate enough money to pay for what the RCMP must do.

"The difficulty for me was, what do you give up?" Inkster said, recalling the dilemma he faced when confronted with the prospect of government cutbacks in the early nineties. "I took the decision when I was there to get rid of something as insignificant as the migratory-bird enforcement co-ordinators, of which there were nine in the country. You wouldn't believe the letters I got from Ducks Unlimited and so on and so forth, saying this was absolutely abominable. It became a terrible political football. The police shouldn't be making those decisions. That's what governments should be doing. That's why they exist. The real difficulty for the RCMP is that, while the government is saying, 'You're going to be all things to all people,' they're also saying, 'You're going to do it with $600 million less than you had five years ago.' It's pretty tough."

The amount of the financial cutbacks to the RCMP may seem reasonable to the average Canadian taxpayer. The force was being asked to shed an average of $173 million per year out of its $1.9-billion budget, or less than 10 per cent. The RCMP was just doing its fair share of belt-tightening, or so it seemed. But, as taxpayers have come to learn, the government numbers don't tell the whole story. In fact, they masked a series of rather deliberate misrepresentations, not the least of which was that the budget reductions were across the board. In fact, they mainly affected *federal* programs.

To appreciate the significance of such reductions, one must first understand how the RCMP accounts for its spending, according to the force's 1997–98 budget estimates. In the chart that follows, everything is broken down by "business line," in the same way accountants and auditors would deal with a real business. In the chart, Contract Policing Services refers to provincial and municipal policing work that the RCMP "contracts" to do for provinces, territories, and municipalities across Canada. National Police Services includes most technical operations, such as crime databases, fingerprint and DNA labs, and the like, services that are in place for the use of all police forces in Canada. Federal Policing Services enforces federal statutes and laws, such as drug enforcement and immigration.

Gross expenditures by business line	Main estimates 1996–97 ($millions)	Main estimates 1997–98 ($millions)	Planned 1998–99 ($millions)
Federal Policing Services	526.6	452.4	393.4
Contract Policing Services	809.1	817.2	817.3
National Police Services	285.1	284.9	285.1
Corporate Management and Human Resources	304.9	282.6	271.6
Total Gross Expenditures	1,925.7	1,837.1	1,767.4

That's how much the federal government spends on the RCMP, but what tends to be overlooked is that the federal government also earns significant income from the RCMP.

Revenue for government	Main estimates 1996–97 ($millions)
Contract Policing Services, Including Aboriginal Policing	721.2
National Police Services	3.5
Total Revenue	724.7

I have not included charts for 1997–98 and 1998–99, because the revenue numbers currently are, or are projected to be, relatively stable. As one can see, the federal government generates $724.7 million in revenues from selling RCMP services to the provinces, territories, and municipalities. All those revenues are directed back to the government general coffers, and not to the RCMP. Therefore, the federal government does not pay $1.9 billion per year for the RCMP, as it would like to claim, but rather a little more than $1.1 billion.

The government has long seen the RCMP as a business. In a perfect world a police force is designed to be a creature of the rule of law, pure in its vision and independent in its attitude. Yet to ensure its survival, the RCMP has agreed over the years to take on revenue-producing roles and responsibilities that are, in many ways, antithetical to its being a guardian organization. As Jane Jacobs lucidly points out in her book *Systems of Survival*, expecting a guardian agency to run itself like a business is to invite disaster.

The underlying mythology of the RCMP is that it is, and always has been, a classic example of modern public policing, an altruistically motivated meritocracy dedicated to public service. That might have been the case once. The Mounties now are not so much a police force, but a police-services business, a subtle but important distinction. The federal government's long-term plan is for the RCMP to generate even more cash, to pay its own way, as it were.

This brings us to our final chart, the allocation of budget within Federal Policing Services for 1997–98.

Federal Policing Service by sub-activity and business line	Expenditures ($millions)
Executive	0.3
Enforcement Services	151.2
Drug Enforcement	87.9
Economic Crime	36.7
Foreign Services	4.9
Criminal Intelligence	36.9
Protective Services	51.4
Departmental Security	1.5
Technical Security Services	24.7
Airport Policing	53.3
Major Events	3.6
Total	452.4

By breaking down the federal policing-services budget in this fashion, one can instantly see that there are really only four areas which involve criminal investigation: Enforcement Services (enforcing such federal statutes as those concerning customs, immigration, migratory birds, etc.), Drug Enforcement, Economic Crime, and Criminal Intelligence. The rest are essentially protection and guard duties. The total budget, therefore, for federal criminal investigations is $312.7 million, which is about one-sixth of the RCMP's global budget. When the government says it's cutting back on the RCMP's budget, this is the relatively small area that is taking the brunt of the attack. Many might think that $312.7 million is a lot of money to pay for federal criminal investigations, but in a country of thirty million people, it means that slightly more than ten dollars per Canadian per year goes towards such protection.

Each kind of criminal investigation has its own budget, as if each were a business line. Most of those other "business lines" – drugs, customs and excise, taxation – are relatively well funded in relation to the total impact of such crimes on the economy. But when it comes to economic-crime – fraud – investigation, the government has been slicing away at the RCMP's budget for years, to the point at which, today, the budget for economic-crime investigators is laughable. In an era when major frauds are calculated in tranches of tens of millions of dollars, the entire budget for the Economic Crime Unit across Canada is $36.7 million or about *one dollar and twenty-two cents per Canadian per year*. By comparison, due to fraud, Canadian banks alone expect to lose two dollars per year for each credit card issued – more than $80 million annually. The annual loss from all varieties of fraud in Canada is estimated to exceed 1.5 per cent of the country's $800-billion gross domestic product – or more than $12 billion a year stolen from individuals, corporations, and government.

One might have hoped that Norman Inkster would have fought to avoid reducing the federal investigation budget any further, but he says he felt that he couldn't resist. He didn't want to make waves. As round after round of government orders for cuts came down the bureaucratic pipe, Inkster says he felt there was little he could do to defy the government's wishes, no matter how misguided or destructive he thought they might be. "You can say one of two things: 'Is there anything I can do to influence the impact of that decision so that the RCMP as an organization is less affected than other government departments?' Or, you say: 'No, I'm not going to do it, and here's my resignation.' Those are your choices." Inkster chose to stay and comply with the government's demands for change. If the government wasn't all that interested in fraud investigations, neither was he.

•   •   •

As with most business organizations in the late eighties and nineties, change became the operative word for the RCMP. As long as the RCMP was seen to be changing – no matter what those changes might be or their effect – the government was happy with Inkster. Or so it seemed. Bombarded by budget cutbacks, Inkster clearly had little room to manoeuvre. The government made it clear that it didn't want to see reductions to Contract Policing, because it was a significant revenue source. National Police Services was absolutely necessary as a support system for all policing, and it fit into the high-tech aspirations of the business-minded government. Every successful DNA match in the National Police Services labs could be used by the government as an example of taxpayers' money well spent. On the other hand, few taxpayers really had a clue about what the duties and responsibilities of the federal police might be, or why they were so important to the country, especially in the area of economic crime.

Under Inkster, the Economic Crime Unit began to be effectively watered down and emasculated. It must be remembered that, since its inception as the Commercial Crime Branch, the unit always was more than just a typical municipal police fraud squad chasing down sticky-fingered bookkeepers or people who bounced cheques. From the mid-sixties on, the Commercial Crime Unit had much higher aspirations – to deal with organized and white-collar crime (that is, any crime involving business). It attracted the most capable and experienced Mounties in the force. Each Commercial Crime detective was an experienced police officer who became a specialist in a certain defined category – be it bankruptcy, stock-market scams, crimes against the public treasury, or cross-border fraud. The RCMP paid for university courses and professional training. The unit's case list was the stuff of legend as it mounted successful investigations of socially prominent and often politically connected criminals from coast to coast. In the seventies alone, Commercial Crime investigators successfully attacked organized criminals operating on the country's stock exchanges. Its investigations helped bring about the closing of the corrupt Canadian Stock Exchange in Montreal. The Commercial Crime Branch brought charges against politicians, bureaucrats, and businessmen who were dipping into the public treasury, most notably in the Hamilton Harbour investigation, the Dredging Scandal, and the Sky Shops Affair in the seventies. In a country where everyone is supposedly equal under the rule of law, the Commercial Crime Branch investigators were the great equalizers. But all that changed under Inkster, who converted the Commercial Crime Branch into the Economic Crime Directorate, then reduced it to the Economic Crime Unit, a division within Federal Policing Services.

Of all the departments within the RCMP, Inkster seemed to come down hardest on Economic Crime. First he championed promotional and operational policies which appeared to contradict the promise of his own technocratic credentials and goals. For example, at a time when the rest of the world had recognized the value of specialization and knowledge, Inkster headed off in an entirely different direction; specialists were out, generalists were in. As one Mountie put it: "Inkster was of the opinion that a cop was a cop was a cop and that any police officer could do any job. There was no magic." By the late eighties, the de-emphasis on specialization in Economic Crime began to have its effect. Case after case began to blow up in the force's face. Mountie criminal investigators, who had once been renowned for their thoroughness and effectiveness at gaining prosecutions, began to be seen as clumsy, mistake-prone, and even incompetent.

In the early nineties, Inkster made moves to transform Economic Crime from a division based on function to one based on territory. He asserted that any cop can do any policing job. This flew in the face of the original intentions of those who had founded the Commercial Crime Branch. As Inkster's former deputy commissioner, Henry Jensen, put it: "The Commercial Crime Branch was created out of necessity. There was a recognition that criminal business behaviour had spread across the country and across borders. If such units were structured along territorial lines, the likelihood would be that the priority of regional or local commanders in charge of such units would be to police their own areas first. With the structure of the force and budget constraints, there was little or no incentive for them to take the big view."

The result was predictably negative. As Economic Crime members became less and less capable of conducting successful fraud investigations, their track record and reliability in courtrooms diminished. Naturally, with this erosion came a loss of political support for Economic Crime, both within and without the force.

Inkster's policies, however, could not be held solely responsible for what happened. The external forces mounted against the police were formidable. Governments across the country, focused almost entirely on violent crime, never kept pace with the growth and increasing sophistication of economic crime. Fraud was considered little more than a victimless crime. No recognition was given by government or the courts to the real impact of economic crime on a society, which is not the case in many other countries, especially England and France. In those countries there is a greater appreciation for two of the difficulties present in a fraud investigation. By its very nature fraud is based on confusion and deception; and, unlike violent crime, the investigative trail in fraud usually leads from the suspect to the crime, not the other way around. In these countries, not only are the police specially trained to investigate fraud, but prosecutors and judges are also schooled in how to deal with the minefield of lies and half-truths usually found at the heart of any criminal-fraud prosecution. They have recognized in recent years that criminal-fraud cases are more difficult to investigate and prosecute and that special rules and procedures often are required for their successful prosecution.

In Canada, however, there has been little done to strengthen and improve the success rate of federal police investigators, particularly in the area of economic crime. In fact, quite the opposite has happened. Beginning with Inkster, the grand plan was to run the RCMP like a business, and what this eventually meant was that the RCMP began willingly to sacrifice its own federal police investigators, standards, and reputation to make successive federal and provincial finance ministers happy.

As Inkster began to run the force as he thought a business might be run, other questionable decisions were made.

Throughout the mid to late eighties, the RCMP was confronted with a serious problem, which was felt most acutely in the Toronto and

Vancouver areas. The combination of rising house prices and a freeze in wages had brought many Mounties who were assigned to those areas to the verge of bankruptcy. Over the years, Inkster and the force had pleaded with the federal government to allow the RCMP to pay its members in the Toronto area an allowance for having to live in such an expensive area. As it was, the rigid rank structure dictated that Mounties of equal rank, say a corporal on highway patrol in rural Nova Scotia, a corporal doing intricate commercial-crime work in Toronto, or a corporal working the streets in suburban Vancouver, all be paid the same. It didn't seem fair that the Nova Scotia Mountie enjoyed a better lifestyle, but, more importantly, the system was skewing the way Mounties were being deployed and was threatening the integrity of the force. The more-experienced officers were using their seniority to claim jobs in the hinterlands, where it was cheap to live. Detachments in the expensive urban areas, meanwhile, had to fill the resulting openings with less-experienced juniors. The outcome was that Mounties were being deployed across the country in a most inefficient manner, and the situation is even more pronounced today. The force is designed so that most new cadets spend their first years of service in a rural area before moving to a busy, complex urban or suburban detachment. Instead, the young are starting out in places like suburban Surrey and Burnaby, while the veterans are working relatively cushy jobs near fishing holes across the country. The normal practice with most national police forces in the Western world that operate in rural and urban environments is to pay a substantial subsidy to those forced to live in the high-cost areas, where the most sophisticated work is usually done. Nevertheless, the federal government, which has lumped the RCMP in with the rest of the public service, has continually denied the RCMP's request to deal with the inequities, many believe unreasonably so. This has had an effect on the way the RCMP carries out its law-enforcement duties.

Over its first hundred years, the RCMP was a strictly regimental force; the only way to do things was the RCMP way. The force was dedicated to serving the law and the public interest first. The needs and creature comforts of its members rarely received any consideration. In the mid-seventies, political and social forces caused the RCMP to become more civilianized. Barriers to entry for married men, women, and others were all but eliminated. By the eighties, economic pressures meant that the RCMP had cut other standards. Over the past twenty-five years, accommodation to government demands became almost instinctual to RCMP leaders, but none more so than Inkster, who became a master at moving in the direction of least resistance.

Under Inkster, Mounties began to think differently about the force, themselves, and their duties. Across the country, the force became designed to accommodate the personal needs of its employees more than to serve the public interest. This playing down of the sense of duty, almost unfathomable for some Mounties, became relatively common. Since there was a government-ordered across-the-board pay freeze, Inkster allowed Mounties to take on second jobs. Hours of work in many detachments were arranged to accommodate the personal interests or second jobs of Mounties. In some detachments it became, and continues to be, the rule that Mounties come to work to rest after spending most of their week moonlighting in construction, in gardening, or even in long-distance truck driving, to name some of the favourite second jobs. In many ways, the overlapping expectations of the law, the taxpayer, and the real or potential victims of crime became secondary to many Mounties. Selflessness and a sense of duty, once the most valued of attributes in the closed world of the RCMP, became substantially devalued by the nineties. Perhaps the best example of how lax the RCMP had become about the notion of defending the public interest occurred in Toronto, where Inkster "managed" the cost-of-living problem in a classic bottom-line solution.

The RCMP's operations in Toronto had always been located in the downtown core – for the last twenty years on Jarvis Street, a short walk from the financial centre, the focus of much of the RCMP's operations in Ontario. In Ontario, the RCMP is strictly a federal police force.

When confronted with the problem of a cramped building in Toronto and underpaid Mounties trying to survive there in the late eighties, Inkster used modern business thinking to come up with a solution. First, he had the administration component moved to London, Ontario – two hours west of Toronto. The RCMP says it took on a ten-year lease for the building there, paying $2.5 million a year in rent, with an option for a five-year extension.

Then the operations were divided among three sub-detachments. The first was a one-hour drive west of Toronto, in Milton, where the RCMP says it took out another ten-year lease on a building, paying $1.3 million per year. The force says it spent an additional $1.2 million getting the building in shape, and, as of this writing, an officer assigned to Milton describes the building as "totally inadequate, an absolute disaster."

Another sub-detachment was located a one-hour drive north of Toronto, in Newmarket. There the RCMP built a $16-million edifice on land that had been purchased for $1.8 million.

The third sub-detachment was in Bowmanville, an hour's drive east of Toronto. The RCMP says it took out a ten-year lease, paying $586,000 a month in rent, as well as an additional $740,000 to renovate the structure.

In October 1997, the Mounties sold their original Toronto headquarters for $2.5 million to a developer.

Why did the Mounties move so far out of Toronto? The thinking behind the move was that the price of real estate that far from the city would be stable for a number of years. As a result, in 1998 the Mounties are little more than a rumour in Toronto, which in their absence, as mentioned, has become one of the leading centres in the world for commercial crime and other forms of fraud. RCMP members are still scratching their heads about why Inkster did what he did. The head of operations – the person ultimately responsible for federal investigations for Toronto – is based in London, but must spend most of his time in the Toronto area, where the work is. In Toronto, every unit was fractured into three and scattered, yet not one of the new Toronto-area buildings has a boardroom big enough to hold a meeting on any kind of operation involving the three sub-detachments. The RCMP must rent space in hotels for such routine matters.

Prior to the breakup, the Toronto office had within its walls the knowledge base required to do its work properly. In the old Toronto-based days, expertise on any subject could be found somewhere in the office. Today, an investigator in Milton who might be an expert on one area of stock fraud is a two-hour drive from his Toronto counterpart in Bowmanville, who might need his help. The problem was exacerbated even further by the fact that, with the high turnover and mobility of RCMP members, it wasn't long before the Mounties in Milton, Newmarket, and Bowmanville were mostly strangers to each other, so that no one knew any more who was an expert in what field.

Staff Sergeant Ross Kossatz, of the Economic Crime Unit in Bowmanville, said that he once confronted Inkster about the fact that there was not enough travel money in budgets for the RCMP to get to Toronto to do its work. He quoted Inkster as responding only: "That's the price of doing business in the big city."

Staff Sergeant John Bothwell, in charge of Bowmanville's Customs and Excise Section, said he sometimes finds it difficult to get his staff to work in Toronto when their jurisdiction extends to 150 kilometres east of Toronto, in much less hectic and more pleasant physical surroundings. "Every so often we have to put projects together to get the people to go to Toronto."

As another Mountie put it, "No one has any idea how much this all cost the force or if there were any real savings. But I would bet a year's pay that it would have been far cheaper for the Mounties to buy each member in Toronto a brand-new car every year than do what we did."

As for Inkster, all the criticisms seem to be water off a duck's back. Everyone thought the RCMP had moved out of Toronto as part of the government's much grander decentralization program. Inkster says that's not so. "It may have looked like part of the government's decentralization policy, but it wasn't that at all," Inkster says. "We couldn't get experienced people to come to Toronto, where we were dealing with some of the most sophisticated crimes. Young members were actually facing personal bankruptcy because they couldn't afford to live here any more. So what was the answer? You don't need to have an office in downtown Toronto. We put them on the outskirts where they could buy the housing they could afford, come into the detachment and travel to downtown Toronto on government time to do the work." In effect, Inkster resorted to an accountant's trick to give the appearance of saving money and being more efficient. The move also meant a hidden 25-per-cent reduction or so in real work by Mountie investigators, who now were forced to fight rush-hour traffic in and out of Toronto. "Yep," Inkster says, and a look of satisfaction comes over his face. "The members were able to survive. They were able to feed their children and send them to school."

In early 1994, just after Jean Chrétien and his Liberals won a majority government, Inkster announced that he was leaving the force after thirty-six years of service. He says that he had stayed on even longer than he had originally planned. Politicians such as Warren Allmand, who was head of the House of Commons Justice Committee at the time Inkster left, said he believed that, as commissioner, Inkster had headed the force in "the right direction," meaning that it was moving away from its paramilitary roots and becoming an ultra-modern law-enforcement agency. "He was a good man, he did a good job."[2]

Others within the force had a much different opinion, but Inkster doesn't really seem to care all that much about what they think of him. "There were a lot of rumours that I was pushed out, but if I was pushed out, I guess Mr. Chrétien wouldn't have given me the Order of Canada and a couple of other things."

It is also true, however, that while the RCMP that Norman Inkster left behind might well have been held together by so much baling wire and blarney, Inkster cannot be blamed for all that has gone wrong. Other forces have long been at work, more powerful and insidious than any one man. They are almost as difficult to pin down as the notion of accountability in Canadian politics itself, but foremost among these was the popular neo-conservative, neo-liberal notion that there is little real need for public guardians and that the marketplace must rule.

Of all Canada's public institutions, it would seem at first blush that a guardian organization such as the RCMP would be the most resistant to the lure of business-like thinking – but the real RCMP has never really been what Hollywood said it was, and it's not now. To fully understand the inherent contradictions within the RCMP of the present, it is absolutely necessary for the reader to understand how the Mounties got here. On our trip back into history, let's stop first in the late fifties and early sixties in Ottawa.

Chapter Three

•

THE GLASSCO COMMISSION: THE CHANGING OF THE GUARD

OTTAWA IN THE LATE fifties was a dull, stodgy place with an acute aversion to risk-taking. That all began to change around the time Robert Broughton Bryce caught the ear of Prime Minister John Diefenbaker. Bryce, who had been a student of British economist John Maynard Keynes, had long been one of the most influential advisers within the Canadian government. As the *Globe and Mail* pointed out in a 1997 obituary, Bryce was a close adviser to every Canadian prime minister from Mackenzie King to Pierre Trudeau. He was secretary to the cabinet and clerk of the Privy Council under Louis St. Laurent, John Diefenbaker, and Lester Pearson. He was Pierre Trudeau's economic adviser on the constitution and deputy finance minister until his retirement in 1971.[1]

Diefenbaker saw himself as a latter-day Sir Wilfrid Laurier, a leader who might both unite Canada and make it prosper. As philosopher George S. Grant suggested in *Lament for a Nation*, Diefenbaker, unlike his Liberal predecessors and successors, actually believed, naively so, that he could achieve unity in one truly united Canada.[2] The perfect vehicle for Diefenbaker to achieve his dream would be the full implementation of Bryce's Keynesian philosophy. In the 1958 election campaign, Diefenbaker hit the hustings promising the reform of government. "Something must be done to improve the efficiency of national public administration," he said, on his way to winning unprecedented support in Quebec and a surprisingly large majority government.

That something was the Royal Commission into the Organization of Government, called by Diefenbaker in 1960. The three-man commission was headed by powerful and influential Toronto businessman J. Grant Glassco, a former vice-president of Brazilian Traction, Light and Power Co., forerunner of Brascan. In each of the previous four decades Glassco had served on a royal commission, and each time he delivered exactly what the government of the day wanted. What Diefenbaker wanted was simple. As Finance Minister Donald Fleming put it in a Toronto speech in 1960: "The commission will survey the whole structure of our administration with the aim of cutting costs."

The roots of the Glassco inquiry dated back to 1947, when U.S. president Harry Truman appointed former president Herbert Hoover to set up a commission and study the U.S. civil service. Hoover finished his work in 1950, claiming that $4 billion a year in savings could be had – if his recommendations were adopted. In 1953, President Dwight Eisenhower set up a second Hoover Commission. This time, Hoover claimed he could find $8.5 billion a year in savings, although no such savings were ever achieved; in fact, quite the contrary. As the government tried to behave more like a business, its spending went up, and the quality of service down. Diefenbaker and the Canadian business community, nonetheless, picked up on the Hoover Commission ideas, and the chief consultant to the Glassco Commission was, of course, Herbert Hoover.

Whatever Hoover's strengths or weaknesses might have been, he was the embodiment of a school of thought that had been building throughout the twentieth century. The powerful ideas driving the Glassco Commission didn't come to Robert Bryce and John Diefenbaker as they savoured the beauty of the Gatineau Hills from their Parliament Hill offices. They had been building for more than a century.

Since the days of eighteenth-century Scottish philosopher David Hume, there had been an incessant and unrelenting attack on the legitimacy of government. Over that same period, terms such as industrialization, corporatism, and capitalism had been used in such a confusing way that their original meanings had (and have) been fused into a single image, when they shouldn't have been. Much of this was based on a misinterpretation of Hume's famous dictum: "Nothing is more certain than that men are, in great measure, governed by interest." Along the way, the phrase "in great measure" somehow got lost, and Hume joined Adam Smith as a godfather of free-marketers, based on a statement he really didn't make – or believe.

At the turn of this century, along came Émile Durkheim, the father of modern sociology. Taking Hume's philosophy one step further, he predicted that corporations would become the "elementary division of the state, the fundamental political unit." They will "efface the distinction between private and public, dissect the democratic citizenry into discrete functional groups which are no longer capable of joint political action." Through the corporations, "scientific rationality [will achieve] its rightful standing as the creator of collective reality."[3]

By the thirties and forties, it seemed that like-minded thinkers everywhere began to emerge, including Mihail Manoilesco, Alfredo Rocco, and Friedrich von Hayek, and were particularly influential in the United States. As John Ralston Saul points out in his 1995 book, *The Unconscious Civilization*, "What linked them was a religious devotion to the market and an inability to see government as the justifiable force of the citizen. That is, their inability to see the human as anything more than interest driven made it impossible for them to imagine an actively organized pool of disinterest called the public good."

At the same time, there was another stream of thought developing about the way the world should work. Perhaps the most influential work of the time was that of John Maynard Keynes. In *A Treatise on Money* (1930) and *The General Theory of Employment, Interest and Money* (1936) Keynes expressed his belief that a government could plan its economy by manipulating its own budget. This manipulation could be achieved by cutting taxes or increasing government spending in order to stimulate growth in the private economy. It made sense to some, and the philosophy gained some legitimacy during the Second World War.

Historians J. L. Finlay and D. N. Sprague succinctly described the times in their 1979 book, *The Structure of Canadian History*:

> The war bonanza seemed conclusive evidence that a modern government
> could orchestrate the peaks and troughs out of the business cycle. . . . The

important point was the apparent efficiency with which government took control of effective resources and seemed to manage them completely for the shared goal of victory. Naturally, many people came to the conclusion that if a country could spend billions fighting wars and plan the economy for the good of that cause, the same bureaucracy might also control production to ensure peacetime prosperity and promote the general welfare by adding other social security programs to unemployment insurance.[4]

Keynesian economics had taken hold in the United States with Franklin D. Roosevelt's New Deal, and the pressure on Canada and other Western countries to align themselves economically with the United States was intense. Enter Glassco, the agent of such change in Canada.

After holding a series of public hearings, the Glassco Commission dribbled out the five volumes of its report in 1962 and 1963, capturing headlines with one bureaucratic horror story after another. One of the best descriptions of the commission's findings and philosophy was summed up in the lead paragraphs of a front-page-story in the *Ottawa Citizen* by Southam News Services writer Charles Lynch, who wrote on November 27, 1962:

> The Glassco Royal Commission today pictured the government service as a sick colossus dominating the Canadian economy, and it prescribed large doses of private enterprise as a remedy.
>
> In the second volume of their report on government organization, the commissioners continued their tale of mismanagement, misconception and self-induced blindness in the public service, operating not only to the detriment of government but to the community at large.
>
> In almost every case, the methods of Big Business were recommended, and in many areas the commission advocated that the government wind up its own activities and farm the work out to private concerns.
>
> As in the first volume, published in September, there was no evidence of corruption – but evidence of inefficiency filled almost every one of the report's 421 pages.

Something entirely unforeseen had happened along the way in Canada, similar to what had occurred in the United States. Diefenbaker and Bryce had set out to run the country along Keynesian lines, but the Glassco Commission extrapolated this to recommend that the country should in future be run like a business, which was not what Keynes himself had ever intended. In the welter of ideas swirling around in the forties, Keynes's ideas had become fused with those of the free-marketers. The British economist had provided a seemingly viable scenario whereby government could behave like a business. In the view of the Glassco Commission, it made perfect sense that politicians and bureaucrats see themselves in a different light. They were now managers empowered to run the economy like a business, but soon they would start to *think* like businessmen too, rather than guardians whose primary role was to protect the greater good and the public interest.

As popular and appealing as such a hybrid may be, what was lost in the hoopla is that government and business are entirely different beasts. To mix them, as Jane Jacobs argues in *Systems of Survival*,[5] is to invite catastrophe. By their natures, businesses take risks, while governments are cautious. Businesses that don't take risks and governments that do are doomed to fail; such businesses will wither and die, such governments will usually become involved in horrible wars and other catastrophes.

In an effort to achieve its goal of transforming the Canadian government, a key Glassco recommendation was that the powers of the comptroller general be curbed. The comptroller general was a bureaucrat whose office was responsible for spending. He approved everything going out the door, while the auditor general made sure afterwards that the money had been spent properly. A check and a balance. Glassco believed the country needed to be more efficient and less bureaucratic. It recommended – as did many political scientists at the time – that politicians be held accountable for all public spending, which suited the politicians just fine. Not one party challenged that idea at the time, nor does any today. When the comptroller general's power to control spending was eliminated in 1965, nobody even wrote a story about it. The government was now going to be run like a business, which seemed like a very good idea until the hard realities of the arrangement sunk in. The accumulated deficit went from zero in 1965 to $610 billion in 1997. During the same period as this movement took hold internationally, deficits continued to rise, yet private enterprise continued to call for government to be even more "business-like."

The other main thrusts of Glassco's 257 recommendations were clearly political, and had little to do with economic efficiency. These included decentralization of federal government activities and the implementation of a program to include more French Canadians in the federal government, along with official bilingualism.

Diefenbaker was determined to find a place for Quebec in the federal government, and thus cement his Laurier-like aspirations, but he never got the chance. He was turfed out of office before Glassco's final report was made in 1963, and replaced by the Liberal Lester Pearson, who came to power with a minority government. The Liberals were propped up by a rump of six Quebec nationalists known as the Créditistes. The price of their support for Pearson was the implementation of policies favourable to Quebec,[6] and the Liberals, themselves concerned about Quebec, went along. In spite of the turmoil, all federal parties wholeheartedly agreed with and accepted Glassco's recommendations, for each could readily see the obvious advantages in this new order. The politicians would gain more control over spending, more powers would be given to the provinces, and there seemed to be enough left over to appease Quebec. Whatever Diefenbaker's plans might originally have been, they somehow got lost in the translation.

Over the years, the Glassco Commission has been treated by Canadian politicians and media as a mere matter of improved housekeeping, but the impact on Canada was much more profound than that. In a 1992 interview, Cliff Kennedy, an old Justice Department lawyer, was the first to point out to me some of these effects. "A lot of what Glassco did made sense, but what bothered most of us senior public servants at the time was the way Glassco had loosened the chains of accountability. When they took away the powers of the comptroller general, accountability was placed in the hands of the House of Commons which, as they liked to put it, 'allowed it to perform its traditional function as custodian of the purse,'" Kennedy mused. "You know what happened next."

What happened was what Kennedy and other knowledgeable senior bureaucrats feared might occur. All the forces combined – Keynesian economics, the growth of the corporate mentality within government, the decentralization of powers, and the desire to appease Quebec with new policies – meant that the floodgates of the public treasury were opened. Politicians and bureaucrats alike had come to see themselves as entrepreneurs, but they were entrepreneurs unlike any in the private sector. They had the right to spend the public's money while standing as guardians of the federal treasury, an obvious conflict. Successive governments began to invest wildly in real estate, people, and programs. By the time John Turner resigned as finance minister in 1975, corporate tax breaks were saving companies close to $1 billion a year more than they were five years earlier. The government could mint its own money, and never really have to pay for its mistakes. No matter how large the risks a government might take, everyone knew the government could never go bankrupt – a businessman's heaven, as it were.

By the late eighties, the effect of this runaway spending on the economy seized the political agenda, and there were cries for reform. Inspired by the free-market policies of Margaret Thatcher and Ronald Reagan, the prescription for success was that governments should be even more businesslike in their thinking and behaviour, far more than even the Glassco Commission had ever contemplated. The plan now was for the government to put the brakes on spending, come to a full stop, put the pedal to the floor, and speed off in the opposite direction.

The promise of lower taxes sounded like a great idea, and the electorate bought into it. But, as we will see in upcoming chapters, nobody seemed to have a clue about what all this really meant for Canadians. Corporate principles and strategies were going to be applied to government, which presumes that commercial enterprises and public guardian organizations are one and the same, which they most assuredly are not.

A guardian organization, as mentioned, is by its very nature the antithesis of a business. A guardian organization, such as government or the police, is an *un-business*, as it were.

A successful business is driven by the profit motive, which is achieved by minimizing the costs of production and maximizing the sale price of a product. A business invests money to make more money. The risk is that, if it fails, a business may go bankrupt and die. A successful guardian organization is driven by its the ability to serve the needs of the public. In the corporatist view, the product of a guardian organization is service, while the measure of its profit is the theoretically ever-reducing demands on the taxpayer. The only way to increase this "profit" is by cutbacks on services to reduce spending, an entirely negative proposition.

The differences between corporations and guardians are even more profound than this, however. As Jane Jacobs points out, again in *Systems of Survival*, a successful commercial enterprise "must shun force, come to voluntary agreements, be honest, compete, collaborate with strangers and aliens, respect contracts, use initiative and enterprise, be open to inventiveness and novelty, be efficient, promote comfort and convenience, dissent for the sake of the task, invest for productive purposes, be industrious, thrifty, and optimistic." While a business entity might have a moral or ethical code, businesses by their nature are not necessarily moral or ethical. A business may claim to believe in tradition, loyalty, and honour, but it's usually only paying lip service as a way to improve sales. This is not intended as a slight toward business. That's just what business must be: the bottom line is the bottom line.

Guardian organizations, on the other hand, Jacobs says, "must shun trading, exert prowess, be obedient and disciplined, adhere to tradition, respect hierarchy, be loyal, take vengeance, deceive for the sake of the task, make rich use of leisure, be ostentatious, dispense largesse, be exclusive, show fortitude, be fatalistic and treasure honour."[7]

When a guardian tries to think or act like a businessperson, his message gets confusing and distorted. A businessman can say he is going to "kick butt" and not offend anyone, because he is speaking only for himself and his business. When a politician – or a police officer, for that matter – talks tough like a businessman, the words, backed by the power of government, come out stronger than he might like. The more a guardian tries to act like a businessperson, the greater he risks, at best, unpopularity, and, at worst, a revolution. The more government cuts back services to make its "profit," the angrier the electorate becomes with the declining quality of the "product" government is offering.

In the thirty-five years since the Glassco Commission made its recommendation that government think more like a business, the most ironic effect has been the way government now views itself. As it thinks more and more like a business, government likes itself less and less. In the sixties, the hippies demonized the public sector: government, bureaucracy, and the police were called, among other things, pigs. By the late nineties, as government began to think more like a corporation, and encouraged more and more privatization, what in effect it did was demonize itself and the rest of the public sector. Government began to paint itself as the enemy of the people and the public good, and point to private enterprise as a saviour. While in this mode of self-flagellation, public institutions created to protect the greater good, such as the Royal Canadian Mounted Police, have come to see themselves as a drain on the economy. In the interest of "pulling their weight" in the new corporate world of government, decisions are made and policies are implemented that defy the public interest. But they go unquestioned because the public interest is defined only in terms of the bottom line – tax savings. As John Ralston Saul writes in *The Unconscious Civilization*:

The most powerful force possessed by the individual is her own government. Or governments, because a multiplicity of levels means a multiplicity of strengths. The individual has no other organized mechanism that he can call his own. There are other mechanisms, but they reduce the citizen to the status of a subject. Government is the only organized mechanism that makes possible that level of shared disinterest known as the public good. Without this greater interest the individual is reduced to a lesser, narrower being limited to immediate needs. He will then be subject to the other, larger forces, which will necessarily come forward to fill the void left by the withering of the public good. . . . By demonizing the public civil servant they are obscuring the matter of the citizen's legitimacy and of the public good which only that legitimacy can produce. People become so obsessed by hating government that they forget it is meant to be their government and is the only powerful public force they have purchase on. This is what makes the neo-conservative market forces so disingenuous. Their remarkably successful demonization of the public sector has turned much of the citizenry against their own mechanism. They have been enrolled in the cause of interests that have no particular concern for the citizen's welfare. Instead, the citizen is reduced to the status of a subject at the foot of the throne of the marketplace.[8]

• • •

Business-like thinking by government beginning in the mid-sixties set the stage for the current problems facing the Royal Canadian Mounted Police. Back then, most people, never mind the Mounties, did not recognize the potential long-term implications of the Glassco Commission findings. The RCMP could never imagine itself running as a business or even being all that affected by business-like thinking. But there was no escape.

One of the first things the federal government did in the mid-sixties was to turn its attention towards Quebec. In the past the federal government had taken the position that the separatist movement in Quebec was not a serious problem. It wasn't as if the entire province was up in arms. But no business – especially one as large as Canada hoped to be – could market itself successfully without appearing to bring all its units together in one happy enterprise.

In 1968, Pierre Elliott Trudeau was elected prime minister, and immediately his government set in motion the reinvention of Canada over the next sixteen years. Without a comptroller general, the Trudeau government had unprecedented access to the public treasury. The size of the federal government soon appeared to be growing at a fantastic rate – for example, federal expenditures on goods and services rose to $13.9 billion by 1980 from $4.5 billion in 1970. But the federal government wasn't growing in relation to the provinces. In fact, Trudeau had taken another of Glassco's recommendations – decentralization of powers – and divested much federal power to the provinces. Between 1962 and 1978, the federal government's share of public revenues dropped from 47 per cent to 32 per cent. Between 1970 and 1980 federal transfers to the provinces rose to $36.5 billion from $8.4 billion. Even though there were some strings attached, the theory was that the devolution of powers to the provinces brought with it the potential to appease Quebec. Finally, Trudeau brought more Quebeckers to Ottawa and implemented policies, such as official bilingualism and "Francization" in 1974, which put them on the fast track to positions of power. Quebec was going to have its say in Ottawa, and become a true and full partner in Confederation, which, most would agree, seemed to be a fair and rational turn of events.

While most of the political debate during this period and up to the present has been about the devolution of powers to the provinces, there has been little real debate about the impact of all this transition on the police and the justice system. The tendency has been to treat each of them as mere social programs, when, in fact, they are much more than that. In a democracy governed by the rule of law, the police and the justice system are the spine of the country. But this somehow all got lost in the marketing effort for the new and improved Canada, in which the federal government devoted much of its time to appeasing the provinces in the name of national unity.

Beginning with Trudeau, the Royal Canadian Mounted Police began to have a visible Quebec problem, which dovetails perfectly with the fact that Quebec and Quebeckers were being given a greater say over the force and the justice system. That there was friction between the RCMP and Quebec should have come as no surprise. Since its founding in 1873, the force has always been viewed suspiciously by Quebec.

If Canadians had only known about the history of the relationship between the RCMP and Quebec, they might have collectively chosen another course of action.

Chapter Four

·· ● ··

QUEBEC VERSUS THE MOUNTIES

ON MAY 10, 1873, ten wolf hunters from Fort Benton, Montana, crossed into Canada seeking revenge against a band of Assiniboine Indians they suspected of having stolen some horses from them. Lawlessness was the order of the day, and the international boundary was just a line on a government map. The wolf hunters found the natives about sixty-five kilometres south of Medicine Hat and killed thirty-six of them, kidnapping and raping some of the squaws. A few days later, word reached Ottawa about what came to be known as the Cypress Hills Massacre, but the Dominion of Canada was just six years old, and hadn't yet got around to setting up a police force west of Ontario.

The entire North-West, as it was called, had effectively been run by fur-traders as a huge company town until 1869, when Canada purchased the rights and privileges to the land for £300,000 from the London-based Hudson's Bay Company. In 1870, two militia battalions and a detachment of British regulars had been sent west to appease both sides in the aftermath of the rebellion by French-speaking Métis settlers who had not been told about the land sale. Under their leader, Louis Riel, the Métis had set up a provisional government, published a bill of rights, and, as a way of asserting authority, executed Thomas Scott, an Ontario Orangeman, on charges of disorderly conduct, insubordination, and open opposition. With the creation of the province of Manitoba that year, the situation was extremely delicate. John A. Macdonald, Canada's first prime minister, did not want to inflame the already tense religious-racial situation by taking any action which might be construed as anti-French. There were

3.5 million Canadians at the time, three-quarters of whom lived in Ontario and Quebec. French Canadians were already outnumbered two to one in the country, and were beginning to feel threatened by the growing numbers of English speakers.

But the 1873 Cypress Hills Massacre forced Macdonald's hand. Thirteen days after the killings, he introduced enabling legislation authorizing the creation of the North-West Mounted Police. Macdonald, who also served as justice minister, wanted to establish a federal government presence in the North-West which would bring the rule of law to the area, but would also impede any thought of territorial expansion by the United States and protect the aboriginal population.

There was already one federal police force in central Canada, originally known as the Western Frontier Constabulary, established in 1864 by the United Provinces of Canada "to patrol the whole frontier between Toronto and Sarnia." One year after Confederation, in May 1868, the organization had become known as the Dominion Police Force, and its headquarters were moved to Ottawa. Now, the North-West Mounted Police, for a time nicknamed the Manitoba Mounted Rifles, were to be a unique hybrid, a body that combined the mobility of the United States Cavalry with the organization and civil responsibilities of the Royal Irish Constabulary. The legislation dictated that it would be a small, mobile mounted force, with no more than three hundred men – a temporary measure until settlers arrived. The force's jurisdiction extended over most but not all of what is now western Canada, the Yukon, and the Northwest Territories. There were only 275 members, each of whom was paid seventy-five cents a day for his work.

Heading out from Dufferin, the force mounted the Great March West, splitting along the way into different divisions. From the outset the force's mandate was clear; as historian James J. Boulton, put it, "pacifying the Indians and dealing with the refugee Sioux streaming from across the border, policing the illegal whisky trade, and representing some Government offices."

The North-West Mounted Police set up their headquarters in what is now Regina, and continued to grow along with the rest of the North-

West. By the late 1800s, when the total population of Canada was nearing five million, the original restrictions on the size of the force had been amended to meet the demands required, so that the NWMP had been allowed to grow to one thousand members, each an expert horseman of medium height and build. About one-third were French Canadians, about the same proportion as in today's force. The success of the NWMP in dealing with wolf-fur and whisky traders soon earned them a reputation in the United States for always getting their man,[1] but in the rest of Canada they were not so popular. The Mounties were fortunate to survive to the turn of the century, because Canada's economy was a wreck.

A mild depression in 1893 had set off fears of economic doom which were fanned by concerns about the country's rising public debt. The minister of finance in 1895 demanded that unnecessary government spending be eliminated. "Dominion expenditures have risen from $23-million to $38-million," the *Hamilton Times* reported somewhat hysterically in June 1896, adding that the additional new debt from the previous year being the equivalent of "475 wagon loads of one ton each of silver. . . . The total debt now is 17,555 tons of silver . . . a treasure procession over 133 miles long or about as far from Hamilton to Chatham."

Provincialism was rampant, led by Ontario. As historians John Moir and D. M. L. Farr noted in their 1969 book, *The Canadian Experience*:

> The Fathers of Confederation deliberately strengthened the federal government at the expense of the provinces to overcome the sectionalism that had cursed the Provinces of Canada and to avoid the 'states' rights' issue that had caused the American Civil War. . . . Yet, after Confederation the Ontario Liberal party, feeding on many of the prejudices of Upper Canada tradition, spearheaded a movement for 'provincial rights' which, within twenty-five years, upset and partially reversed the balance of power established in 1867. . . . The Toronto *Globe* put the basic assumption of this theory succinctly: 'The Dominion is the creation of these Provinces.'[2]

The paper still propounds this view today.[3]

Decentralization was a key plank in the platform of Wilfrid Laurier, the Liberal leader in the federal election of 1896. Laurier hoped that, by appeasing Ontario and, to a lesser extent, Quebec, he might be successful in his attempt to become the first French Canadian to lead Canada, a difficult proposition for the times. French Canadians were angry with the federal government, especially with the Mounties, who bore much of the resentment over the trial and execution of Métis rebel Louis Riel eleven years earlier.

The French-Canadian antipathy to the federal government was also fuelled by an ongoing debate in Manitoba over the rights of Catholic students to study in separate schools. Then there was the highly charged issue of compensation to the Jesuits, the Catholic religious order, whose vast land holdings and properties had been wrongfully expropriated by the government years earlier. Finally, the last free land had been doled out in the United States west, and covetous eyes were still being cast across the border at "The Last Best West" on Canada's relatively empty prairies. Canada would have liked to have settled that land with people from Great Britain and France, but few of them were interested in taking up the offer on the cold, bleak flatlands. Canada began to seek immigrants from the rest of Europe.

The prospect of all these new Canadians set off a wave of nationalism in Quebec, where it was felt that the new immigrants would tilt the delicate balance of the country towards the English side. Both in the House of Commons and in the Quebec National Assembly, politicians lamented that Canada was not heading in the direction they had envisaged. Instead of a Canada in which French and English would be equal, Manitoba had become another largely English-speaking Ontario rather than another largely French-speaking Quebec. According to historian H. Blair Neatby: "It was clear to French Canadians that their form of Canadian society was not welcome in the Western province."[4]

To win the 1896 election, therefore, Laurier had to tread ever so lightly on the fragile sensibilities of the electorate. As a Liberal and a Catholic, he already had two strikes against him. Both Protestant and Catholic clergy warned their congregations that they risked eternal damnation if they voted Liberal, the Protestants because he was Catholic, the Catholics because he was Liberal. But Laurier's policies appealed to a wide constituency in Ontario and Quebec, partly because of his promotion of a key Quebec-driven issue: increased provincial rights. Shrewd and always ready to compromise, Laurier fashioned a solid electoral victory over the Tories led by Charles Tupper.

Long forgotten in the mists of history is another key plank in Laurier's winning platform: his promise to disband the North-West Mounted Police. In such hard times, the move made economic sense. The country already had the Dominion Police in Ontario, and there existed ample precedent for disbanding a police force. In 1845, an entity called the Mounted Police Force had been raised to quell disorders among workers enlarging the Welland and St. Lawrence canals. It was later decommissioned. In 1849, the Elgin Riots in Montreal, during which the Parliament Building of the United Province of Canada were burned, caused the central council to raise a temporary police force of fifty men, which was called the Mounted Constabulary Force.

The Dominion Police were small and isolated, confined largely to Ottawa. The Mounties, on the other hand, were large and getting larger. Quebec nationalist leaders such as Henri Bourassa were harassing Laurier about Quebec's treatment within Confederation and the diminishing prospects for French Canadians in a more pluralistic country. As the Mounties became more entrenched as a federal institution, the force clearly represented a potential impediment to the consolidation of provincial powers. Ottawa and the provinces had never come to terms about the administration of the law. While Ottawa had the sole right to enact criminal law, the provinces had always demanded the sole right to enforce those laws. The Mounties were created to enforce federal laws and regulations, and not the Criminal Code or Quebec Civil Code. With immigrants flocking west, it was inevitable that the Mounties would continue to grow and expand their reach, duties, and responsibilities. Ontario and Quebec didn't want the federal police force to grow but, at the same time, were reluctant to set up their own full-fledged police forces, relying for the most part on volunteers and private security firms. From Laurier's perspective, for the purpose of ensuring national unity – such as it was – it undoubtedly would have been better if he could have disbanded the Mounties and encouraged the provinces to create their own police forces, which Ontario and Quebec would eventually do, many years later.[5] But Laurier's plan to disband the Mounties became a political impossibility in 1896, oddly enough, because of an ongoing manhunt for an escaped prisoner.

In 1895, a twenty-one-year-old Cree by the name of Almighty Voice had been arrested for killing a steer owned by the Indian Department, near Duck Lake, between Saskatoon and Prince Albert.[6] He eventually escaped custody. He was tracked to Kinistino, eighty kilometres east of Prince Albert, by Sergeant Colin C. Colebrook, the six hundred and fifth man to join the Mounties since 1873. Using a double-barrelled shotgun, Almighty Voice killed Colebrook, who became the nineteenth Mountie to die in the line of duty, making Almighty Voice Canada's Public Enemy Number One. The resulting two-year manhunt ended on May 30, 1897, with a spectacular shoot-out, in which the Mounties used field guns to kill Almighty Voice. Two more Mounties, John R. Kerr and Charles H. Hockin, were slain during the incident.

The case might well have been closed, but renewed fears of a native uprising forced Laurier to postpone his plans for disbanding the Mounties, plans which were, as it turned out, overtaken by other events. Despite opposition from Quebec, a Mountie contingent was sent to fight in the Boer War in South Africa. Their stellar performance resulted in King Edward VII honouring the entire force the next year, by conferring upon it the status of "Royal." It now became the Royal North-West Mounted Police.

It is important to appreciate that Laurier, who one historian has called "the architect of Canadian unity" for his conciliatory policies towards Quebec, was no hero to Quebec nationalists. In the context of the times, the fate of the Mounties might have been a rather minuscule issue, but Laurier's failure to deliver on that and larger issues, caused him to be regarded as a traitor by many in the Quebec political elite.

The next important step in the evolution of the Mounties occurred when Alberta and Saskatchewan were created in 1905. Each province entered into an agreement with the newly named Royal North-West Mounted Police to provide provincial policing. This contract gave the Mounties a guaranteed visible presence in the West, and the much-needed means to expand the organization, something that couldn't be done within the narrow confines of its federal allowance.

The arrangement was to last just twelve years, however. When Alberta and Saskatchewan decided in 1917 to adopt Prohibition, Mountie Commissioner Aylesworth B. Perry unilaterally cancelled the policing contracts with the two provinces. In this day and age he might be considered reckless, but Perry was a man of principle: he thought, and rightly so, that the laws were unenforceable and would bring the administration of justice into disrepute. Alberta and Saskatchewan ploughed ahead, and each set up its own provincial police department, plunging the Mounties back into tricky political waters. The First World War had drained away both members and recruits, so that, in the early years of the war, the numbers had dwindled from 1,200 members to only 303 Mounties on duty in Canada. In 1917, a Mountie contingent was sent to Russia to assist in the international intervention in the Russian civil war.

At the end of the First World War, the notion of eliminating the Mounties was, once again, on Ottawa's agenda. Arguments were made that, since the Mounties were essentially a paramilitary organization, it made sense that the organization be absorbed as a militia into the Canadian army. That's what Quebec wanted, but the province didn't have much influence on the Union government of Conservative Robert Borden, especially after the controversies caused by Quebec's reluctance to participate in the war effort. Borden saw to it that the Mountie strength was restored to 1,200. That and another timely event, to be explained below, helped save the hide of the Horsemen, once again.

After the war, the state of policing in Canada could be described as a virtual free-for-all, similar to what was happening in the United States. Public police forces had begun to spring up in urban centres around the country. In those places law enforcement was easy to define – constables patrolled the streets with a view to preventing crime and protecting public and private property. When crimes were committed, the police investigated, made arrests, laid charges, and brought suspects to court.

The great fear of the day, soon after the Russian Revolution, was a Bolshevik-inspired revolt by the workers, a battle between capitalism and communism. The public police were poorly paid and scattered around the country, with many geographical gaps in between. Police and security agents from Canada, the United States, and even Great Britain crossed each other's borders, conducted investigations, and made arrests at will. Vigilante groups sprang up everywhere. In the United States, for example, the American Protective League was formed in 1917 as a business-supported volunteer agency with quasi-official status as an adjunct to the Department of Justice. By 1918, it had 250,000 part-time spies lurking around North America ferreting out other spies, communists, and draft dodgers for a bounty of fifty dollars a head. Private-investigation and policing agencies such as Pinkerton were being used not only by private citizens and corporations. The Dominion Police themselves used them as secret agents and spies in Canada.

The Dominion Police operated as both a law-enforcement agency and a counter-intelligence service, which was the normal practice for federal policing agencies in most countries then – and is still the case today. During the 1919 Winnipeg General Strike, the Dominion Police were in charge of counter-surveillance, hunting communists. The Mounties were brought in for law enforcement. But it is important to note that the Mounties were a breed apart from other police forces, a paramilitary organization so regimented that they were more like soldiers of the law than peace officers.

What then transpired in Winnipeg brought to a head the issue of the use of private security firms to perform public-policing and counter-intelligence duties for the government. Both the Dominion Police and the Mounties hired private security firms to infiltrate the labourers' movement and serve as spies for them. It was later learned that these secret agents provided the police with a distorted view of what was happening, with tragic consequences. On June 21, a Mountie troop charged into a demonstration of strikers. Firing ensued. Two strikers were killed and twenty wounded in what would come to be called Bloody Saturday. The débâcle startled the government into action. The use of private security firms to do the dirty work of the public police had to be stopped immediately. Days after Bloody Saturday, the federal government passed an order-in-council expanding the scope of duties of the Mounties in all of Canada west of Ontario.

Eight months later, on February 1, 1920, the Mounties merged with the Dominion Police. The new force would be known as the Royal Canadian Mounted Police, and it took over the former Dominion Police headquarters in Ottawa. At the time of the merger, the Dominion Police was empowered to protect the government buildings in Ottawa, the dockyards in Halifax and in Esquimalt, B.C. – and nothing in between. The counter-intelligence wing of the Dominion Police was transformed into the RCMP Security Service. The Dominion Force also had its own fingerprint bureau, the predecessor of today's RCMP National Police Services laboratories in Ottawa.

Prime Minister Borden kept the merger so quiet that Quebec didn't learn about the news until well after the RCMP Act had received Royal Assent. Immediately, Quebec Premier Sir Jean-Lomer Gouin fired back to Parliament a letter, dated February 4, 1920, which read, in part:

I have to state that we made no request in connection with police assistance to the Federal Government and that we do not anticipate that any condition will arise necessitating our having recourse to the Federal Police. . . .

I have always considered that police matters, in the province, are within the exclusive attributes of the provincial governments as being part of the administration of justice, of municipal and local matters in the province.

I have grave doubts as to there being any jurisdiction at all in the Federal authorities in this connection . . . I am inclined to believe that the numerous encroachments upon Provincial rights and powers of which the Federal Government and its commissions have been guilty during the past four or five years have also given them the idea that Provincial rights exist no more.

I can assure you that we feel capable of coping unaided with everything that occurs in this Province in the way of administration of justice
and the protection of the life and property of its inhabitants.[7]

While Gouin was stating the obvious about provincial rights, the underlying message in his letter was apparent: the Mounties have no place or
role in Quebec.

Quebec's opposition aside, and in spite of the fact that they were still
concentrated in the West, the RCMP now could officially call itself a
national police force, reporting only to the federal government. But with
the change came a series of complications. Forty-seven years earlier, when
they had been first formed, the Mounties had started out with what
seemed to be a relatively clear vision of their mandate, which was to
provide policing services and represent the federal government in the
West and the territories. But in absorbing the Dominion Police, the
Mounties also assumed the duties of the Dominion Police as a preventive
and counter-intelligence service. Their domestic security duties included
the vetting of all civil servants. The present-day U.S. Federal Bureau of
Investigation, like most federal police forces around the world, continues
to be similarly constructed.[8]

Five months after sending his letter to the House of Commons, Gouin
resigned as premier of Quebec, after fifteen years in the job. Gouin was
the son-in-law of Honoré Mercier, a former premier who had been forced
out of office in the 1890s because of corruption in the Baie des Chaleurs
Railway scandal. While seen as a progressive industrialist, Gouin was
often described as a tool of powerful financial interests. He once stated
that he would rather have been chairman of the Bank of Montreal than
premier.[9] He also – interestingly, in light of our discussion – has been
described as an ardent federalist, because of the views he expressed in the
Francoeur Debate in 1918, after an anti-conscription riot ended with four
civilians being killed by soldiers in Quebec City. In the 1921 federal election, Gouin ran as a Liberal for a seat in Parliament and won.

Prior to the election, Borden had attempted to address Quebec's
concerns about the justice system and the RCMP. He had made himself

justice minister. On October 1, 1921, Borden's successor, Arthur Meighen, appointed Guillaume-André Fauteux to the subsidiary post of solicitor general in charge of policing. But the tactics were to no avail as Liberal Mackenzie King was elected with a majority government.

Prime Minister King appointed Sir Jean-Lomer Gouin as justice minister, a position he would hold until January 1924, making the man who did not believe in the validity of the Mounties as a federal police force the top law officer in the country. It was an important precedent. Until the watershed year of 1982, when the Constitution was repatriated from Great Britain and the Charter of Rights and Freedoms was enacted, French-Canadian politicians dominated justice portfolios. Between 1921 and 1982, under mostly Liberal rule, the attorney general's office was usually reserved for the prime minister's Quebec lieutenant. In that sixty-one-year period, French Canadians held or controlled the post for forty years. The solicitor general was French Canadian for forty of the sixty-one years, as well. Since 1982, with the three brief exceptions of John Turner, Joe Clark, and Kim Campbell, the prime minister has hailed from Quebec.

Controlling the growth of the federal justice system and the spread of the federal police was always on the mind of Quebec and, to a lesser extent, on that of Ontario. For example, Quebec premier Alexandre Taschereau and Ontario premier G. Howard Ferguson proclaimed the "Compact Theory" of Confederation at the Dominion Provincial Conference in 1927. In *The History of Canada*, Kenneth McNaught describes this as "a position which would give near autonomy to the provinces and which saw federal powers being merely delegated to Ottawa by the provinces."[10]

The implications for federal policing were serious. The Criminal Code is designed to protect property and individual rights within society. Each case stands on its own, and it makes implicit sense that the provinces be responsible for enforcing the Criminal Code in their respective jurisdictions. Federal police, on the other hand, enforce laws and regulations that are designed to protect the greater good. The simple way to understand what federal policing entails is to consider the duties of any federal department. The Mounties investigate crimes against the public treasury, as well as enforce acts affecting areas such as customs, immigration, taxation, drugs, the environment, the protection of wildlife, and the combating of organized crime, which covers only a small portion of the range of their duties and responsibilities. These are laws which validate the presence and role of the federal government in our everyday lives. Many Quebec nationalists object to these laws on principle, no matter how sound and useful they might be, and to the police force empowered to uphold them. Meanwhile, Ontario, today, doesn't mind the RCMP presence, but the course of events since 1920 has caused the force to develop as an almost invisible presence in the province.

For the RCMP to grow from 1920 to the present, it had to do so in a manner that may best be described as a negative response to the early opposition of Ontario and Quebec. It had to find alternative ways of proving its worth. Like a plant prevented from reaching its natural height, it began to sprout branches in a wide and awkward fashion, straining for stability.

In 1928, cash-poor Saskatchewan realized that it could no longer afford the luxury of its own provincial police force. It asked the RCMP to come back into Saskatchewan and police the province on contract. On June 1 of that year, the Mounties absorbed the Saskatchewan Provincial Police and embarked on a tangent that proved to be both the salvation of the force and its Achilles heel. The contract with Saskatchewan dictated that the Mounties operate a police force on a turnkey basis. The federal government subsidized the province on the grounds that the Mounties were providing federal law-enforcement services as part of their duties. Without a formidable or credible presence in central Canada, the Mounties were desperate to be visible and, as it turned out, proved to be rather good at the job of provincial and municipal policing. However, in setting out down this road, the Mounties saw their purity of purpose become a little more distorted and often difficult to define. All Mounties in Saskatchewan reported to two masters. In terms of administration and operations within the province, the Mounties took direction from or reported to the provincial attorney general or his equivalent. The province paid the bills. But, no matter who paid the bills, for every

Mountie the RCMP commissioner in Ottawa came first. He controlled their ultimate fate.

In 1932, in the midst of the Great Depression, the federal government cut similar deals and the RCMP absorbed the provincial forces in Manitoba, Nova Scotia, New Brunswick, Prince Edward Island, and Alberta, as well as the Preventive Service of the National Revenue Department. In 1950, a year after Newfoundland joined Confederation, the Mounties took in the Newfoundland Rangers and, in the same year, the British Columbia Provincial Police. Before long, the force began taking on municipal-policing contracts, as well.

In 1950, the RCMP had slowly doubled its size to become a force of 2,350 men, distributed across the nation, with one huge exception – the heartland of Ontario and Quebec. Having the Mounties police their provinces would have been anathema to them. In Ontario and Quebec, the Mounties would continue to be seen as outsiders, mostly Western farm boys, known more for their Musical Ride and splendid uniforms than for their role as an important and relevant agency responsible for the enforcement of federal laws and regulations.

Over the first forty-five years of its existence, therefore, the RCMP had pretty well been held in check and never presented much of a threat to Quebec sovereignty. Ironically enough, that began to change in the wake of the Glassco Commission, which urged modernization and business-like thinking. Quebec would soon have its back up about the Mounties.

George B. McClellan, the twelfth commissioner of the RCMP, took office on November 1, 1963, just as the Glassco Commission made its final report. McClellan, an old-fashioned street cop, interpreted Glassco's findings in his own way. If he was going to be an entrepreneur, his product would be law enforcement Canada had never before experienced. McClellan realized that the RCMP had become a bit of a caricature of itself. The strict regimental attitudes, necessary in the war-like atmosphere of the Old West, were now an anachronism. For example, after the Second World War, the boom in personal automobiles forced the Mounties to expand its own fleet. As vehicles became smaller and sleeker, individual Mounties found it difficult to get in and out of the cars, since the force dress code dictated that each officer must wear his full uniform at all times, including felt hat, breeches, and long boots. McClellan changed the dress order, simply replacing those items with a cloth cap, blue trousers, and ankle boots or oxfords. The outcry was so great one might have thought he had committed treason. Former Mounties and politicians up to former prime minister John Diefenbaker decried the change, arguing that it sullied the splendid traditions of the Mounties, but McClellan ignored them.

McClellan persevered in more substantive areas, as well. The RCMP had developed as a monolithic entity dominated by police officers with street experience and horse sense, most of whom had some kind of military background. McClellan wanted the Mounties to be more sophisticated, like the federal police in the United States. There, in such agencies as the FBI, the U.S. Postal Inspection Service, and the Bureau of Alcohol, Tobacco and Firearms, investigators were considered specialists. Many had university degrees, even law degrees, as a prerequisite for entering their respective forces. McClellan and his advisers also realized that, whereas each specialized U.S. agency had a clear mandate and vision, the Mounties were having trouble focusing on what exactly they were supposed to be doing. The force had begun as a federal policing agency, but it was hardly that now. The impetus to survive and become credible had forced the RCMP to expand its reach and power base. It now did every kind of policing imaginable in cities, provinces, and at the federal level. It was guarding politicians, diplomats, and other dignitaries, and operating a counter-intelligence service, among many other things. There was no simple answer to the question, What does a Mountie do? There had rarely been a moment in almost a century when the RCMP had not found itself on the defensive, trying to prove to governments just how valuable and important it was. In a relatively short period of time, it had been transmuted into a rather bizarre hybrid – an organization that took on almost everything under the sun so that it could justify calling itself a national police force as opposed to just a federal one.

McClellan recognized that the force had not been keeping up with the times. His ambition was to strengthen the federal policing area, which most Canadians tend to assume is the *raison d'être* of the RCMP. He was convinced that specialization was the remedy to much that ailed the force. He wanted the best investigators, technicians, and scientists, so that the RCMP would be recognized as one of the most sophisticated police forces in the world.

In the mid-sixties Canada, as today, was being swamped by a wave of fraud. Banks, insurance companies, individuals, other police forces, and the federal bureaucracy itself were up in arms about the high degree of lawlessness to be found in the commercial world. The laws and policing had not kept up with the developments in the criminal world. McClellan wanted to change that. It was at that point the Commercial Crime Branch was organized, as an elite investigative unit founded on function rather than territory. Based in Ottawa, it would investigate major fraud any-where in the country, and thereby not be subjected to local controls or corruption.

The Commercial Crime Branch began conducting investigations in 1968. Under the direction of commanding officer Henry Jensen, it soon attracted the best Mounties to its ranks, and before long became the most prestigious unit within the RCMP, the launching pad for future leaders of the force. McClellan and his followers instilled a sense of mission in these men. In the ensuing years, Crime Branch members led the charge in turf wars against all potential rivals, blocking initiatives by other agencies to set up other federal services with full policing powers in areas such as the treasury, taxation, customs and excise, immigration, and the post office. But, as the Mounties charged ahead with their new mandate, no one seemed to realize that, ultimately, the seeds of the intended demise of federal policing had already been planted. As large and powerful as it might have appeared to some, the RCMP was not particularly well designed or organized to defend the public interest, and was extremely vulnerable to a political attack.

First, there had been the Glassco Commission, with its recommenda-tions about decentralization, bilingualism, and government operating more like a business. Next had come the Royal Commission on Bilingualism and Biculturalism, one of the first actions taken by Liberal

Lester B. Pearson after he was elected prime minister in April 1963. Pearson, who had won the Nobel Peace Prize in 1957 for his part in settling the Suez Crisis, was a career diplomat. According to his biographers, he was the kind of man who was never sure of himself and could be easily influenced, especially by people he felt were more experienced than he.[11] Pressed by the six Quebec nationalists propping up his minority government, Pearson (who had already expressed sympathy to the issue) announced the B & B Commission, as it came to be called, on July 22, 1963, in the heat of separatist threats. Ten days earlier, the Queen Victoria monument in Montreal had been destroyed by a terrorist explosion. The political consensus at the time was that Canada was passing through a major crisis in its history and that something had to be done urgently to prevent the country from breaking up.

On April 6, 1966, Pearson had responded to the B & B recommendations, announcing that his government had taken the first steps to make the federal civil service bilingual. In *Lester Pearson and the Dream of Unity*, Peter Stursberg wrote:

> In his statement to Parliament Mr. Pearson said that it was important that all Canadian citizens, whether English-speaking or French-speaking, should have a fair and equal opportunity to participate in the national administration and to feel at home in Ottawa, the national capital. . . . Beginning in 1967, university graduates recruited for the civil service, would have to be bilingual or be willing to acquire a reasonable proficiency in both official languages. By 1975, promotion would depend on bilingual proficiency or willingness to acquire it. . . . However, Mr. Pearson pointed out that bilingualism was required only for positions where a need existed for both languages.[12]

Although bilingualism was not departmental policy until almost the mid-seventies, a wave of French Canadians began flooding into Ottawa and making their presence known. From today's perspective, most Canadians seem to recall that the notion of bilingualism was widely accepted, with the only criticisms coming from rednecks and the like. But that was not the case in the late sixties. Many were concerned about the possible implications, including a number of leading Quebeckers.

MP Maurice Sauvé warned that the policy "will not satisfy Quebeckers and will antagonize the rest of Canada." While supporting in theory the concept of official bilingualism, former Quebec premier Jean Lesage observed, "I believe that governments should avoid legislating on two matters – very important matters – which are language and religion. The history of the world tells us that there always has been more harm than good that came out of any legislation touching either language or religion." Former Ontario premier John Robarts, who later became part of the B & B process, stated, "Bilingualism and the language question was perhaps the focus but . . . I saw few problems between French-Canada and the rest of Canada that a good 15 per cent increase in the standard of living wouldn't cure."[13]

In the context of the times, Pearson's implementation of official bilingualism and biculturalism in 1966 seemed morally, ethically, and politically correct. From the outset, however, Pearson's policies failed to bear the intended fruit for the federal government, as Sauvé had warned. No matter how hard Ottawa tried to appease Quebec, all the efforts seemed wasted. There was virtually no indication that the bilingualism policy was having any positive effect on separatist attitudes towards federalism either. In fact, the response was quite the opposite: the more Canada tried to embrace Quebeckers, the more the separatists lashed out at the federal government.

In the late sixties the battle rose to new heights, climaxing with the October Crisis of 1970. Pierre Trudeau, who had become prime minister in 1968, invoked the War Measures Act and called out the army after British diplomat James Cross and Quebec cabinet minister Pierre Laporte were kidnapped. Laporte was later murdered.

Then everything then seemed to go quiet for a few years. In the meantime, Commissioner McClellan, the hard-nosed, old-style cop, had retired in 1967, to be replaced by Frank Lindsay (1967–69) and then by Len Higgitt (1969–73). Each was considered to be a weaker leader, without much vision and more amenable to the views of government.

Higgitt's background was in the counter-intelligence Security Service wing of the force.

RCMP employees attached to the Security Service were considered agents of the government and not peace officers. As in similar services around the world, a Chinese Wall existed between the two sides of the force, and the police in the RCMP and the Security Service members didn't have much truck with each other. The popular perception was that the police side was made up of straight-ahead, by-the-book coppers, while the Security Service attracted the more intellectual types. The Security Service had two main operational duties: detecting Soviet agents operating in Canada and, beginning in the early sixties, keeping an eye on the Quebec separatist movement. A 1968 royal commission chaired by Maxwell Mackenzie had recommended that the Security Service be split off from the RCMP, but Trudeau sat on the recommendation. The RCMP had successfully argued that it would be wrongheaded to do so and potentially dangerous for the federal structure and security if such a division were to take place.

In the next few years, the animosity between the RCMP and Quebec would reach war-like levels, but not in the way most people remember.

What Canadians tend to remember about the RCMP and Quebec in the seventies are controversial counter-intelligence operations by the Security Service, such as the burning of a barn and a break-in at a suspected separatist newspaper. But again, it's important to remember that the Security Service members were effectively agents of the government and not law-enforcement officers.

Canadians tend to forget what the RCMP police were accomplishing in criminal investigations during the same period, especially after the October Crisis. Throughout the sixties, Quebec had become recognized as a bastion of organized criminal fraud in North America. The provincial government, the Justice Department, and the courts seemed oblivious to or uninterested in the crime wave, and the record shows that police forces had become so corrupted that they served more as security guards for the criminals than as protectors of the public. Around 1970, the RCMP Commercial Crime Branch was involved in a series of controversial investigations, the most spectacular of which had one common denominator – Quebec. It seemed that no matter where in Canada the Mounties began a serious fraud investigation – on the stock exchanges, in Hamilton Harbour, or in some obscure company's files – the trail would inevitably lead back to some of the most prominent business leaders and politicians in Quebec, including Premier Robert Bourassa himself. As one investigation led to another, the skeletons were tumbling out of Quebec closets faster than the doors could be bolted shut. By the events that followed, it appeared that Quebec – the nation – was desperate for relief, for a way to harness the Mounties and neutralize what it must have perceived to be a federal attack on its integrity.[14]

Since the time of Laurier, Quebec had been searching for ways to neutralize and even dismantle the RCMP. In July 1974, the issue of the Security Service finally exploded in the form of an actual bomb. Robert Samson, a member of the Security Service, was injured after a device detonated prematurely outside the Montreal house of supermarket executive Melvyn Dobrin. Samson was arrested and charged over the incident, and it was soon learned he was doing freelance work for a Montreal crime boss who wanted to send a message to Dobrin. Samson was charged with the crime and dismissed from the Security Service.

When Ottawa had begun to beef up its French-Canadian contingent after the Glassco and B & B Commission recommendations, one of the first to answer the siren call was Samson. He joined the Mounties during the height of the October Crisis, benefiting from the lowering of standards that occurred as the RCMP rushed to increase its French-Canadian representation. "A few years earlier Samson wouldn't have even got an interview," says one former high-ranking Mountie who knew him. "But there was a demand for French Canadians to serve as counter-intelligence agents in the coming 'war' in Quebec, so he got hired." After training, Samson was assigned immediately to the Security Service. He was never a police officer.

At his trial in 1976, Samson blurted out that, while in the Security Service, he had broken into the offices of a left-wing newspaper, *L'Agence Press Libre*, to steal a list of the names of militant separatists. He said he had accomplices from the Security Service, the Montreal police, and the Sûreté du Québec. The admission resulted in the Quebec government setting up a public inquiry under lawyer Jean Keable, who provoked a confrontation with Ottawa over the incident, demanding access to federal government files. The Quebec Department of Justice eventually laid charges against one member from each force – for authorizing a search without a search warrant. The three pleaded guilty, were given unconditional discharges, and returned to their duties. Then the tensions seemed to die down a bit, but it was the calm before the storm. On November 15, 1976, René Lévesque led the separatist Parti Québécois to victory over Bourassa's Liberals in the provincial election. Now in control, the separatists were going to turn up the heat on Canada.

In May 1977, two Security Service malcontents, Donald McCleery and Gilles Brunet, surfaced, complaining about their dismissal from the force four years earlier. They were let go after RCMP police investigators reported to the commissioner about their suspicious activities and association with undesirables in the Montreal area. McCleery and Brunet brought their case to federal deputy attorney general Roger Tassé and his assistant, Louis-Philippe Landry, part of the growing French-Canadian cadre with the federal public service. The appeasement of Quebec was the number-one item on the political agenda of the day, and Quebeckers were entirely in charge of what was going to happen. Responding to the rather thin allegations by McCleery and Brunet, and the recommendations of Tassé, Landry, and Solicitor General Francis Fox (a Montrealer), on July 6, 1977, the federal government called a Royal Commission of Inquiry Concerning Certain Activities of the Royal Canadian Mounted Police. It was headed by Mr. Justice David C. McDonald of the Alberta Supreme Court.

Conducting their inquiries contemporaneously, McDonald and Keable unearthed story after story about the Security Service. One of Keable's findings included the 1972 burning of a barn located on a farm at Sainte-Anne-de-la-Rochelle in the Eastern Townships of Quebec. The farm was owned by relatives of Jacques and Paul Rose, two of the FLQ kidnappers involved in the October Crisis. McCleery said that he had had information that the barn was going to be the site of a meeting between the FLQ and the militant U.S. group the Black Panthers. The Mounties found they couldn't put a listening device in the barn, so they decided to burn it down and so thwart the meeting. The meeting never took place.

Other revelations about the Security Service's activities soon emerged. Agents had opened the mail of suspected terrorists, which security agents in most democratic countries can legally do with a court order. A phony communiqué had been sent to discredit an FLQ member, another normal tactic of counter-intelligence agents. There had been break-ins, including one at the headquarters of the separatist Parti Québecois in search of a list of supporters – again, not unusual as a pre-emptive strike in a potential civil war. The problem for the Security Service was that Canadian law had never anticipated such a situation. There were no precedents or legal remedies or protection for the Security Service, so sometimes the members resorted to drastic measures to carry out their duties and protect the integrity of their country. Over the years the Security Service had been particularly effective in infiltrating and neutralizing Quebec terrorists, especially the FLQ. At times poor judgement had been exercised by Security Service members. A potential informant had been kidnapped, and some electronic surveillance had been illegal.

From their inceptions the Keable and McDonald inquiries and most of the media covering them rarely distinguished between the police, the Security Service, or the RCMP, using all three interchangeably in their public statements. Outside Quebec, naturally, despite the headlines in some papers, the majority of the public were only mildly concerned about what the Security Service had done. Across the country, however, opposition politicians and civil libertarians, along with Quebec separatists, were whipping themselves into a frenzy about the problems with "the police." The RCMP were called anti-democratic and abusers of the rule of law, leaving a lasting impression that the Mounties had been corrupt, dangerous, and out of control.[15]

In the end McDonald, and even Keable, were forced to conclude that, on balance, the RCMP as an organization hadn't done anything seriously wrong. They found that every action taken by Security Service agents had been done in response to a situation and without the knowledge or approval of headquarters. They had been acting on their own initiative. McDonald made a series of recommendations in 1981. He suggested that the Security Service be removed from the RCMP and civilianized and that the RCMP implement a system of checks and balances to ensure that its members weren't running off on their own any longer. The stated intention of the controls was the proper supervision of Security Service agents. The effect was something else. The RCMP police investigators, who were not part of the Security Service or party to their actions, were brought under entirely new constraints, even though policing was not a part of McDonald's original mandate, nor had there been any complaints about the performance and integrity of the RCMP police services.

It wasn't until a dozen years later that what might have been the most interesting news about the entire affair came out. In 1993, CBC television journalist Victor Malarek reported that Gilles Brunet, the ex-Security Service member who started the "Security Service scandal," had been a paid agent of the Soviet Union. His job was to destabilize the Canadian government. The news didn't come as much of a surprise to most members of the RCMP. "He was booted off the force in the first place because we knew there was something wrong about him. Brunet lived a lifestyle in the early seventies that I couldn't afford today," said one senior officer. Yet others voiced deeper suspicions that the traditional tensions between Quebec and the RCMP had reached a new level. "Most who knew about him in the Mounties think he wasn't just working for the Soviets, though. His real masters were in Quebec City."

While it's not outside the realm of possibility that Quebec was running a counter-intelligence operation against the federal government and its police force, the reality of the situation was that the RCMP was made vulnerable because Canadians themselves don't understand what the force represents in society. The reason for this is largely that so many Canadians themselves seem to be confused by the term *federalism* and what it really means in Canada.

Chapter Five

.... • ....

THE TRUDEAU EFFECT: FEDERALISM AS A BUSINESS

IN ANY CONSIDERATION of what the Royal Canadian Mounted Police are or might be, one must first come to understand what Canada is or seems to be. The name Canada defines a single political entity under one flag from the Atlantic Ocean to the Pacific. The Canadian government is elected to represent the interests of all the people. It is by definition a big government whose view is the big picture; that is, the government, its bureaucracy, and the justice system collectively serve as guardians whose role it is to protect the public – they are defenders of the greater good.

If only it were all so simple, but when it comes to Pierre Elliott Trudeau, nothing is ever as simple as it first appears.

Over the past four decades, the politician who has come the closest to personifying this description of Canada is Trudeau, prime minister from 1968 to 1984.[1] As prime minister, Trudeau is usually best remembered for three major accomplishments:

1) Expanding the size of the federal government;
2) Facing down the Quebec separatist movement during the October Crisis in 1970; and,
3) Repatriating the Constitution from Great Britain and enacting the Charter of Rights and Freedoms.

The legacy of Trudeau as an ardent federalist and a great Canadian nationalist seems assured and secure. I even helped contribute to this reputation in my previous book, *Above the Law*, when I recounted a number of incidents in which Trudeau defended the Royal Canadian Mounted Police, and protected their power base as a federal police force. In one instance he blocked an initiative by the Treasury Department to have its own investigators sworn in as peace officers to investigate phony bankruptcies and other financial crimes. Trudeau accepted the argument put forward at the time by the RCMP that splitting off jurisdictions might not be in the best interests of the RCMP or the country. This precedent was used to help defeat other such initiatives along the way, from the post office, revenue, immigration, and customs and excise. In another incident in the mid-seventies, Trudeau comforted beleaguered RCMP commercial-crime investigator Rod Stamler during a controversial investigation involving the Hamilton Harbour commissioners, which seemed to be leading back to a Trudeau cabinet minister, influential politicians in Quebec, and powerful business friends of the Liberal Party. Trudeau took the unusual step of meeting in his House of Commons office with Stamler to assure him that neither he nor any one of his ministers would ever interfere in the federal police investigation. During that meeting, Trudeau told Stamler that, in a democracy, politicians must never know what the police are investigating. If the practice were otherwise, then the rule of law might be usurped by the rule of politicians, and the democracy endangered.

Trudeau appeared to be not only a great defender of Canada as a strong, national entity, but also, in many ways, a living symbol of the country. Impressions, however, as powerful as they might be, can be misleading, sometimes very much so.

When I first conceived the idea for this book and began to conduct research for it, my intention was to try to understand why the RCMP was failing to serve the national interest in its federal policing capacity. Canada is one of the richest countries in the world, but the federal government was claiming that it didn't have enough money to properly finance its major police force, so that it might conduct thorough and much-needed national and multinational commercial-crime investigations. My underlying assumption was that Trudeau, the great defender of the rule of law and protector of the RCMP, would never have intended that the federal police force fall into such disarray.

Like many Canadians, my own memory of Trudeau was that he was both a statesman and a political idealist who stood for a strong, central government. In my research, however, I found to my surprise abundant evidence that my own interpretation of what Trudeau stood for had been mistaken. I thought of Trudeau as a great federalist, which, to me, was synonymous with him being a great Canadian nationalist. Such a conclusion seemed logical under the circumstances. In the great, ongoing battle between federalists and separatists, I had come to identify federalism with both Trudeau and the accompanying notion of a strong, central government. I didn't appreciate that, when Trudeau used the word *federal*, it did not mean the same as it did to me.

When the Dominion of Canada was founded in 1867, our first prime minister, John A. Macdonald, described the federalist structure of Canada this way: "A general government and legislature for general purposes with local governments and legislatures for local purposes." The intention of the founding fathers was that there be a strong, central government and Parliament, but with an ample measure of autonomy and self-government for each of the federating communities. The federal government would serve the interests of all Canadians – "peace, order and good government" – while the local level would administer "property and civil rights." In other words, the federal government was the protector of the "Greater Good," while the provincial and local governments were more concerned with day-to-day matters. That's an accurate general description of how the federal system works today in the United States, but not in Canada.

In Canada, the definition of *federal* has changed. This started in Macdonald's own lifetime, originating with decisions in the courts and strong opposition from the provinces, especially Ontario. In latter days, it accelerated, especially because of what happened during the Trudeau years, between 1968 and 1984. In this quiet "evolution," the provinces seized a greater share of revenues, responsibilities, and power from the federal government. As federalism changed, so did the guardian role of the federal government and its institutions, such as the Royal Canadian Mounted Police. Today, the RCMP's role as a federal police force is clearly under attack from the federal government, odd as that might seem. As pointed out in Chapter Two, each Canadian is paying only a little more than ten dollars per person for federal policing by the RCMP, and just $1.22 each for commercial-crime investigation, and even those paltry budgets are scheduled to be reduced. There is no public pressure on the government to weaken the RCMP's federal policing capacity; in fact, it is quite the contrary. In the face of the spectacular rise in multi-provincial and international commercial crime, Canadians want more and better police investigators. Yet the federal government seems oblivious to the lack of logic in its actions and remains reluctant to change course. Instead it continues to encourage the "privatization" of much commercial-crime investigation and the virtual decriminalization of commercial crime, in the name of efficiency or budgetary restraint.

In an era of unprecedented private wealth, these rationalizations don't wash. It doesn't make sense that, while the mandate, responsibilities, and powers of the federal police are slowly being strangled, the federal government can remain virtually unconcerned about the RCMP's gasps for breath and the serious public-policy implications that lie therein. There is clearly more going on here than meets the eye. The RCMP is the most visible and – other than Parliament – the most important federal institution linking the country sea to sea, yet the federal government is reluctant to provide enough financing to maintain the organization as a strong, independent public guardian. Why is the government so hard on the RCMP's federal policing role?

As difficult as the struggle to survive has been for the RCMP since its inception in 1873, life has never been more difficult for the Mounties as it has been in the wake of the policies and decisions made by the Trudeau governments, beginning in the late sixties. Much of what is happening to the RCMP today is a logical extension of the course Pierre Trudeau set for the country as a whole. When Canadians think of Trudeau, they may see a great federalist. But what did Trudeau mean by the word *federal*?

Trudeau was first elected as a Member of Parliament in the 1965 federal election, in which Lester Pearson was returned for his second and last minority government. In 1965, the final recommendations made by the Glassco Commission were being implemented. As discussed earlier, the key recommendations of the commission were that the federal government should devolve some of its powers to the provinces, the federal government should act more like a business, politicians and not bureaucrats should be held accountable for spending, and room should be made for more Quebeckers both in Ottawa and in the federal civil service across the country.

Trudeau was one of the leading thinkers in Quebec, and the Glassco Commission recommendations in many ways dovetailed nicely with the new political and economic philosophies popular in Quebec. Until the fifties, Quebec had been a rather insular place, where the dominant force in society was the Catholic Church. Quebeckers weren't all that interested in Canada, which to many was distant and foreign. By the sixties, with the Quiet Revolution and the explosion in modern communications and multinational businesses, Quebec began to shift away from an almost feudal society controlled by the Church to a more secular one. With the demise of the Church's influence and the growth of the branch-plant economy, the entrepreneurial spirit which had long been an important component of the Quebec psyche rose to the surface. It is important to remember that the educated Quebec elite had read the same books and articles as everyone else, including the members of the Glassco Commission: the writings of Hume, Durkheim, and Keynes, and their apostles. In Quebec, however, these ideas struck a slightly different chord than they had elsewhere. In Quebec during the fifties, the dominant theme of higher education was that the only way Quebec could survive as a distinct nation was if it were to be economically and, many argued, politically independent.

Neither of these thrusts were new to the province. Laurier, the first prime minister from Quebec, fought – unsuccessfully – for greater provincial rights and freer trade with the United States at the turn of the century. But in the late fifties and early sixties, the talk of freer trade was back, with a few twists. The popular sentiment was that government should operate more like a business, with the result that Quebec would someday become wealthy enough to protect its own culture, and, if necessary, separate from Canada, if it wished to do so. Second, as a society now freeing itself from the stern and unforgiving rule of the Catholic Church, Quebec wasn't much interested in the government as a public guardian. Quebec's future was business, a means to an end, and nothing would stand in the way.

In the previous chapter we saw how Pearson, the Nobel Prize-winning conciliator, had decided to appease Quebec by implementing a policy of bilingualism and biculturalism, which was not met with all that much enthusiasm from those on either side of the debate. Nevertheless, Pearson believed that giving official recognition to the concept of two equal founding nations in Canada would help stave off the separatists. It is important to note that Pearson explicitly did not want to rush the country blindly into a possible public-policy nightmare. Pearson's plan was to move slowly and cautiously and to gradually introduce bilingualism and biculturalism, *where needed.*

Pearson's three key political advisers during this period were a powerful triumvirate of important Quebeckers in Ottawa: Trudeau, Marc Lalonde, and Michael Pitfield. They went along with Pearson's plodding until Pearson resigned and was replaced by Trudeau in 1968. Once Trudeau was named prime minister, Pearson's three Quebec advisers had an extraordinary influence: Trudeau ran the government, Pitfield the civil service, and Lalonde the Liberal Party. No sooner was Pearson out the door, than the three seized the moment. They brought with them to Ottawa made-in-Quebec solutions to the problem of Quebec separatism, and were breathtakingly persistent in implementing their plans.

On July 25, 1969, the Trudeau government pushed the Official Languages Act through Parliament, making English and French the official languages of Canada. Trudeau's intention was that such a prerequisite would create the conditions for Quebeckers to land jobs easily in the federal civil service. But things didn't quite work out that way, as former RCMP deputy commissioner Henry Jensen notes: "At the beginning of bilingualism there were all kinds of special programs for English to learn French and French to learn English. It was an exciting time. People were flying everywhere across the country. There were all kinds of language exchanges. Dollars didn't matter, because most people were behind the government's initiative. By the early seventies, however, it became clear that English Canadians were adapting quickly to the new reality and starting to build up their French-language proficiency."

As English-speaking Canadians jumped at the opportunity to learn French and reconcile their differences with their Quebec cousins, their very enthusiasm and success began to undermine the Trudeau government's plans. Not enough Quebeckers were making it to Ottawa or, once there, rising through the ranks as quickly as had been intended. So Trudeau came up with another measure to increase the number of French Canadians within the federal bureaucracy. In 1973, a new policy was implemented which stated that bilingualism alone would no longer be the measure for promotion, but rather "francophone participation." That is, French Canadians – the vast majority of whom were native Quebeckers – would be given designated positions in the government and its institutions. "Trudeau delivered the message in spades to the members of the RCMP," Jensen said.

The wave of Quebeckers entering the federal bureaucracy became a tsunami. Who could complain? It seemed like the right thing to do. The grand plan was for all Canadians to be treated equally, which meant, for the most part, that they would get service from the federal government in the founding language of their choice. Few challenged the logic, because the overriding concern was that something be done to keep the country intact.

While the Trudeau government might have been excited about official bilingualism, it didn't care at all for the other half of Pearson's vision, biculturalism. Trudeau believed that adopting such a policy "could be interpreted as lending support to the 'two nations' view of Canada, and might be seen to be playing into the hands of separatists."[2] That sounded like a good argument for a federalist to make. In 1971, Trudeau adopted and energetically promoted an alternative policy – multiculturalism – which, to many Canadians, seemed once again like the right idea for the times. Trudeau's stated intention was that "such a policy should help break down discriminatory attitudes and jealousies. National unity, if it is to mean anything in the deeply personal sense, must be founded on confidence in one's own *individual* identity; out of this can grow respect for that of others and a willingness to share ideas, attitudes and assumptions. A vigorous policy of multiculturalism will help create this initial confidence. It can form the base of a society which is based on fair play for all."[3]

But multiculturalism, as implemented by the Trudeau government, brought its own pitfalls. The program was set up in such a way as to provide a power base for the Liberals among ethnic communities across the country. The biggest problem with multiculturalism was that, no matter how good the plan might have sounded to the rest of Canada, it landed with a thud in Quebec. Since Laurier's day – and Trudeau, Lalonde, and Pitfield, all scholarly men, had to know this – Quebec nationalists feared such policies, because their very success automatically diminished Quebec's influence within Canada. If anything, Trudeau's multiculturalism policy inflamed Quebec nationalists of all degrees. This is an important consideration because, as more and more Quebeckers moved into positions of power within federal institutions, many must have come with an agenda that implicitly contradicted what the federal government said it was hoping to achieve. Considering the history of multiculturalism and Quebec, one had to wonder what the Trudeau government was thinking.

•   •   •

Now, let's leave the biculturalism and multiculturalism thread and pick up another one, which we have already seen affecting the RCMP, the issue of government operating as a business. The Quebeckers who came to Ottawa in the mid-sixties – among the key ones, Trudeau, Marc Lalonde, and Michael Pitfield – described themselves as technocrats. To a man they were far from idealists. They were among the leading advocates of a school of thought in Quebec that promoted business-like thinking and scientific innovation in government affairs. Once in Ottawa, the record shows, they saw themselves as modern managers determined to bend the entire, stodgy federal bureaucracy to their collective will.

As we have seen, when Trudeau became prime minister in 1968, the floodgates of the public treasury were wide open, courtesy of the Glassco Commission's recommendation that the guardian powers of the comptroller general be abolished. That happened in 1965, and from that point on, federal politicians had no independent bureaucratic overseer of their spending. They could virtually mint their own money and spend it at will. The high-minded technocrats in the Trudeau government were perfectly positioned. Their mandate was that the government should operate more like a business, and to conduct itself in this fashion, the government would have to "invest" in the means of production.

It didn't take long for the Trudeau government to appreciate the potential of this confluence of events and philosophies. It began spending public money like no other government in Canadian history. The sheer magnitude of the spree gave many Canadians the distinct impression that the prime minister was a strong Canadian nationalist, because his government was spending so much federal money. The government splurged on expensive programs, real estate, and employment. Across the country, and especially in Ottawa, federal buildings began to sprout from the ground. Between 1964 and 1975, the membership of the federal civil service expanded from 200,000 to 300,000. "In 1969, the last year of a balanced federal budget, and after a century that included two world wars, the federal debt was about $20-billion. By 1984, after fifteen years of peace, during which spending on national defence had declined from 20 per cent to 10 per cent of the total, the deficit was $38-billion (54 per cent of revenues) and the debt was $200-million."[4]

But all this spending tended to mask something more insidious: the federal government wasn't getting stronger, it was getting fatter. It was the provinces who were bulking up on muscle – and none more so than Quebec. The Glassco Commission had advocated the decentralization of powers, and Trudeau came to power with precisely that idea in mind.

What most Canadians have failed to appreciate is that the bedrock of Trudeau's political beliefs from his earliest days as a writer was the decentralization of power. As such, his arguments are not much different than those of Robert Bourassa, René Lévesque, Lucien Bouchard, or even Preston Manning. Controlling and limiting the powers of the federal government to link the country east to west has always been at the heart of various provincially based reform plans for the federal government. The public record is quite clear on this about Trudeau, as well. From his earliest days as a public figure in Montreal, Trudeau never portrayed himself as anything but an advocate of stronger provincial powers. He may have called himself a federalist, but read his description of what he meant: "Federalism is by its very essence a compromise and a pact. It is a compromise in the sense that when national consensus on *all* things is not desirable or cannot readily obtain, the area of consensus is reduced in order that consensus on *some* things be reached. It is a pact or quasi-treaty in the sense that the terms of the compromise cannot be changed unilaterally."[5] In other words, Trudeau says, the federal government can only be as strong and visionary as the provinces allow it to be.

Almost from the moment he replaced Lester Pearson, Trudeau began devolving powers to the provinces, but mostly to Quebec. Many Canadians may well have missed that crucial point, but his biographers and most historians didn't, although this confusion was understandable, given the firm tone Trudeau took towards Quebec. In reporting on Trudeau's first election campaign, George Radwanski wrote:

> On both the Quebec issue and the general nature of his campaign, Trudeau walked a precarious tightrope by simultaneously appearing to do one set of things and loudly insisting that he was doing something else. He quite consciously used his firmness toward Quebec's constitutional aspirations as a major element of his campaign, thereby feeding assumptions he was a prime minister who could "put Quebec in its place." But at the same time, he kept insisting, quite truthfully, that he should not be mistaken for a Quebec-basher and that his intention was to increase, not diminish, the role of Quebecers in Canada's life.[6]

Ron Graham, in his 1986 book, *One-Eyed Kings: Promise and Illusion in Canadian Politics*, took it a step farther when he wrote about how Trudeau fought "on the letter of the law and matters of principle . . . but [gave] in to provinces on demands for money. On the one hand, he wanted to safeguard the rules and powers necessary to keep the country prosperous and together. On the other hand, he thought that the provinces could do as good a job as Ottawa in many fields and that their electorates would keep them honest." Graham went on to write:

> Many people saw Trudeau's hard-line defence of the national interest as a cause of strain in federal-provincial relations. Certainly, the vicious logic of his debating techniques, which never admitted wrong and rarely pulled back from a kill, infuriated the premiers who were almost always at the losing end of his arguments. Some of them came to despise him; most of them approached a negotiation with him in the spirit of gladiators going into the arena with a lion. . . . By the end of the Seventies, however, a good case could be made that the real strain had been caused by Trudeau's decentralizations. Between 1962 and 1978, Ottawa's share of public revenues dropped from 47 per cent to 32 per cent. Billions of dollars were handed over to the provinces to help them fulfill their responsibilities in areas such as medicare and post-secondary education, all without conditions so that Ottawa wouldn't interfere in their jurisdictions. As a result the federal government sacrificed most of its abilities to establish national standards.[7]

Even so, many Canadians still see Trudeau as an advocate of a strong, central government, based mainly on his performance during the October Crisis and his government's implementation of the short-lived and highly controversial National Energy Program in 1980–81. Upon closer examination, however, each is not what it seems.

During the highly charged days of the October Crisis, many Canadians recall Trudeau's comment – "Just watch me" – to television reporter Tim Ralfe, about how far the prime minister was prepared to go to fight Quebec separatists. Trudeau sounded like an independent-minded federal leader defending the national interest – the greater good – but the proof of what he really meant was in the details. Most Canadians recall that the next day Trudeau invoked the War Measures Act and called in the army in what seemed to be a unilateral declaration by a strong, federal leader. That's the legend. The reality seems to be less clearcut.

In his *Memoirs*, Trudeau describes exactly what happened: "The Canadian Armed Forces were called in, at the request of the Quebec government, in 'aid to the Civil Power.'" Trudeau took such drastic action *only* after a formal request had been made by Quebec premier Robert Bourassa for the federal government to use the army. This was an important and often-forgotten distinction, which was not lost on Trudeau, himself.[8] This might well have been a courtesy, but it is also possible that it was a reflection of Trudeau's own political belief that the provinces have the ultimate control over federal powers, especially such extreme ones as martial law. Perhaps Trudeau and the federal government didn't feel they had the right to defend the national interest without the prior consent of the provinces.

Then there was the National Energy Program of 1980–81, whereby Ottawa tried to assert its control over the oil and gas industries across the country. But the National Energy Program wasn't conceived so much to make the federal government stronger as to redirect wealth to Quebec. On the surface, at least, Trudeau, and his key cabinet ministers, Marc Lalonde and Jean Chrétien, among others, were using their power to back up their belief that Quebec must be appeased, and the way to appease the province was to make it richer. In the early days of the National Energy Program débâcle, this was articulated by Jean Chrétien, who stated proudly in the House of Commons debate of April 17, 18, and 21, 1980: "Quebec will receive in 1980 more than 50 per cent of the whole equalization program . . . the energy policy of this government has saved the province of Quebec no less than $6 billion since 1974; . . . Quebec pays at most 22 per cent of federal taxes; Ottawa pays 55 per cent of the Quebec health budget; Quebec received 35 per cent of the funds allotted to public welfare schemes in Canada; 75 per cent of the family allowance cheque to

Quebec mothers comes from the federal government; . . . Quebec gets more family allowances and tax credits than it pays out in taxes."[9]

That's the dollars and cents of Trudeau's federalism – increasing the ability of the federal government to generate revenues, so that a disproportionate percentage of those monies might be diverted to Quebec. At the end of the day, the provinces, especially Quebec, would have more say about where Canada was headed than each might have enjoyed in the past. Now let's leave that thread for a moment and pick up another one.

•　　•　　•

While it is evident that the Trudeau government was dedicated to appeasing Quebec at almost every turn, it would be wrong to suggest that this was done entirely for political reasons. There was business logic at work here. If the Trudeau technocrats were going to run the country as if it were a business, they had to comport themselves like businessmen. Everyone had to be on the same page – business people don't brook dissent. Therefore, satisfying and enriching Quebec made good business sense in the long run, no matter what the long-term public-policy implications might have been.

But there was something else that the Trudeau government did, something less obvious, which struck at the heart of the guardian role of the federal government and its institutions. In his first two governments, including the minority government from 1972 to 1974, Trudeau's major public-policy accomplishment was probably limited to official bilingualism. The Quebec technocrats who had hoped to accomplish so much had actually done very little since coming to Ottawa in 1965. Having won a new majority government in 1974, the Trudeau team focused its efforts on making government run more like a business. Governments and public institutions are steeped in rules and traditions. They are by nature cautious, conservative, and take a post-to-post approach in nation-building. The Trudeau government wasn't going to play by those rules any more. It was going to be more business-like, which meant that it would take risks, change the rules as it went, and disdain tradition. If the third Trudeau government was going to be anything, it would be daring and innovative. The time had come for experimentation.

The signal for this new-look government came on May 1, 1974, just as the country was to go to the polls for the federal election that summer. Marc Lalonde, then minister of national health and welfare, introduced in Parliament a working document, entitled "A New Perspective on the Health of Canadians." The paper was intended to address the perceived problem that universal health care was becoming a drain on the economy. The notion of token user fees or a more disciplined system were considered to be politically unpalatable, so Lalonde came up with something different to deal with the conundrum he faced. In "A New Perspective on the Health of Canadians," Lalonde set out a new approach to governing that was clearly based more on the corporate model than on the guardian one. The heart of Lalonde's plan was to combine the power and resources of government with the knowledge and techniques of advertising and marketing in an attempt to re-engineer the way society behaved. As an historical document, "A New Perspective" is important, because it is really the first articulation by any Canadian government about how it might approach its duties in a more business-like fashion. The ideas expressed in the document soon came to be known as the Lalonde Doctrine.

When the Trudeau government was returned with a majority government in July 1974, a new era of governance began in Canada. Armed with the Lalonde Doctrine, the entire notion of the federal government as guardian was turned on its ear.

The first tangible outcome of the Lalonde Doctrine was the birth of the government-financed health-promotion industry. The government began to campaign for exercise clubs, granola, and soda water. Fats, cholesterol, and smoking were among the many enemies. That there was little or no scientific support for many of the health-promotion policies and programs didn't really matter to Lalonde, who wrote in Chapter Nine of "A New Perspective":

The spirit of enquiry and scepticism, and particularly the Scientific Method, so essential to research, are, however, a problem in health promotion. The reason for this is that science is full of "ifs," "buts," and "maybes," while the messages designed to influence the public must be loud, clear and unequivocal. To quote 1 Corinthians, Chapter XIV, Verse 8: "If the trumpet gives an uncertain sound, who shall prepare himself to battle?"

The scientific "yes, but" is essential to research but for modifying the behaviour of the population it sometimes produces the "uncertain sound" that is all the excuse needed by many to cultivate and tolerate an environment and lifestyle that is hazardous to health.

The intention of the Lalonde Doctrine was in parts noble, practical, and politically beneficial. The government would use its guardian power to make the world a safer and better place, while, theoretically, controlling expenditures from the public treasury. At the end of the day, the ruling Liberals hoped to reap rewards for their genius at the polls.

The use of the Lalonde Doctrine by the government led immediately to some beneficial public-policy decisions in the health and safety field. For example, automobile seatbelt legislation was enacted, even though there was not much scientific evidence at the time of the efficacy of such equipment. But there is a fine line between health promotion and scare tactics, with the result that needless public panic was created from time to time.

Government health-promotion advertising and marketing soon became a huge and thriving industry, which in many ways changed the way Canadians lived their lives and thought about themselves. But to what end? In Canada governments are voted into office with a certain mandate to manage programs. Usually the government is seen to be a source of credible information. The Lalonde Doctrine implicitly condoned and, in fact, encouraged the government's sacrifice of objectivity in order to advocate policies in which it believed, regardless of whether these policies actually could be supported by credible evidence.

Behaviour modification and re-engineering became the government's agenda.[10] On the surface it appeared that the government was behaving like a guardian, defending the greater good, but increasing numbers of Canadians naturally found themselves confused, sceptical, and, largely uninterested in what government was doing because it became more difficult to separate the government's true defence of the public good from its mere good intentions. Government had begun to see itself as not unlike a sales-based private-sector organization, created to generate revenue and feed the bottom line by saving the government money.

Lalonde Doctrine thinking had been evident in the Trudeau government prior to 1974, but afterwards it became rampant. Ottawa did what it wanted because there was never enough time to wait for enough proof to support one course of action over another. For example, the Trudeau government was determined to build second airports in Montreal and Toronto, despite a spate of studies that showed they were not needed. Ottawa, nevertheless, charged ahead with opening Mirabel Airport, an hour's drive northwest of Montreal. In 1997, the airport was finally closed to passenger service because of lack of use, but not before billions of taxpayers' dollars were lost.

When credible scientists argued that cod stocks on the East Coast were endangered, and more scientific study was required, the Liberals said they couldn't wait for a definitive opinion. The federal government charged ahead and expanded the fishery – with the result that, a few years later, mature cod had all but disappeared from the waters, and thousands of fishers were put out of work, causing entire fishing communities to die out.

The examples are endless, but the point is that, as the government started to think like a business, it viewed itself differently as well. As it began to shed its pure guardian role, it also began to lose its guardian instinct. It was no longer cautious, sceptical, or as "on guard" as it once had been. During the Trudeau government, there emerged another kind of Big Brother: corporate paternalism at its most powerful, making moral judgements for people, denying choice, stigmatizing its enemies, and, most importantly, discouraging normal scientific – or for that matter, political – dissent. The Lalonde Doctrine had served to legitimize the practice of propaganda by the government, and eventually paved the way for, among other things, such dubious enterprises as government-sponsored casinos and gambling being advertised as a good thing for society. Since Trudeau, experimentation within government has been the order of the day.

Of all the experiments initiated by the Trudeau government, however, none was grander than the one involving the justice system.

The Trudeau government always treated the justice system as just another social program, part of his "Just Society." But the justice system is much more than any social program. In a democracy such as ours, the justice system is the spine of the country. The intention of Trudeau's experiments with the justice system was to bring equality to all Canadians, as if equality had never before existed. However, the effect of the changes brought by Trudeau were crippling to the federal justice system, and no single institution better reflects the negative impact of these changes than does the Royal Canadian Mounted Police. The RCMP is Trudeau's child – as close to a spitting image of what Trudeau envisaged a "strong" federal institution to be as exists in Canada today.

The old saw is that hindsight is twenty-twenty, but when one tries to explain why the RCMP is what it is, one can't help but stumble over the various policies and decisions made by Trudeau and his governments over the years. And the more one looks at them, the more suspicious one becomes about what Trudeau's ultimate plan might have been. Take, for example, the following three areas: Trudeau's determination that the RCMP be the sole federal policing force in Canada; the expectations of Quebec and Quebeckers for the RCMP; and the effect of the Constitution and the Charter of Rights and Freedoms on federal law and institutions.

As I described earlier, Trudeau had always stood by the RCMP when it fought off competitors for its powers. As the size of the federal government – and its statutes – blossomed during the Trudeau reign, so did the requirements for federal law enforcement. But the RCMP, as a federal police force, was never able to keep pace with the inflation in federal responsibilities. Yet, throughout this period, with the help and consent of the Trudeau government, the RCMP had vigorously fought off all potential competitors seeking policing powers, including the treasury department, revenue, transport, and the post office, to name the leading contenders. At the urging of the RCMP itself, Trudeau even resisted the recommendation of the Mackenzie Commission in 1969 to hive off the Security Service from the RCMP to create a separate organization. In winning these bureaucratic skirmishes, the RCMP thought it was doing itself and Canada a favour, but not any more.

"At the time it seemed right that the RCMP should be the sole provider of federal law-enforcement services across the country, and that the Security Service should be maintained as a protective service within the RCMP. Trudeau's support in these areas was much appreciated by the force," says former deputy commissioner Henry Jensen. Jensen, who left the force in 1990, was one of those who led the charge within the RCMP to maintain the exclusivity of the force in the federal policing area. "But now," he says, "I tend to see things differently. I think we made a big mistake. Trudeau agreed that the Mounties would be the only federal law-enforcement agency, but a few years down the road, the federal policing capability of the force has been severely compromised. The Mounties are one of the last institutions linking the country. I think it would have been wiser back then if we had encouraged the development of other federal police forces. Instead of one thin line holding the country together, there might have been four or five. Moving in that direction would have made the country and justice system stronger, not as weak as it appears to be today."

Did Trudeau simply make a mistake or were his good intentions overtaken by events? Whatever the case may be, the impact of the influx of Quebeckers into the inner sanctum of Ottawa's public-policy mechanism cannot be reasonably ignored. When the Quebeckers arrived en masse in Ottawa, not only did the language of politics change, but so did the thinking, because many of them landed jobs as advisers and policymakers. Many of the Quebeckers saw Canada through a markedly different prism than had their federal government predecessors. To many of these Quebeckers, as history has clearly shown, the federal government and federal institutions were not as sacred as they were to other Canadians. Trudeau knew this, and had written extensively about this attitude of Quebeckers.

Put yourself in the shoes of a Quebecker, new to the federal government. Demands were being made to create additional federal law-enforcement agencies to compete with the RCMP. Throughout history, Quebeckers have fought specifically against federal law enforcement in their province, as was the case throughout the seventies, with the pitched battles being fought against the RCMP over both the Security Service and the Commercial Crime Branch. By now it should be clear to the reader that the vast majority of Quebeckers, nationalists and federalists alike, favour decentralization and enhanced political power for the provinces. So, given the opportunity to create more federal law-enforcement agencies or maintain just one, the likely approach of Quebeckers in administrative and advisory positions in Ottawa would be to maintain a single force. It's not only common sense, but it conforms absolutely with Trudeau's prescription for federalism, in which the provinces were to expand their powers and Quebec was to be appeased. There was no room for more federal institutions, and those that did exist were ripe to be challenged. And that's what happened.

In 1978, Trudeau floated the idea that the RCMP be renamed Police Canada. His intention was that such a name might both translate more easily into French and, in the process, eliminate the apparent link to the British Crown, doubly appeasing Quebec. This was the corporate approach to the naming of public entities, which already included, among others, Trans-Canada Airlines being renamed Air Canada and the Department of National Revenue becoming Revenue Canada. Such names were sold to the public as simple, direct, and business-like. However, the Police Canada idea was smothered at birth because of a public outcry, mainly from the West, the birthplace of the RCMP. The Royal Canadian Mounted Police was not only one of the most visible federal institutions in the country, it was seen to be a symbol of the country itself. It was successfully argued that to delete the name would weaken the fabric of the country. Trudeau relented on renaming the RCMP, but pressed ahead with his agenda for the justice system.

The ultimate goal for Trudeau was the repatriation of the Constitution and, more importantly, the implementation of the Charter of Rights and Freedoms in 1982. The Charter served to propel Canada farther down the road to decentralization of federal power. Until the implementation of the Charter, the balance in Canada had been tilted in favour of the collective; now individual rights would take precedence. This elevation of individual civil liberties helped to create an incredible imbalance in the justice system.

After the Glassco Commission, government had taken accountability for spending away from bureaucrats – the public's servants – and vested it in elected politicians. With both the Constitution and the Charter of Rights and Freedoms, political accountability was now removed from the politicians and placed in the hands of virtually unaccountable judges. The entire system was being turned on its ear. Trudeau promised the Charter would bring freedom, but the Charter also narrowed many options for Canadians, because what was truly accomplished was a transformation from democratic rights to constitutional rights – the difference between the rule of law and the rule of lawyers.

In accepting the Charter, Canadians might have thought that they were moving from the British system of justice to something closer to the U.S. model, but they were getting neither. The Canadian system had evolved into a hybrid. In Great Britain, for example, the tradition has been that the chief law officer – the attorney general – of the country is not part of the political process; he or she doesn't sit at the cabinet table. The British system is built on one thousand years of common law and traditions, and the police are agents of the law and answerable only to the law.

In the United States, there is a system of checks and balances between the executive, legislative, and judicial branches. Judges, for example, are subjected to public scrutiny before being appointed. As in Britain, the chief law officer of the United States, the attorney general, acts independently, and will, as history has shown, even mount prosecutions against the president, if given sufficient grounds to do so. In Great Britain and the United States, the guardian role of government is well defined, but not so in Canada, and especially in the province of Quebec.

In Canada, not only is the justice minister an integral part of the political process, the prime minister appoints judges unilaterally (after they have been discreetly vetted by their peers); there is no avenue of debate or appeal. Once on the bench, the word of those judges is law. Once a judge is appointed, it is all but impossible to remove him.

If all the changes wrought by Trudeau didn't give Canada the best of either the British or American justice system, then what did Canada get? As odd as it might seem to some, the Canadian federal justice system has come to resemble the justice system of its greatest internal opponent – Quebec.

In Quebec, politics have always played a large role in the justice system. The Quebec premier and his minister of justice have historically exercised control over not only the administration of justice but its execution as well. The political level has its hand in everything from the appointment of judges to the laying of charges against an individual. There are none of the checks and balances one might expect to find in a U.S. court, for example. There has never been much pretence in Quebec that the province is governed by the rule of law – that is that all people are subject to the law and equal under the law. In Quebec, from Premier Honoré Mercier through Duplessis, from the governments of Robert Bourassa to the current problems of wrongdoing within the province's major police departments, corruption has been a constant. The elite of business, society, and politics are treated differently in Quebec than they would be within the Canadian justice system.

Before long, attitudes about the law and policing which had long been commonplace in Quebec began to be adopted by the federal justice system. Foremost among these was the way the police would come to view commercial crime and corruption, the two areas of crime which strike at the heart of the integrity of a country's economic and political systems.

The Charter of Rights and Freedoms made the job of the police almost impossible, because it made a wider range of defences available to corporations in criminal cases, thereby also making it more difficult to investigate and prosecute offenders. As had long been the case under the Quebec Civil Code, corporations were given basically the same rights as individuals under the law, no matter how flimsy, rootless, despicable, unethical, or corrupt the corporation might be. Fraud was difficult enough to prove as a criminal offence under ordinary circumstances, but the Charter of Rights and Freedoms had stacked the deck in favour of anyone with money enough to outlast the will and resources of the justice system.

As a result of the Charter, the concept of commercial crime, except for the most heinous and difficult-to-ignore cases, was effectively downgraded to a civil matter. This is similar to the way such crimes are treated under the Quebec Civil Code. In Quebec, commercial crime has been treated almost exclusively as a breach of the civil law – merely a flawed business transaction – requiring mediation between the parties and a financial penalty against offenders. Commercial crime is virtually an alien concept under the Quebec Civil Code, which is based on the nineteenth-century Napoleonic Code. With the changes created by the Charter of Rights and Freedoms, the federal justice system began to take on the appearance and attitude of the Quebec justice system, especially with regard to commercial crime. This meant that injury and punishment alike would be guided by dollar values. The likelihood of jail time for commercial crime was all but eliminated across Canada.

In implementing the Charter of Rights and Freedoms, Trudeau assured that the construction and mandate of the country's Supreme Court would reflect this ideal. Quebec judges on the Supreme Court, for example, with their background in the Quebec Civil Code, were given jurisdiction over civil matters, a neat closing of the circle. The effective decriminalization of commercial crime and the rise of individual rights for corporations gained even more momentum as ex-defence lawyers, such as John Sopinka, were called to the bench. They began to make rulings that challenged the power of the state at almost every turn, while upholding the rights of private enterprise. Each precedent-setting case over the next fifteen years had a common theme – the guardian role of government was under attack. During this period the underlying philosophy of the Supreme Court seemed to be that public power must be held in check at every turn, while private power was not considered a threat to democracy. The Napoleonic Code had been subtly slipped over the shoulders of Canada's British-based laws.

Few noticed what had happened, but one of those who did was Osgoode Hall law professor Michael Mandel. In his 1995 book, *The Charter of Rights and the Legalization of Politics in Canada*, Mandel argued that Canadians were misled about the intentions of the Charter and that they should be concerned about its effects. He pointed out that concepts were entrenched in the Charter which were profoundly ambiguous. The Charter refers to the supremacy of the rule of law, but as Mandel points out, "It can be democratic or authoritarian. But it can only be democratic if the law that rules is really *our* law. This means that it has to be made by us or by people genuinely accountable to us. And then it has to be applied faithfully and not distorted by those administering it. The democratic sense of the rule of law requires that the authorities, too, are restrained by law, with no exemptions for judicial authorities."[11] Those who supported the implementation of the Charter thought it would enhance popular power, but in fact, it has done the opposite. As has always been the case in Quebec law, the rights of the system itself were protected, and not those of the public.

•   •   •

In 1984, Trudeau resigned as prime minister and slipped out of the limelight, occasionally bursting back on the scene to argue for his version of federalism. His abiding legacy is that, since he arrived in Ottawa in 1965, no province has controlled the federal government more than has Quebec. The Glassco Commission had recommended that more francophones and Quebeckers be brought into the federal government to address obvious imbalances, but Glassco never anticipated having a man like Trudeau in the prime minister's office. Trudeau had indeed seized the moment, as had the Quebeckers who went to Ottawa because of him. By 1997, for example, more than 75 per cent of RCMP employees in Ottawa were French Canadian, the majority of them Quebeckers, according to senior officers within the force. In terms of the entire force, just one-third are French Canadian. Those in Ottawa control the centre – the administrative and policy functions.

But that's the way it has become in Ottawa. Since the Trudeau years, the Canadian political landscape has been dominated by the never-ending debate about the future of Quebec within Canada. During this period, the federal government has been headed, with three brief exceptions, by Quebeckers – Trudeau, Brian Mulroney, and Jean Chrétien. As Jack Aubry of the *Ottawa Citizen* discovered through an access to information request in August 1998, Trudeau knew he had made serious mistakes, especially with regard to the implementation of bilingualism as a solution to the unity crisis. The revelations were found in cabinet minutes from March 17, 1977, and in a discussion paper on co-ordinating government activities to strengthen national unity. At that time, Trudeau admitted to his political colleagues that his belief from 1966 to 1976 that Quebec could be kept in Confederation by ensuring significant francophone participation in decision-making at the federal level had not worked. Therefore, Trudeau decided, the next best thing was opening up the Constitution and decentralization. But the damage had been done. Trudeau and his successors, Mulroney and Chrétien, never conceded the error, and charged on. All, with subtle variations and to varying degrees, have believed in the same thing – the continuing decentralization of federal powers and the belief that government should operate more like a business.

While this debate between Quebeckers in Ottawa and Quebec City has captivated the entire nation, fundamental changes to federal institutions have been taking place without much, if any, public input. The rest of Canada has been reduced to a passenger in the drive down the road to a dramatic restructuring of the country – and much of this has been allowed to take place outside the realm of everyday politics and public debate. Quebec and, to a lesser extent, the other provinces, have got much of what they want quietly, incrementally, through government budgeting policies or administrative decisions.

In all the confusion, the Royal Canadian Mounted Police continues to be driven by the most basic instinct – survival. When a police force thinks this way, its guardian mentality becomes corrupted. The rule of law is jeopardized, because serious and possibly politically sensitive prosecutions are treated differently than they should be. Today, when it comes to RCMP federal investigations – in Quebec, especially – a shudder is felt right up to the commissioner's office. It's not something the Mounties like to talk about, but Quebec politicians have bloodied the nose of the Mounties so many times over the years – from the Dredging Scandal in the seventies to Airbus in the nineties – that the force has become gun-shy about investigating high-profile or politically connected individuals or corporations. When it comes to such investigations, it is not unusual these days to find Mounties sitting on their collective thumbs, creating thick and endless files, but rarely building a prosecutable case. The joke inside the force is that when it comes to these kinds of important cases, the RCMP nowadays acts more and more as if it were a Quebec police force. It prefers to do nothing.

"I've always thought that Canada created the RCMP to be a great national police force," says Michel Thivierge, a former RCMP assistant commissioner who was in charge of the force's Quebec operations when he retired in the mid-nineties. "But now I've come to see that it was put together pretty well by accident, and there was no grand plan. It took me thirty-three years on the force to realize that was probably the real intention all along."

Armed with this history and analysis, you have enough of a context to understand how the RCMP got into the mess that it is in. Now, let's hit the road and take a look at the Mounties from the inside, starting in Ottawa, where many of these issues come together.

Chapter Six

A TALE OF TWO FORCES

IF THE JOB OF managers, as philosopher John Ralston Saul put it, is to try to remove contradictions or, at least, the appearance of contradictions, then RCMP commissioner Philip Murray has done his job well. He has managed to make most Canadians believe that the RCMP is a strong, unified, national police force.

The RCMP is still one of the most popular brand names in the world and, in an age of information, the RCMP have become masters of public relations and self-promotion. A few times a day the force fires out press releases to the media around the country. Each one describes another Mountie accomplishment – perfect, easily digestible fodder for time-pressed reporters. There's the usual round-up of drug-trafficking suspects in Montreal, the seizure of prohibited weapons on a native reserve, the smashing of an immigrant smuggling ring in Ontario, or the tracking down and shooting of a man-killing bear in the Rockies. To the average consumer of the six o'clock news, the RCMP appears healthy. But if that is the case, why is it that almost since the day he was appointed commissioner, insiders say, Murray has been hanging on to his job by his neatly manicured fingertips?

"The general feeling is that Murray has two strikes against him and the third could come any day," one veteran RCMP insider said in the summer of 1997. "If it hadn't been for the Somalia affair, Chrétien would have gassed him by now. But he couldn't take out the head of the army and the head of the RCMP in the same round."

Since being appointed on June 23, 1994, Joseph Philip Robert Murray has found himself pinned down from all sides. Fifty-one when he became commissioner, Murray has never known anything but policing since he joined the Mounties right out of high school in Ottawa in March 1962. He was nineteen years old, almost to the day. He spent the next ten years in Saskatchewan in general policing, served a term as a staff-relations representative for Saskatchewan, before winning a transfer back home to Ottawa, which he never left again. Along the way he concentrated on management and business administration. He received his Bachelor of Adminstration (with Great Distinction) from the University of Regina in 1977, having been awarded the University General Proficiency Scholarship in both 1975 and 1976. In 1978, he received his Certificate in Business Administration from the same university.

In other times, a person with Murray's credentials would have been the perfect adviser, a well-schooled technocrat, who would sit at the right hand of a leader, someone with the inside knowledge or entrepreneurial vision to drive an organization and make it thrive. But in the eighties, things changed. In most organizations the visionaries and entrepreneurs were shuffled aside and replaced, in large measure, by just such professional managers and accountants.

In 1996, when the Somalia scandal broke over the killing and torture of prisoners by Canadian troops on a peacekeeping mission, Murray was still in Jean Chrétien's doghouse over a November 1995 break-in at the prime minister's official residence at 24 Sussex Drive. An intruder had slipped around the RCMP guard stationed on the grounds, broken into the house, and reached the door of Jean Chrétien's bedroom before he was finally apprehended after frantic calls for help from Aline, the prime minister's wife. Chrétien was said to be furious over the slip-up. That was the first strike against the commissioner.

The second was the explosive and ultimately disastrous Airbus affair. Airbus is worth a brief digression, because there were actually two investigations, and each paints a poignant picture of the state of the federal police under both Inkster and Murray.

The Airbus case arose after the 1988 purchase by Air Canada of thirty-four commercial jets for $1.8 billion from Airbus Industrie, a then-fledgling European consortium. Allegations were made that kick-backs had been paid to unknown high-ranking Canadian politicians. What is a kickback? A kickback is achieved when the selling price is inflated by a certain amount, and those monies are then returned secretly to the purchasers or their agents. In other words, a kickback is a well-orchestrated theft. In a transaction involving public money, like the Airbus deal, the victim is the public treasury. An accounting eventually showed that the size of the kickback in the Airbus transaction was at least $12 million. That's how much money – crumbs in a deal that size – mysteriously fell off the table between Ottawa and Airbus's bankers. It has never been traced.

Flesh was added to the persistent rumours in 1988 when Seattle-based Boeing Industries, the world's largest commercial jet manufacturer, complained to the U.S. government about the deal. This sparked the first RCMP investigation by the Special Federal Investigations Unit, which began that same year. The elite four-man unit – two inspectors and two sergeants – came out of the Commercial Crime Branch. The unit was charged with investigating complaints regarding Parliament and the House of Commons. The unit had originally worked out of "A" Division headquarters in downtown Ottawa, but Commissioner Norman Inkster had moved the unit to the force's Alta Vista headquarters in order to keep a closer eye on its activities. During the Mulroney government's tenure, the unit conducted more than thirty serious investigations, but Airbus was the most difficult of all.

The initial investigation was conducted on the most treacherous of ground, as the Mounties found themselves having to play cat-and-mouse with their own superiors. Investigators tried to mask the Airbus investigation by mixing it in with a number of others they were conducting. One of those involved allegations that a secret commission had been paid to a high-ranking member of Mulroney's office over the leasing by the government of office space in Ottawa from U.S.-based Metropolitan Life Insurance Company.[1] The subterfuge was necessary, because Commissioner Inkster, who, like his immediate predecessor Robert Simmonds, held the political title of deputy solicitor general, was reporting to the solicitor general in the Mulroney government on a weekly basis the nature of all high-profile criminal investigations. This unusual procedure, as mentioned, had arisen from the flawed recommendations made by the McDonald Commission in August 1981.

The Airbus controversy also broke at an especially critical time for Canada: the negotiations leading up to the signing of the Free Trade Agreement with the United States. Mulroney had been elected partly on the promise that he was not in favour of free trade, but once in power Mulroney took the opposite tack. He eventually revealed himself to be, like almost every Quebec political leader since Sir Wilfrid Laurier, a champion of freer trade relations with the United States. In April 1988, at the very moment the Mounties were setting out to track down the people who might have received the Airbus kickbacks, Canada was only days away from a final agreement with the United States on the free-trade pact.

On April 22, 1988, Mulroney received a surprise visit from the U.S. treasury secretary, James Baker, and the U.S. ambassador to Canada, Thomas Niles. At a private meeting they raised the issue of the Airbus allegations with Mulroney. No one who attended the meeting will discuss openly what happened that day, but a certain amount is known. According to Mountie sources two things occurred shortly afterwards.

First, the Metropolitan Life case against the high-ranking Mulroney government member collapsed, because documents which had been seized in the United States as part of the police investigation were suddenly no longer made available to the RCMP. Second, Boeing was soon allowed to purchase the assets of de Havilland Canada, a venerable Canadian manufacturer, which had been propped up for years by government money. To its credit, de Havilland appeared to have just turned the corner with the success of its new Dash 7 and Dash 8 short-takeoff-and-landing aircraft. The moment Boeing took over de Havilland, it withdrew its complaint about the Airbus deal. Free trade went ahead. The RCMP investigators were left high and dry, without a complaint to investigate, and their investigation had to be shelved. "The whole thing left a bad taste in the mouth of a lot of coppers," said one Mountie close to the Airbus affair.

But, five years later, the Airbus case resurfaced. Mulroney had resigned, and the Tories were subsequently obliterated at the polls in November 1993, reduced to two seats in Parliament. Fresh allegations were raised about Airbus and the Mulroney government in an hour-long documentary by the CBC program *the fifth estate*, as well as briefly in my first book, *Above the Law*, published in 1994. Following up on the powerful and convincing *fifth estate* story, the RCMP reopened its Airbus file. This time they were looking directly at the possible involvement of Mulroney himself in the deal, as well as the role played by Karlheinz Schreiber, a Canadian who lives in Europe.[2]

In the midst of all this, Philip Murray took over as RCMP commissioner. Although he continued to hold the title of deputy solicitor general, Murray was determined not to follow the McDonald Commission recommendation about reporting high-profile criminal cases to the political level on a weekly basis. Murray told his confidants within the force that the practice was improper. He simply stopped briefing the government about investigations, and no one in the new Liberal government challenged him. Solicitor General Herb Gray didn't even acknowledge this important change. Unlike his predecessors in the Mulroney government, Gray didn't want to know what the police were doing in their investigations, which is the way democratic governments should behave.

As well-intentioned as Murray might have been, however, he clearly didn't appreciate just how weak federal police operations had become. He and other superiors also hadn't learned from history about the difficulties that the RCMP had faced in conducting investigations into the affairs of leading Quebec politicians. To take on Mulroney and the predictable counter-attack from Quebec, the RCMP had to acknowledge to itself that there was a "Quebec problem," but it couldn't do that, for other reasons, as you shall soon see. For the Airbus investigation to be successful, the RCMP also had to put its best and most highly qualified investigators on the case. But that's not what happened.

Staff Sergeant Fraser Fiegenwald, who was a relatively junior member of the RCMP to undertake such an assignment, headed the second Airbus investigation. In the heyday of commercial-crime investigation by the

RCMP in the seventies and early eighties, such a case would have been handled by at least an inspector, the next rank up from staff sergeant. Due to cutbacks in staffing and "downsizing," the RCMP had eliminated layers of supervision to create a more "efficient" and "streamlined" force. As a result, Fiegenwald was mounting the biggest case of any Mountie's career without any real support or guidance from his superiors. Even so, he was making progress.

In his investigation, Fiegenwald identified a Swiss bank account which had allegedly been opened by Karlheinz Schreiber on behalf of Mulroney. To get access to the account, he needed the help of lawyers within the Justice Department, because the police are not allowed to have their own independent legal advisers. On September 29, Justice Department lawyer Kimberly Prost sent a letter to the Swiss government, in which she referred to "an ongoing scheme by Mr. Mulroney (and others) to defraud the Canadian Government of millions of dollars." Another part of the letter said: "This investigation is of serious concern to the Government of Canada as it involves criminal activity on the part of a former Prime Minister."[3] The feds would eventually withdraw the wording and apologize, but how they got to that position is interesting. Mulroney used the convenient cudgel of the Quebec civil system to beat the RCMP and the federal Justice Department into submission.

The letter to the Swiss bank was somehow leaked to *Financial Post* reporter Philip Mathias and *Globe and Mail* editor William Thorsell, a long-time friend of Mulroney. After stories were published in those papers, Mulroney mounted a well-publicized counter-attack against the Mountie investigators. He hired Roger Tassé, the former Justice Department mandarin, who was partly responsible for the setting up of the McDonald Commission. Tassé lobbied the government and Commissioner Murray about the case. Many of those who learned of this have inferred that Mulroney believed that he could manipulate the workings of what is supposed to be an independent justice system. He was a lawyer by training, had served as prime minister, and clearly knew the law.

Tassé, however, was rebuffed by both Justice Minister Allan Rock and Commissioner Murray. Each said that he did not wish to interfere in an ongoing investigation, which is how the law is intended to work in Canada.[4]

Having received no satisfaction from Rock or Murray, Mulroney then launched a $50-million libel suit in a Quebec court against the government of Canada, Commissioner Murray, Fiegenwald, and Prost. In taking such action, Mulroney chose the well-travelled path that so many of his fellow Quebec politicians had found reliable over the years when under investigation by the RCMP. They sought refuge and relief in the relatively safe confines of the Quebec justice system, where a sense of *noblesse oblige* has always pervaded the courts. Dating back to the days of Premier Honoré Mercier in the 1890s, there is a long history of favourable decisions and judicious miracles having been produced for members of the social, business, and political elite.

What happened in the Mulroney case was a good example of how differently the elite are treated in the Quebec civil justice system. The unwritten rule in Quebec courts is that a judge who presides over a preliminary hearing is replaced by another judge for the trial to assure a fresh view of the facts. In Mulroney's case, the rule was waived by Lyse Lemieux, chief justice of the Quebec Superior Court. Mr. Justice André Rochon was designated to handle both cases. From the outset Rochon made it clear that Mulroney would be given special privileges by the courts to expedite the case, including being allowed an office in the courthouse and the use of telephones. Rochon then made a number of key legal rulings which were extremely advantageous to Mulroney. Although Mulroney was claiming extreme damages, he did not have to disclose his financial statements, including income-tax filings. The government wanted to examine Mulroney's long-distance telephone bills to find out who he might have been talking to in the weeks leading up to the leak of the government's letter to the Swiss. That seemed to be a reasonable request, considering there was a controversy over who might have released the documents to the media. However, Rochon ruled that Mulroney's telephone records would remain confidential. "The court can't see how that requested document could add anything to the debate at this point."[5] As the case proceeded through the court system, the RCMP and the Justice Department had been placed in a near-impossible situation.

To successfully conduct a criminal investigation, the police must do its work in a confidential and often surreptitious manner. That's the nature of policing. That's what the law demands. The final blow came from Mr. Justice Pierre Denault of the Federal Court of Canada, who ruled that the RCMP could not invoke international relations as a reason to deny Mr. Mulroney the opportunity to ask questions about the way the letter was handled by the Swiss. This meant that the RCMP would have to testify about what it knew before its investigation was completed or before it was ready to lay charges.

Clearly looking for a way out of the mess, the federal government found one when it learned at a last-minute meeting before trial that Sergeant Fiegenwald had confirmed information for Stevie Cameron during the course of the investigation. A scapegoat had been found, and the government beat its retreat on the courthouse steps in January 1997. Fiegenwald was charged with violating the RCMP's internal code of conduct and his oath of office, charges which were dropped when he left the force voluntarily later in the year. But Commissioner Murray refused to pay his estimated $30,000 in legal fees.

Meanwhile, Alan Gold, former chief justice of the Quebec Superior Court, was brought in to mediate a settlement. He awarded Mulroney $3.4 million, a staggering amount under the circumstances, considering that the largest libel award in Canadian history was $1.6 million, granted to Ontario Crown attorney Casey Hill in 1995, only after a jury trial and an appeal.[6] Mulroney was reimbursed not only for his lawyers' expenses in Canada and Switzerland, expert opinions, translations, travel, and hundreds of pages of transcripts, but also for his public-relations expenses. He had spent $600,000 documenting each slight to his reputation and managing the media. Mulroney called it a great day for Canadian justice, and, once again, the RCMP was ridiculed and embarrassed by Quebec politicians.

So, to review for a moment, when he stepped up to bat Commissioner Murray had two huge, well-known strikes against him: the embarrassment of the break-in at the prime minister's residence and the Airbus débâcle. But as significant as some made them out to be, they each paled in comparison with the difficulties caused by the profound and deepening English–French split within the force.

At a time when Murray is preaching that the force must be transparent – "open to all Canadians; we have nothing to hide" – the English–French divisions in the force are real and nearly irreconcilable. Over the past six years of dealing with Mounties from coast to coast, he has found the distrust between the two sides readily apparent, and the tensions sometimes explosive. As a result, as powerful as Murray appears to be as commissioner, he has been reduced to dealing with a force that is a public-policy minefield. He never knows when he might trip a hammer and blow himself up.

The closest Murray has come so far to detonating the hidden bomb may well be over the issue of regionalization of RCMP operations, the latest manifestation of the long-forgotten Glassco Commission decentralist recommendations from the early sixties. This means that central control of the force has been largely dispersed to four areas across the country. Although that may sound like a normal evolution in an organization, for the RCMP and Canada the implications of regionalization are serious.

From the days of the Great March West in 1874, the RCMP had spread out to cover much of the country like a blanket, and perform services at the federal, provincial, and municipal level. True to its paramilitary origins, the RCMP operated along divisional lines, each division having its own commanding officer, administrators, and staff. In most cases the reporting structure in each division was split – to the commissioner on RCMP matters, to the federal solicitor general on federal policing, to provincial solicitors general on provincial matters, and to local councils in the areas where the force performed municipal policing duties.

Until recently there were seventeen divisions, divided roughly along provincial lines, most being identified by a designated letter: "A" Division was Ottawa, "C," Montreal, "O," Ontario, "E," Vancouver, and so on. With the loss of the Security Service and some modest restructuring over the years, the number of divisions was reduced to fourteen, plus headquarters, in the early nineties. In 1996, there were fifty-two sub-divisions and 707 detachments across the country.

The Mulroney government had imposed severe budget cuts on the force, reductions which were continued by the Chrétien government. This forced commissioners Inkster and then Murray to re-evaluate the existing structure, particularly the thinning of federal policing, which distressed Murray much more than Inkster. After all, as we have seen, federal policing services were costing Canadians ten dollars each a year, but that amount, government said, was more of a burden than Canadians were willing to bear.

As Inkster has said, and as Murray has found, the commissioner had two choices: he could try to help the government implement its policies in the best possible way, doing his best to protect the interests of the RCMP, or he could retire. In other words, play ball or die, not much of a choice for anyone who has spent more than three decades of his life working towards the top job.

Because he is deputy solicitor general, the commissioner of the RCMP serves at the pleasure of the prime minister. To stay in favour with the prime minister, who is intent on cutting budgets, the commissioner must show in some concrete fashion that he is introducing change – any kind of change. The RCMP evolved as a command-and-control operation, the traditional mode of policing, in which regimental order and discipline are deemed crucial; everyone was on a short leash. Murray chose to move away from this model to its near-antithesis, creating a force that is almost entirely driven from the bottom. This involved cutting out layers of administration, loosening the rank structure, and pushing authority for decision-making further down the command structure, which naturally meant moving power away from headquarters in Ottawa. The Mountie on the street was not only being put on a long leash, in some cases there would be no leash at all.

To accomplish this, however, Murray faced a conflict between his RCMP heritage with its revered traditions and the technocratic persona he had honed to help win him the commissioner's job. Murray is still a regimental man at heart. He likes the pomp and circumstance of the Mounties, the red serge and the Cuban-heeled Strathcona high-dress boots. When RCMP members speak on television, Murray sometimes is less concerned about what they say than with what they are wearing. Memos have gone out criticizing members for not wearing a hat on camera, even if the hat might have been lost or misplaced during a rescue effort, as once happened in British Columbia. In Ottawa, when a news story breaks out, the force's media spokespersons, who usually dress in civilian clothes, can often be found running madly to get into their uniforms in the event they might be photographed. In every way, Murray is a stickler for appearances and tradition, but when he puts on his managerial hat, as distressed as he claims to be, he seems as willing as any outsider to cut corners and make sacrifices.

Regionalization, no matter how one cuts it, goes entirely against the grain of what most Mounties see as their traditional mandate – being a national police force with huge federal responsibilities. Many Mounties wondered how such a force could not have centralized national direction. Nevertheless, Murray charged ahead.

The entire plan has many facets, some of which will be investigated in upcoming chapters, but the sales pitch Murray used to sell decentralization both to the Mounties and to the government was designed to assuage the fears of both sides. He argued that decentralization would make the RCMP more efficient and better for individual police officers, a win-win situation for the government and the force. This plan to get rid of unneeded layers of bureaucracy would give the cops on the street more freedom to do their job. The bonus was that the leaders of the force would be brought closer to the field personnel, making them more sensitive to what was going on in the real world and more accountable. As with so many other well-intentioned initiatives of the past, who could argue against it?

The regionalization plan was unveiled at a conference called by Murray, held on March 13, 1996, in Aylmer, Quebec, an Ottawa suburb. Four new regions were created, in addition to headquarters: Atlantic, Central Canada, North West, and Pacific. Each region would be run by a deputy commissioner, positions that would be removed from the Ottawa executive roster. All federal programs, which had been run out of headquarters, would now be moved to the regions, under these separate commanders. In the rush-rush atmosphere of the present-day RCMP, the implementation of the regionalization concept was set for April 1, 1996, just eighteen days after the announcement. The force hadn't worked out any details; that would come later. Murray's intention in holding the open meeting at Aylmer, and elsewhere afterwards, was to show the rank and file how "transparent" the force would be under his leadership. But as transparent as it all might have been, the regionalization plan was a *fait accompli* – there was no room for dissent.

Grumbling soon began everywhere. Many Mounties couldn't understand how Murray hoped to achieve any more efficiencies. In fact, they saw the creation of the regions as the *addition* of a layer – a layer that would come between existing divisions, which would continue to operate, and headquarters. "If you wanted to be more in touch with what was going on, it would have made better sense to move the divisional commanders to Ottawa and make them part of the executive committee," was the substance of what more than one Mountie said in interviews. By devolving to the regions, the main concern among the rank and file was that headquarters was now going to be cut out of everyday operations and become even more distant and removed from reality than it already was.

But the real problem for Murray came from RCMP members in Quebec. By mid-1996, sites had already been chosen for the other regional headquarters – Halifax, Regina, and Vancouver – but the Central Canada (Ontario and Quebec) headquarters was trickier. It would see the combining of "A" Division in Ottawa, "C" Division in Montreal, and "O" Division in Ontario, a volatile mix.

When he heard about this plan, Assistant Commissioner Odilon Emond, who was based in Montreal and responsible for Quebec, went wild: He demanded an emergency meeting with Murray. Soon afterwards, a delegation from the Montreal detachment was in the waiting room of Murray's third-floor office at RCMP headquarters at 1200 Vanier Parkway in Ottawa. The Quebec members told Murray that, if there was to be an amalgamation of the three divisions, then all Central Canada federal policing operations would *have to* be supervised out of the Montreal office. Quebec would accept nothing less, Murray was told.

While Murray won't comment on the meeting, sources close to him say that he took the demand from the delegation under advisement, to ponder his next move. For more than a year, Murray didn't make that move. With the ever-present national-unity debate bubbling on the political agenda, Murray knew he had to be extremely careful not to give the separatists some opening to exploit. At the same time, there was no way that the commissioner could give in to such a demand. The visit by Assistant Commissioner Emond only served to accentuate the fundamental and deep divisions within the force.

In Central Canada – Ontario, Quebec, and especially Ottawa – the RCMP is seen by Mounties to be a largely Quebec-influenced police force, while in the rest of Canada there is a more traditional mix of ethnic backgrounds, though white males continue to dominate. Because of previous policies by which French Canadians were recruited and then fast-tracked to federal positions, mostly in Central Canada, resentments and disparities have been created. The typical Mountie in Western Canada or the Maritimes also has a markedly different background than the typical Mountie in Central Canada when it comes to law-enforcement experience. In Central Canada, the only investigative work the Mounties perform is federal policing, while in the rest of Canada the Mounties serve as municipal, provincial, and federal police officers.

But the differences are even deeper than that. In Central Canada, the majority of Mounties are Quebeckers who have grown up in a different society, with different expectations of police, and a different interpretation of the rule of law. Quebeckers control the centre and a majority of the key jobs, particularly the development and implementation of policy, even though many of them have very little if any basic police training. Under commissioners Simmonds and Inkster, many Quebeckers were recruited, trained in the theory of policing, and then shipped to Ottawa so that the force could meet employment quotas set by the government.

In late 1997 in Ottawa, there were 834 regular members assigned to headquarters, 591 in "A" Division in Ottawa, 939 at "C" Division in Quebec, and 1,107 in "O" Division in Ontario. That is, 3,471 Mounties were stationed in what has become the Central Canada region. Since 1994, the number of designated bilingual positions in the entire force has risen from 3,331 to 3,376, the majority of them located in Central Canada, with a relatively small proportion in New Brunswick and elsewhere across the country where there is a demand for French-speaking police officers. The designated bilingual positions aren't all occupied by Quebeckers and other French Canadians, but the numbers strongly reflect the proportions. Some Quebeckers hold down jobs that aren't subject to bilingualism policy, but the numbers don't lie. More than 75 per cent of the Mounties in Ottawa are Quebeckers or French Canadians from other areas, whereas only 18 per cent of the general population of Ottawa–Carleton region reports French as a first language, according to Statistics Canada.

Across the force, bilingual capability has come to matter more than policing ability. The fact that Quebeckers do not rise to the highest levels of the force is seen as incidental, because they control the middle. As others in the force see it, their real power lies in their ability to shape policy and advise the force's leaders about which course of action they should take.

As a result, the rest of the force feels bitter and cut off. Antagonism and mistrust are rampant. There is a strong feeling within the force – even at the highest levels – that Quebec has used the Trojan horse of bilingualism and equality to take the force over from within. In short, many of the Quebeckers who have risen to the upper middle and top of the RCMP are considered by their fellow Mounties to be too political when it comes to initiating investigations, building cases, and laying charges.

As the brass at headquarters are being forced into public-policy contortions by their own advisers, what's going on in the field in Quebec is even more destructive. No matter where they might be within the RCMP, Quebec-born Mounties tend to march to their own beat – Quebec's beat – and no more so than in Quebec itself.

Former assistant commissioner Michel Thivierge saw the problem firsthand while serving as commander of the RCMP in Quebec from 1993 to 1995. The rumpled, erudite Thivierge, popularly known as Mike, was extremely well regarded within the force, and his sudden resignation stunned and disappointed Commissioner Murray.

In Thivierge's view, the Quebec problem poses a serious threat to the integrity of the RCMP. He believes there is a fundamental lack of understanding at the highest levels of the force about what makes Quebeckers tick: "Ottawa has never understood Quebec. In the top strata of the force there is not one real Quebecker. The force has always been based in the West and has been biased by a Western anglophone mentality. In recent years the commanding officer in Quebec has not been a native Quebecker. They have usually been French speakers from the West. They might sound the same as all French Canadians when they open their mouths, but they're not the same. They're not part of the group. Therefore, for the commanding officer, it's a lot like trying to run the foreign legion. Everybody pays lip service to your ideas, but nobody really listens. To be a leader in that situation is extremely difficult."

Having said that, however, Thivierge adds that, while the brass in Ottawa may well be out of touch with Quebec, the problem is exacerbated by the fact that most Quebeckers within the RCMP don't seem all that interested in what Ottawa has to say.

Thivierge was sent to Quebec in 1993 to clean up the incredible mess that had accumulated in the eighties and early nineties, culminating with the in-office suicide in December 1992 of Claude Savoie, the former head of the force's drug squad in Montreal. Savoie's superiors had discovered that he had received bribes totalling $200,000 from the notorious West End Gang, an established Montreal organized-crime group. Thivierge found there was more to the corruption than the Savoie case, but he won't elaborate. "On the whole in the RCMP there is very little corruption," Thivierge says. "It is a proud force and the members are dedicated, honest, and hardworking. The record is quite clear on that. There have been a few bad Mounties over the years, but they were the exception. On the whole, in my opinion, the RCMP system and training makes most Mounties virtually incorruptible."

During his time in Quebec, Thivierge, who is proud of his French-

Canadian roots, found that Quebec was a foreign world, surprisingly, for him, even within the seemingly safe and friendly confines of the RCMP itself. Born in Moncton, New Brunswick, he spent his first twelve years in Montreal, where his father served with distinction as a Mountie, having also retired as assistant commissioner in charge of Quebec. "Even though my father was born in Quebec and I am a French Canadian who grew up in Montreal, I'm not considered to be a Quebecker by Quebecker standards, especially by Quebeckers inside the force." In other words, being French Canadian and being from Quebec were not the same thing, an important but often overlooked distinction.

Thivierge believes that the corruption problem in Quebec arose because the RCMP does not operate the same way in the province as it does anywhere else in Canada. The normal practice in the RCMP is for members to be moved around from detachment to detachment, and often province to province, on a regular basis. Members don't have time to get too familiar with corrupting forces in their communities. In Quebec, however, that's not the case. Over the years, RCMP members tend both to come from Quebec and to serve their entire careers there. There has been little if any movement because, outside of Ottawa and New Brunswick, there are few places where many French-Canadian officers feel welcome in the country. "That creates a dangerous situation, because a police force by its very nature is a closed society," says Thivierge. "Quebec itself is also a closed society. To be a police officer in Quebec means that one is trapped in a doubly closed society. There is a very narrow view. Everyone on the inside becomes too familiar, while all outsiders are treated with suspicion. Corruption is inevitable."

In Thivierge's experience, the RCMP is caught in an uphill battle in Quebec. The force still faces resentment that has its roots in the execution of Métis rebel Louis Riel in 1885, and it's seen to be commanded in Quebec by "outsiders" – like him. Therefore, many of the changes Thivierge tried to implement in the RCMP's Quebec operations were resisted by his underlings. "In Quebec, they clearly play by a different set of rules. I wouldn't call the majority of the members in Quebec dyed-in-the-wool separatists, but they are generally proud of their origins. Quebec is a

French-speaking world, where people see the world in terms of the province, and not on a national level," Thivierge says. "It's not all that unusual, really. How many people don't want to leave New Brunswick or Manitoba or the mountains of British Columbia? The difference in Quebec is that their feelings are just that much stronger. The RCMP members from that society might best be described as soft federalists. They resist policies. They do their own thing rather than fall in line with Ottawa's thinking. In the end you can make all the changes you want, but as soon as you leave, they will revert back to what they are doing, unless you change the culture of the force entirely."

Commissioner Murray tried to solve these Quebec problems in a most subtle way in 1995, without arousing any media attention. Most Mounties didn't realize what he had done either. Until the Trudeau years, Mounties had to serve in provincial and municipal detachments before moving up to federal policing and jobs in headquarters, but that policy was largely abandoned to accommodate government-imposed quotas on hiring. Murray quietly implemented a new version of this rule: all new cadets must serve at least five years in a contract-policing position to learn basic policing before being able to apply for an opening in federal policing. As logical and practical as such an order might seem, the implications for the force were enormous.

After Pierre Trudeau's "francophone participation" program was implemented within the RCMP in 1974, the RCMP had recruited as many French Canadians as it could find, the vast majority of them from Quebec. The first assignment for many of these new recruits were in the traditional RCMP contract postings, in British Columbia, the West, and New Brunswick. However, two things happened. In the mid-seventies, the force began to get complaints, from places such as Surrey, B.C., about the number of RCMP officers on the streets who couldn't speak English. Meanwhile, many of the French Canadians in these positions were frustrated, angry, and homesick. At the first opportunity, many transferred to Quebec.

Commissioner Inkster, first as the force's personnel director in the early eighties, then later as commissioner, decided that it would be prudent if the force just skipped the basic training in contract policing and sent Quebec recruits directly from cadet school to the highly complex world of federal policing. This meant that most if not all Quebec recruits would go to Toronto, Ottawa, or Montreal, the hub of federal policing in Canada. Soon these new recruits, pushed by the double advantages of language and favourable promotional policies, began to flood into head-quarters, eating up job opening after job opening. Meanwhile, English-speaking cadets continued to be sent to contract work in the West and the Maritimes, where they were schooled en masse in an entirely different kind of work – street policing.

It is no coincidence that during this period, the RCMP has been quickly transformed from a top-notch federal police force into one so ineffective that it might be considered comical, if the issues involved weren't so critical to the country. During this time, the RCMP has become organized in such a way that it is almost incapable of performing a guardian role. Embarrassment after embarrassment has become the norm. As the Mounties failed, the government demanded more reforms. But as each reform was implemented, the spiral continued, and the inves-tigative capabilities of the force continued to decline.

Former deputy commissioner Henry Jensen, who remains close to the force, expressed the concerns within the RCMP this way: "The RCMP had evolved into two distinct police forces, with different experiences, identi-ties, and approaches to law enforcement. In the contract provinces, all the Mounties had basic training and experience as police officers, and most of them spoke English. In Central Canada, in particular Ottawa, the force was French-speaking, which in and of itself was not a problem. The problem was that most of those French-speakers had no basic policing experience, but they had risen through the ranks to the point where they were devising and implementing policy or even running investigative units. Some of those running investigations had never even served a search warrant or testified in a criminal case. Is it any wonder that federal policing by the RCMP began to fall into disrepute in the 1990s?"

In 1995, when Murray blocked new cadets from moving directly into federal policing positions, the message he sent was the equivalent of the first shot in a civil war. To the Quebeckers it was clear that Murray was going to try to seize back the centre of the force in an incremental way. He was going to play the long game. In that light, the 1996 regionalization program was seen by the Quebec members as the next logical step in the silent battle. But word of Assistant Commissioner Emond's visit to Murray, demanding that "C" Division run all investigations in Central Canada, caused an equally angry backlash among non-Quebec members, most of whom were stationed in Ontario.

After the Aylmer meeting in March 1996 and Emond's call on Murray, the force held a regional information meeting in Cornwall, Ontario. The intention of the meeting was for the force to get input from the rank and file, but the everyday Mounties knew the force had already made up its mind. Those who attended the Cornwall meeting said the atmosphere was charged from the beginning. Then it turned nasty.

Informal minutes taken by members who attended the meetings report some of the following comments, which reveal the sort of bitterness and prejudice that has grown up among the rank and file and the problems with morale: "Quebec is the most corrupt place in Canada. . . . Olympic Stadium. . . . Everyone's dirty. . . . The only place in the country the RCMP has a problem with corruption in its own force is in Quebec. . . . They are all separatists. . . . It's suicidal. . . . They're trying to kill the RCMP, and we're giving them more power? . . . If Murray does this he's signing the RCMP's death warrant. We'll never have another successful investigation. We might as well just close up shop. . . ."

Meanwhile, English-speaking administrators, based largely in the Toronto area, who were in contention to head up the Central Canada division, echoed the above comments. Some said that they would prefer not to have to live in Quebec, and that they would rather see the Central Canada adminstration located in Ontario.

In late summer 1997, Murray finally made his decision on where the Central Canada headquarters would be located – in Ottawa, in a separate building from RCMP headquarters. He presented the decision to the force as a worthy compromise between the two "extreme" positions.

Ontario investigators were not placated and continued to be chagrined by what was taking place. As far as they were concerned, having the Central Canada headquarters in Ottawa wasn't going to be much different from having it on Quebec City's Grande Allée, a stone's throw from the National Assembly.

What may well have been the most telling about the commissioner's decision was that the government of Quebec never complained for a moment about the RCMP's intention to move its brass to Ottawa. This is a province that has caused federal-provincial ruckuses over much, much less. Quebec's very silence, though, was also a clue to the real controversy about regionalization. As has been the case down through the years, Quebec ultimately got what it wanted. While the federal government was arguing about national unity, at the same time, by virtue of its economic imperatives, it was weakening a key federal institution.

Concerned Mounties point to the fate of Dorval Airport as an example of the potential problems the country faces with downsizing and regionalization of the RCMP. One of the outcomes of these programs was that the RCMP federal police would no longer be policing federal airports in jurisdictions where there were other police forces. In Toronto, for example, the suburban Peel Regional Police took over patrolling the airport. Even in Vancouver, there is concern in some quarters of the RCMP that airport policing being handled by the Mounties' own Richmond municipal detachment is not up to the standard of the federal police. "They just don't have the same perspective or interest," says one high-ranking Mountie familiar with the situation. But it is in Quebec where the greatest concern lies. The very prospect of having the Sûreté du Québec in charge of Dorval sent alarm bells ringing in the corridors of a number of federal government departments in the fall of 1997. No one in government had appreciated that forcing the RCMP to downsize could have such potentially disastrous consequences.

"Dorval is still a federal jurisdiction, but Ottawa, in effect, just handed it over to Quebec," said one high-ranking government insider. "With the Sûreté guarding the airport, God knows what's going to happen. That airport is one of the main routes for drugs and smuggling, areas of federal jurisdiction. The Sûreté has no interest in enforcing federal laws. Christ, they don't enforce their own laws. It's absolutely scary to contemplate what's going to go on there. The one thing you can be sure of is that, when passengers arrive in Montreal, they will be greeted by the fleur-de-lis. There won't be a maple leaf in sight."

During the Mulroney era, a concern within the RCMP had been that the force had fallen under political control. As we have seen, Commissioner Murray addressed that problem by not reporting to the political level about high-profile criminal investigations. But what everyone seemed to fail to see was that political control of the police was ultimately being exercised by budget controls that dictated the direction the police would take. By drastically cutting federal policing budgets, the government put the problem of downsizing and reorganization into the hands of the police themselves.

Some RCMP federal investigators fully believe that the defederalization of the force is intentional. They believe that was the game plan all along, and for that reason they see regionalization as a near-fatal blow to the force's federal policing capabilities, because now there is no commander of investigations in the country who has the mandate for the big picture. There are now four commanders, each in charge of his own budget and kingdom.

"Who is going to be there to look out for the big view?" asks former assistant commissioner Michel Thivierge. "I know Ottawa will say that everything will be co-ordinated. That's fine in theory, but that's not what happens in practice." Thivierge speaks for many others who worry that the RCMP is creating the circumstances for its own embarrassment. He cites the creation and operations of the Special Federal Investigations Unit in the early eighties as an example of what is likely to go wrong. "All major investigations relating to government corruption or that touched upon national security were handled by the special unit at headquarters. The unit had the best people, the most experience, good qualifications, and what-not. They made sure all the proper steps were taken. There was a whole series of checks and balances. One of the things that started to happen after a period of time, and it started under Inkster, was that they began to dismantle sections like Special Federal

Investigations in the name of decentralization. But in sending out these responsibilities to the regions, what they were doing was that they weren't sending out the people or developing new people. In other words, people were on their own."

The key to decentralization is the notion that anyone in the RCMP can do anyone else's job, despecialization, as it were, and that a manager is a manager is a manager. No distinction has been made between what should have been decentralized and what shouldn't have been. "There are certain types of key investigations that need very close supervision and qualified people," Thivierge continues. "It doesn't make sense economically to start having these units all over the place. You might only have one or two or three events per year, and so, if you have a group located somewhere, you can make sure the proper controls are in place. They can work out of anywhere, but you need one central area, whether it's there to coordinate or actually deal with the problems in an investigation. With the massive decentralization that has taken place, they have thrown out all these controls. Now the regions and divisions are running around doing their own thing, making their own contacts overseas, travelling all over the place, and the old structure that was in place, making sure that everything was being done properly, has disappeared into the wind. It is a recipe for disaster. In such a climate it is inevitable that another problem like the one they had with Airbus is going to happen."

Thivierge is also extremely concerned at another level about the future and integrity of federal policing. "In the contract provinces, the commanding officers report to the local justice minister or solicitor general. In the provincial policing contracts, the agreement is that the federal government will pay for 30 per cent of the cost of each officer, because that's how much federal policing they expect they might do. In municipal contracts, the federal government picks up 10 per cent of the cost for the same reason. But in every province there are also pure federal police officers. What has happened in the past, and it's a major problem, is that the local commander will constantly draw on these federal resources to carry out his provincial or municipal duties. They are driving down these federal resources to satisfy their ministers at the local level, because they know they won't get any heat from Ottawa for doing that. Their whole *raison d'être* is to satisfy the local minister. As a result, federal programs have been limping along, because federal investigators are out there investigating rapes, murders, and other local problems, mainly because the provincial governments and municipalities aren't willing to pay for the number of police officers they really require. Regionalization will just exacerbate that problem."

Thivierge speaks for dozens of Mounties who hold the same opinion.

One of them, Inspector Gary Nichols, is currently assigned to federal duties in Newmarket, Ontario. "The biggest problem in Canada right now is the influx of organized crime. Almost every problem police face at the street level is the result of organized crime – drugs, fraud, prostitution, you name it. To make a lasting impact on crime, we as a country need to focus most of our attention on this organized crime. We can only fight organized crime if the police force is organized along national and international lines. In my opinion the RCMP is going in exactly the opposite direction. It's driving down all its resources to fight street-level crime. If we do that, we're just spinning our wheels."

Among the rank and file and RCMP officers such as Nichols, there is a feeling that the tall foreheads at RCMP headquarters are lost somewhere high in the clouds over Ottawa. Although their intentions may well be pure, Mounties wonder why Murray and his administrators can't see the obvious effects and negative implications of their decision-making. How could Murray and all his trusted advisers have been so blind?

In *Voltaire's Bastards*, John Ralston Saul provided one possible answer: "A society which teaches the philosophy of administration and 'problem solving,' as if it were the summit of learning, and concentrates on the creation of elites – whose primary talent is administration – has lost not only its common sense and its sense of moral value but also its understanding of technical advance. Management cannot solve problems. Nor can it stir creativity of any sort. It can only manage what it is given. If asked to do more, it will deform whatever is put into its hands."[7]

Chapter Seven

•

POLICE LTD.

THE NATURE AND VERY health of the RCMP took a turn for the worse in October 1990, when the Mulroney government tabled in the House of Commons a forty-seven-page discussion paper entitled, "Police-Challenge 2000: A Vision of the Future of Policing in Canada." While it seemed like a good idea for the times, many in the RCMP saw it as a trojan horse which finally broke through the barricades of the institution. "Everything we have become today can be traced to that little document," says RCMP Inspector Rod Knecht, a federal police officer based in Newmarket, Ontario.

The author of "Police-Challenge 2000" was Solicitor General Pierre Cadieux, who credits André Normandeau, a criminologist and professor at the Université de Montréal, as the driving force.[1] The discussion paper was larded with the kind of American technocratic ideas and Harvard Business School buzzwords and phrases that have been so seductive to the business elite over the years: "total quality," "core values," "empowerment," "partnerships," "excellence," "risk-taking," "conflict resolution," "ownership," and "user-pay systems."

"Police-Challenge 2000" was the culmination of three years of activity and "innovation" by the Mulroney government to transform and modernize policing across Canada, at the local, provincial, and federal levels. Cadieux advocated that more police jobs be civilianized and that more routine police and security duties be privatized. He saw private policing "as the dominant mode of policing in Canada." In Cadieux's vision, the role of the public police should be to work with private police and to

125

provide armed backup when "real crime" occurs. Cadieux's impassioned plea for the new trend for the force, "community-based policing," was met as a breath of fresh air by police reformers, but few outside the inner circles of the RCMP recognized what was really going on. While "Police-Challenge 2000" waxed eloquent about how every police force in the country would take on an increasingly complex role, its result was the virtual elimination of the RCMP's federal policing role in Canada. One paragraph in particular stands out. Cadieux wrote:

> Although police organizations will remain locally based, because of the increasingly non-local, inter-connected, international nature of white-collar crime, they will co-operate with forces in other countries on issues such as drug trafficking, computer fraud and financial fraud. Thus the role of Interpol and similar agencies will become more important. Federal policing will be responsible for relatively few federal statutes, while federal agencies will be concerned mainly with standards of police services, accreditation of police forces, audit and evaluation of service delivery against national standards, and accountability. Like much of the criminal justice system, regional and local policing will be community-based and integrated into a local support and self-help system. Police professionals will engage in multi-disciplinary task forces and inter-agency co-operation.

That single paragraph in "Police-Challenge 2000" articulated the direction in which the RCMP would head in the nineties. Cadieux recommended the partial dismantling and disempowering of the RCMP as a federal law-enforcement agency. The new and improved RCMP would be reduced more or less to a police-services business providing laboratory and forensic services for police forces across the country – as it does now – and contract police services to provinces and municipalities.

Cadieux's recipe for success was one which might best be applied to the problems experienced in the inner cities of the United States, where radical tax-cutting measures crippled municipal police forces. In fact, much of what was in "Police-Challenge 2000" was relevant to the problems faced by American *municipal* police forces – and not even state or federal investigative services. There were two obvious and fundamental problems with adopting the same approach in Canada.

First, the crime-control problems facing Canada now aren't the same as they are in the United States, where there is, and will continue to be, a plague of inner-city ghettoes and guns, lots of guns. Second, and this is even more critical, there are significant differences in the police structure and justice institutions in the two countries. The United States has a strong and diverse federal structure and justice system, with a myriad of overlapping and vibrant law-enforcement agencies; Canada doesn't. All Canada has are the Mounties.

The RCMP's federal jurisdiction is the enforcement of legislation relating to the Food and Drug Act, customs, excise, income tax, bankruptcy, and unemployment insurance. Their mandate includes everything from the national investigation of organized crime to telemarketing schemes and, as former commissioner Norman Inkster alluded to earlier, such obscure legislation as that involving the protection of migratory birds. If it is the intention of the government that the Mounties not be there to enforce federal laws, then who will? The provinces? The municipalities? Private police? Not likely.

There was no provision made by Cadieux for any police force, public or private, to be empowered to enforce these laws, laws which are designed in the national interest, to set national standards and in defence of the greater good. In an age of globalism, Cadieux's plan was based entirely on community policing, fixing neighbourhood problems at the sidewalk level, as if there were no link between organized crime and dangerous neighbourhoods. Such links, as we shall read about in later chapters, are well known and well documented. Cadieux's reliance on Interpol as an alternative to federal policing was a joke: Interpol is not a police agency, but an information service, and will continue to be so.[2]

The calm, business-like approach Cadieux took to the justice system and federal law enforcement was guaranteed to please Quebec – and, one could argue, the United States. In effect, the Mulroney government had shredded the RCMP's federal role, all but breaking another link holding the country together. Forcing the Canadian police into more of a north-south axis than an east-west one was billed as inevitable, a better way to manage policing. But no Canadian asked for this to happen – or were told about the implications. There was no pressing need. The government just kept moving the force in that direction, incrementally, decreeing what was best, and using its power and publicity machine to make it so. The public interest was what the government declared it to be, damn the facts and larger arguments, which, as the Lalonde Doctrine suggested, was proper behaviour for a modern government.

Like a well-drilled marching band stuck behind a malevolent drum major, hardly missing a beat along the way, the RCMP followed the government's lead into a blind alley, the ranks eventually piling one by one into a brick wall, leaving the force utterly dazed and confused.

• • •

Today, if any Mountie cares to know what the brass upstairs is thinking at RCMP headquarters, the answer lies on a wall of the cafeteria in the basement. In the lineup for the hotplate, every hungry Mountie at 1200 Vanier Parkway must pass the Law Enforcement Research Centre bulletin board – all sixteen feet of it. The board is a running catalogue of the bedside reading of RCMP administrators. On one particular day in 1997, the colourful dust jackets from fifty-seven hardcover books were pinned into the cork. The dominant themes, represented by forty of the titles, were leadership and business management in books mostly by American authors such as Peter F. Drucker, Richard M. Hodgetts, Dean R. Spitzer, William E. Schneider, David M. Messick, and Ann E. Tenbrunsel. Prominently displayed are the hits of Harvard Business School alumni and their numerous imitators: *Managing in a Time of Great Change*; *Leader of the Future*; *Leading with Soul*; *Codes of Conduct: Behavioral Research into Business Ethics*; *The Re-engineering Alternative: A Plan for Making Your Current Culture Work*; *Competing by Design: The Power of Organizational Architecture*; *Light Bulbs for Leaders: A Guide Book for Team Learning*; *The Practice of Empowerment*; and that all-time favourite, *Corporate Executions*.

Stray away from the RCMP cafeteria and it doesn't take long for the listener to hear echoes of the ideas contained within those books. In the national fingerprint identification lab, the talk is about "efficiencies," including a project designed to "cut down on keyboard strokes" to save time. Over in the firearms lab, director Michael Foran fingers a compact disc produced by his department. It is a unique registry of every firearm ever made, a product in demand by police forces all around the world. "It's all about cost recovery today," Foran says. RCMP scientists are constantly hunting for new, better, and cheaper ways to do their work. A relatively cheap dentist's tool has been redesigned to identify phony credit cards. An industrial machine is converted to lift fingerprints from plastics, which used to be virtually impossible. Robots designed to climb stairs and break down doors are being constructed from scratch. A secondhand 1994 recreational vehicle is transformed into a command post. Others are working with business and industry to solve security and technical problems. In many respects, all these are the RCMP's core "businesses."

"We are not going to learn by looking at other police departments, we are going to learn from successful companies," Commissioner Murray told his management team, shortly after taking over his post in June 1994. Soon, RCMP senior officers were flying around North America visiting U.S.-based multinational corporations such as IBM, 3M, and Motorola to learn the management strategies that helped make them all profitable. A few short years later, the language of business is the language of the RCMP, at least within sight of 1200 Vanier Parkway.

No matter what a Mountie administrator is doing these days, he sounds like a chip off Lee Iacocca's block. Assistant Commissioner Cleve Cooper, who runs community, contract, and aboriginal policing services, talks about the new initiatives being promoted by the force, "all premised upon the new service-delivery model." These include everything from "partnering" and community-based policing to an alternative system for young offenders called Family Group Conferencing. Cooper talks so much about the influence of concepts such as "the aboriginal holistic world view," one almost forgets that a policeman is in the room. "In my thirty-five years, I've never seen as much change as I have in the past two years," says Cooper. "There has been tremendous change taking place, coupled with all the difficulties associated with change. We're getting away from the military approach."

Assistant Commissioner Joop Plomp, in charge of technical operations, talks about invention and risk-taking and joint ventures. Money may be tight in Canada, so the RCMP figures out innovative ways to do things. It likes to see itself as the development and testing wing for many larger and richer U.S. forces. Plomp says the members are driven by their own pride in the force to excel, even though the budget is tight. "We have the ideas," Plomp says, "and the FBI finances the solutions."

This notion of invention and efficiency extends right down to the Special Emergency Response Team. Take bomb-squad members Sergeant Sheldon Dickie and Corporal John Bureaux. They hadn't received a pay raise in five years, but each of them feels privileged to have the opportunity to be a Mountie. "The government's got to get the debt down. We all have to do our part; we each have to pull our weight," says Dickie. On this day Dickie and Bureaux demonstrate a new anti-blast suit they helped design, in a joint venture with an Ottawa company. The suit is now being sold in a hundred countries. "We were able to make a better suit because we're part of the design process," says Dickie. "We are both front-line operators" – they actually go out on bomb calls and defuse bombs – "and liaisons with industry. We're unique that way. We've even formed alliances with the Defense Department and Transport to help cut costs." The squad is most proud of its ability to invent new systems and policing aids. In concert with a U.S. company, for example, it helped develop a stable of bomb-proof vehicles that are a wonder to behold, taking the brunt of a car bomb without cracking.

Beneath the scarlet veneer every Mountie in Ottawa comes across as a businessman in disguise, the kind of public servant who would make a tax-fearing, government-hating citizen proud. It seems that everyone who matters at headquarters has a business or commerce degree. To get to such a high level in the force, having a business degree is the second prerequisite for any Mountie with ambitions to be commissioner someday. The first, of course, is being fully bilingual.

Dawson Hovey, the chief spokesman for the commissioner, talks about project renewal, structuring and restructuring, and such tried-and-true business concepts as economies of scale. "The RCMP has lost 2,300 positions since 1993 and $173 million from its budget. Administration has been cut out. We have only one administrative staff for every ten police officers. In the army, there are five support people for every soldier," Hovey says, proudly. "We're flattening the organization and moving away from the military model – the command-and-control structure. It's too rigid. We've had to change our way of business. The plan is that there will be no more than two layers between a commanding officer and the lowest member under him. We're using the savings to help provide more and better front-line services."

All the RCMP seems to want to talk about is front-line services – what it's doing on the streets – mostly in police cars, mostly in small towns across the country. What the RCMP doesn't want to talk about is federal law enforcement, which, most Canadians believe, is the precise reason the RCMP was created and continues to exist.

•   •   •

The final push towards RCMP Ltd., as it were, began in the mid-to-late eighties. Since the Glassco Commission's recommendations in 1963 that government should operate more like a business, the RCMP had, in large measure, successfully resisted going in that direction. In some respects, with its contract-policing services, the RCMP has operated like a business for a long while. But it never really thought like one. Contracts were a means to an end – that is, to give the force a national reach and scope. Another reason the RCMP didn't think like a business was that, until the mid-to-late eighties, few understood how a police force could possibly be treated as a business.

That began to change in 1987, when one key incident occurred which gave the Mulroney government all the leverage it needed to overcome the weight of the traditions, myths, and public support that the RCMP enjoyed, and to eventually enforce its political will. At a regular meeting of the solicitor general's committee on Parliament Hill, Commissioner

Robert Simmonds found himself sandbagged by Quebec members over his inability to speak French. This moment and the ensuing headlines embarrassed James Kelleher, the solicitor general of the day. He immediately promised the public that the next commissioner would be bilingual.

Kelleher had been appointed solicitor general a few months earlier as a reward for being the first Conservative to win the riding of Sault Ste. Marie, Ontario, in the 1984 general election. Mulroney had received pressure from within the party to honour this achievement, and he did so by appointing Kelleher solicitor general, a relatively minor portfolio in the scheme of things. Spurred on by Simmonds's faux pas, Kelleher argued that the force needed a makeover. The way to do it, he believed, was to convert the RCMP from a paramilitary operation into something more like a modern business. In Kelleher's modernist view, the RCMP was "a bit of an anachronism in that it has been steeped in the past by a military structure and outlook. That kind of structure might very well work in a war or with military people, it doesn't lend itself in today's society to the way a police force should operate."[3] A second problem affecting the force, Kelleher said at the time, was the number of masters it tried to serve at the federal, provincial, and municipal levels. Something had to be done.

Simmonds had served as commissioner for ten years, one of the longest terms in the history of the appointment.[4] He had commanded the force through the McDonald Commission and its aftermath, and by the time Kelleher arrived, the shell shock from that experience had still not worn off, as Simmonds continued to wrestle with the flawed recommendations of the commission. McDonald had urged the government to add extra layers of administration to the force, the checks and balances that it believed were needed to avoid repeating another barn-burning incident by the Security Service. Simmonds implemented some of the recommendations, resisted where he could, and tried to look after everything himself. A seasoned and successful investigator, he was a hands-on administrator who ran the force as if he were a corporal running three constables in a contract detachment in some prairie town. His desk was piled high with files as he worked every night late into the evening, ruining his marriage in the process. Every one who knew him generally agreed that while

Simmonds's heart was in the right place, there was more to running the RCMP in the eighties than trying to do the right thing for both the force and the government. The search began to replace Simmonds.

Kelleher had some clear goals. "What we decided we wanted was a commissioner who could bring the force into the twenty-first century," Kelleher recalled in a 1997 interview. "We had nothing but police officers in the RCMP. Police officers did everything. They were secretaries, filing clerks; you name it, they did it. They weren't trained and they didn't know anything about business methods or running a large organization. Their management skills were sadly lacking."

Kelleher set up a committee comprised of himself, deputy clerk Jack Manion, and John Tate, the deputy solicitor general, and they conducted a competition across the country to search for the right man. "Whoever it was going to be, I wanted him appointed right away, and I was going to give him an office right beside mine. I wanted him to sit there for six months and think about how he was going to bring the RCMP into the twenty-first century. I wanted him to be meeting with other deputy ministers. I wanted him to look at management and civilianization."

After all the hunting and searching, Kelleher says his committee fixed its gaze on Norman Inkster, who was already the number-two man in the force, the hand-picked choice of Robert Simmonds. Normally it had been the practice of the RCMP for the commissioner to anoint his successor, with the rare exception of Maurice Nadon's appointment in the mid-seventies. In Kelleher's version of the story, the next significant step he took, after appointing Inkster, was to make one of his own assistant deputy ministers, Michael Shoemaker, deputy commissioner, the first civilian executive manager in the force. That's Kelleher's version of the story, but that's not how Henry Jensen, who was a deputy commissioner under both Simmonds and Inkster, remembers it.

According to Jensen, Kelleher is now putting a spin on the story that masks what really happened. Jensen, who had helped create the Commercial Crime Branch back in 1965, was on the short list to replace Simmonds, along with Inkster and two other senior Mounties, Thomas Venner and Don Wilson. "There was no great search," Jensen says today.

"Kelleher's plan all along was to bring in Michael Shoemaker as the commissioner. Shoemaker was going to be the Great White Knight, a civilian who would come in and show the police how to do their jobs better. When Simmonds got word of what Kelleher was planning to do, he went straight to Brian Mulroney and put a stop to that nonsense. In the end Mulroney supported Simmonds, at least to the extent that Shoemaker wouldn't be commissioner. Instead, he was made deputy commissioner."

Mulroney's motives can be guessed at. He and some members of his government were up to their eyeballs in investigations by the RCMP, with the Airbus case on the horizon. Replacing the RCMP commissioner with Shoemaker, not only a civilian, but one who was also seen to be a political friend, would likely have been political suicide, especially since the next election campaign was just a year or so away. Having Shoemaker a heartbeat away from both Inkster and Mulroney was close enough. In many respects, the intention all along seemed to be that Inkster was there as a token Mountie, as it were, to keep the troops calm as changes were implemented. As Kelleher himself puts it, Shoemaker was brought in as a technocrat, someone who could help the RCMP speak and think in the language of business. In his role as a civilian deputy commissioner, Shoemaker became a contentious figure within the force.

"Shoemaker brought a dimension that was positive, at least in the short term, in that he was able to bridge relationships with the control agencies of government – the Treasury Board and the Privy Council," Henry Jensen says. "Michael had relations with those people, and he was reasonably successful in dealing with them." However, problems arose with Shoemaker over criminal investigations. Although Shoemaker had no responsibilities in the criminal-investigation area, he still was privy to what the force was doing and was suspected of unwittingly being a conduit back to the government.

With Inkster at the helm and Shoemaker as his deputy, the first fumbling steps at running the RCMP like a business were anything but successful. Instead of getting leaner and meaner, the force got slower and clumsier. The civilianization that did take place was limited to the planning personnel within the force. The RCMP was brought more into line with the government way of doing things, and became more, not less, bureaucratic. "As the force became more bureaucratic in its approach," says Jensen, "the government was able to exercise more and more control over the operations of the RCMP. The fact of the matter is that, the more a police force allows itself to be subjected to external conditions in terms of government policy – bilingualism, quotas in hiring, enforcement based on political and social objectives, for example – the more the police move away from being a professional service. Government bureaucracy can live on its own. Bureaucrats feed off each other. Inkster and Shoemaker brought in planners, analysts, and researchers, who in the end delivered nothing in terms of the final product, which is service to the public. But it all consumed a lot of attention and the resources of the organization. My quarrel with Inkster and Shoemaker is not that they made the force more business-like, but they made the RCMP an agency of government. They politicized it. That seemed to be Kelleher's prescription. He was a very unimpressive minister."

However, Inkster and Shoemaker did begin to change the face and thinking of RCMP administration, so that there was little or no resistance within the force to the theories propounded in "Police-Challenge 2000" in 1990. More than any other police force in North America and, perhaps, the world, the Royal Canadian Mounted Police has always had an entre-preneurial side, due mainly to its contract policing duties for the provinces, territories, and two hundred Canadian municipalities that purchase their services. The RCMP got the contract work mainly because it could do it more cheaply than any local force: federal government sub-sidies were paid to any provincial or municipal government that pur-chased RCMP policing services. Ontario and Quebec, which objected to a federal police force, got what they wanted, a force whose law-enforcement role was "national" and largely under control of provincial governments, rather than one that was federal and largely under the control of the federal government.

To keep those contracts, however, the RCMP had to deal with each government on a customer-client basis. Over the years, the force learned that, when it upset a client too much, as it did when Commercial Crime detectives pursued a series of corruption cases in New Brunswick in the seventies, it invited governments to seek out or create competition. In that instance, Premier Richard Hatfield set up the New Brunswick Highway Patrol, a short-lived experiment, to show his anger with the force over investigations of his cabinet ministers, his friends, and eventually himself.[5] Until that time, the RCMP had mostly five-year contracts with provinces, short leashes, which some tried to use to prevent the force from being as independent and effective as it wanted to be. But "Police-Challenge 2000" had an effect on the thinking on all sides. Federal law enforcement was going to be de-emphasized, and the provinces would have a greater say over the RCMP, a notion Commissioner Inkster did not resist. In 1992, in a logical extension of the "Police-Challenge 2000" plan, and at the instigation of the Mulroney government and with its total blessing, Commissioner Inkster entered the RCMP into twenty-year policing contracts with the provinces who wanted such services.[6]

Rank-and-file Mounties themselves didn't resist the twenty-year term, because on the surface it appeared to be the right decision. It was good business. The long-term contract guaranteed stability in planning and gave the Mounties the freedom to enforce the law as they saw fit in their contract responsibilities, lessening the chance of political pressure from their provincial or municipal bosses, whatever the case may be. As much as they were selling their services, the Mounties were still pure in their intentions. They were police officers first, empowered to enforce the laws of the land. But what most didn't appreciate was that the direction for the force was now set down in writing, ensuring that the future of the force would be in contract policing. In the thirty years after the Glassco Commission had recommended that the government operate more like a business, the RCMP had attempted to defy the government. But through time, budget cuts, and the gradual replacement of guardian-type leaders with business-minded ones, the RCMP's resistance was worn down. The era of RCMP Ltd. had fully begun.

When Philip Murray moved into the commissioner's office in 1994, he inherited a force that had been turned into a virtual captive of the government. Inkster had left behind at headquarters a bureaucracy of officials and advisers made up largely of Quebeckers. During his term, that bureaucracy and the government had established ties and procedures that, many Mounties say, gave the government too much say and control over the force. Finally, there was the negative impact on the force caused by a crippling internal promotions policy, which all but guaranteed that the best and the brightest would not rise to the top.

An overwhelming sense of inertia had seized the operation, as the early effects of "Police-Challenge 2000" were being realized, especially the move to de-federalize the RCMP. Tensions from the divisive Quebec–anglo split were rising to the surface, as we've already seen. And the new Liberal government, although more reasonable about the proper distance between the police and government, didn't let up on the budget issue.

Led by Finance Minister Paul Martin, a Montreal businessman, the Liberals proved to be even more fiscally conservative than the Conservatives, their neo-liberal soul-mates. As such, they continued to push the Mulroney government's agenda vis-à-vis federal policing.

In fact, while paying lip service to the beauty and importance of federalism, the Chrétien government hastened the devolution of powers to the provinces. As trans-provincial and trans-national white-collar crime exploded in the mid-nineties, for instance, the government ignored calls for the setting up of a national securities commission to monitor and investigate the growing problem of stock-market manipulation and fraud. With regard to the environment, the federal government consistently moved to distance itself from regulation, although environment is a shared responsibility with the provinces, and federal environment laws are enforced by the RCMP. At the same time, the provinces (as will be shown later) didn't prove all that interested in effective regulation or enforcement. The budget cutbacks seemed mindlessly shortsighted to some, driving experience and expertise out of the public service and sometimes out of the country.[7]

Ordered by government to reduce spending in the federal area of policing, Murray set out to attack the vast bureaucracy built up under Inkster and Shoemaker. If that's all Murray had done, that might have been fine in the eyes of the Mountie traditionalists. But Murray went a step beyond. Many Mounties believe that the essential difference between Inkster and Murray was that, while Inkster made an effort to be business-minded, Murray began to apply business thinking *for real*.

Between 1994 and today, the force has undergone so much change that some say it is suffering from "change fatigue." Winnipeg-based Staff Sergeant Reg Trowell described it this way: "Changes are overtaking changes. We physically can't keep up with the changes."

The Mounties aren't the only ones.

• • •

Since 1990, the message of "Police-Challenge 2000" has swept across the country, so that today the only people appointed municipal police chiefs across the country are those who swear to abide by or implement the concepts set out by Pierre Cadieux. Operating police forces as if they were a business has become an attractive proposition to politicians, and not only to those with responsibility for the RCMP. For example, during the summer of 1997, Bruce Chambers was sworn in as chief of the Vancouver police force. Chambers, who had been the chief in Thunder Bay, Ontario, became the first university-educated person to lead the Vancouver force. This is what the *Vancouver Sun* wrote in a front-page story about his appointment:

> Bruce Chambers has all the credentials of a chief executive officer. He has a master's degree in business administration and a bachelor of arts in politics. But the "company" he'll soon be overseeing is in the business of providing security to the city of Vancouver. . . .
>
> Chambers . . . has thirty years policing experience. But he believes it is his background in business and politics that will be particularly useful in the new job.
>
> "Policing is a service business and many of the skills and knowledge of a business executive are identical to a police executive . . . the principles are the same."
>
> Although unwilling to discuss specifics of how he will tackle long-standing problems such as drug dealing in the Downtown Eastside,

Chambers said he hopes to continue building on the community-based policing philosophy the force began implementing a few years ago.

"It's a vision where the ultimate consumers – the citizens – have an input and will play an active role." Chambers said he doesn't plan to impose any new police initiatives in Vancouver without first seeking community involvement.[8]

In those few short paragraphs reporter Kim Pemberton captured the essence of what may well be the growing controversy and concern within the RCMP, and other police forces, about the concept of Police Ltd. Within months Chambers reported that crime had dropped in Vancouver due to the implementation of his business-like policies, but few on the streets or within the Vancouver police department really believed him.

While politicians, police administrators, and their consultants move to a business model, the world of policing for the rank-and-file police officers, for victims of crime, and for suspects themselves has become so full of contradiction and confusion that no amount of managing can make them disappear. This is as true for local and provincial police forces as it is for the Royal Canadian Mounted Police.

The public has come to see the police debate in general in terms of public security, *only* the men in uniform – the thin blue line between order and anarchy on the streets. The business model for police concentrates almost entirely on the uniformed constable, an easy-to-understand concept that can be quantified and described to the taxpayer or, in the case of private security firms, the client. This is the same approach taken by the vast majority of academic and other experts who study policing and security. Little or no attention is paid to the value of criminal investigations – be they by detectives in a city police force or RCMP federal investigators – because such work is difficult to quantify or qualify.

"Commercial crooks aren't smarter than law-enforcement officers, not by a long shot. But they have a stacked deck," says Ontario Crown attorney Steve Sherriff. "Some of these crimes can't be detected easily or quickly, and they don't have much to fear from an investigation that doesn't have the money to do the job."[9]

There is little *visible* bang for the buck in beefing up detective squads. Therefore across-the-board cutbacks are aimed at these virtually invisible assets, because there is no obvious constituency to defend them, no matter how valuable and important they are in the scheme of things. In an era when Canadians have become captivated by images of U.S.-based real-life television, where street cops chase down poor white trash and minorities, there is an unfounded perception that this is the real world of policing at any level in Canada. Far from it. There is more to policing in Canada than men and women in uniform, but that has been lost in the public and academic debate. As a result, even the police themselves are confused about what they should be doing, while the public and politicians don't seem to have a clue about why the police sometimes seem to be so inept. The conflict in perception is due mainly to logical, moral, and ethical inconsistencies, which have served to cloud the clarity of vision and purpose police require to pursue their duty. For example:

• The traditional role of government in a democratic society is to oversee the police in an administrative way only. The police are servants of the law, and as such should answer to the courts. The tendency in recent years, however, is for government to demand that police administrators be more technocratic and political in their approach. In the selection of leaders, investigative skills have become secondary or tertiary considerations, if they are factored into the equation at all. These bottom-line-driven technocrats are seen to undercut the integrity and efficacy of the police, because they are generally considered to be more conditioned and sensitive to political imperatives than previous leaders might otherwise have been. The duty of the police, first and foremost, in a democracy is to abide not by political or social imperatives but by legal ones.

• The corporatization of police – and this extends well beyond Canada – has meant, as Vancouver Police Chief Chambers pointed out, that the police are seen to be a *service* organization rather than a *force*. Advocates of this position usually refer to the thinking of Sir Robert Peel, who set up the first public police force in England, and who wrote in his *The Principles of Law Enforcement* (1829): "The police at all times should maintain a relationship with the public that gives reality to the historic tradition that the police are the public and the public are the police; the police are the only members of the public who are paid to give full-time attention to duties which are incumbent on every citizen in the interest of community welfare." The intention in making such a distinction between a service and not a force is obviously designed to make the police appear to be friendlier and non-threatening – "the policeman is your friend" – in the most basic and literal fashion. However, the effect of this thinking tends to distort the relationship between police and the public. Neither is sure what the police are supposed to represent. The fact is that the police have, and must continue to have, extraordinary powers within society. They can and must be able to use the law to pry into people's lives, take away their freedoms, and kill them, if necessary, to defend the public or national interest.

• As an adjunct to this police-as-service model, modern police administrators have attempted to instil in its employees the notion that they are providing a service to their clients, as if policing were a real business. This is the true foundation of so-called community policing, the implications of which we will begin to discuss in the following chapters. But who are the clients, the taxpayers or the perpetrators of crimes?

• Finally, all these factors have combined to convince many police officers that they are not public servants, but merely employees of a company. As such, they have no higher responsibilities or duties. Policing is seen to be just another job. That message has been reinforced by society in its insistence on the civilianization of what were seemingly menial policing duties, such as administrative and clerical tasks. "The use of civilians has eliminated positions for injured or slightly disabled police officers," says Mike Funicelli, president of the "E" Division Members' Association in Vancouver, a budding union within the force. "The effect of this is that officers stop taking risks. Many won't go that extra step because the message is clear: Mounties can be loyal to the force and Canada, but the force isn't going to be loyal back. It's just like any other company."[10]

There is no question that attempting to run a police force as a business in a democratic society supposedly governed by the rule of law is to invite contradiction and confusion for everyone. The police are empowered to defend the public interest, but the notion of the public interest itself has been blurred by contradictory social, political, and economic imperatives. It's not a matter of left versus right, but rather democracy versus corporatism. Part of the problem, as discussed earlier, in Chapter Three, is the fusing in the mind of the public of three distinctly different concepts: industrialization, capitalism, and democracy. This ungainly mix of ideas has made it all but impossible for the average person to distinguish the fundamental differences between commerce and guardianship. Business in its essence is not and cannot be a pure moral force in a community. Business organizes capital and the means of production in order to make profits, which are important and desirable for the healthy functioning of a democracy. Government is the people, and is constructed to represent their interests. Government is a moral and ethical force.

When you really think about it, the two are irreconcilable concepts. If a government or its departments operate like a business, what exactly is the profit? As mentioned earlier, profit for a government cannot be measured in dollars earned, but in dollars saved, an entirely negative concept. For government to make a "profit," therefore, it must operate as a business in reverse. Instead of organizing the means of production, it must reduce production and services to make a "profit." For the police, such a reduction means that they cannot enforce the law as fully as they pledged to do when they swore an oath to the Crown. As obvious as the ramifications might well be, politicians everywhere, smitten by what can only be described as a superficial understanding of technocratic theories, have sped down the business highway without their headlights on.

• • •

In the modern business education of the RCMP there have been many gurus, like those found on the dust jackets pinned to the bulletin board in the headquarters cafeteria. But the most recent and important one for the

RCMP is Stephen R. Covey, a Harvard-trained professor of business at Brigham Young University. The current RCMP bible is Covey's best-selling book, *The Seven Habits of Highly Effective People: Powerful Lessons in Personal Change.*[11]

The force's relationship with Covey began in early 1996, when Superintendent Dwight McCallum and Staff Sergeant Jack Briscoe of the Community Policing Branch visited the Covey Leadership Centre in Provo, Utah, where they took a three-and-a-half-day course paid for by the force. Soon the RCMP entered into a licensing agreement with Covey, administered by an Ottawa agent, enabling it to use Covey's materials and techniques to train the members of the force. Briscoe says money for the project was found by reallocating funds through existing budgets.

"Covey is recognized as one of the leaders in the leadership business," Briscoe said in an interview. "He is an adviser to several Fortune 500 companies around the world. The Pentagon uses one of his courses. So do the Roman Catholic Church and large and small businesses everywhere. We are one of the first police organizations to become involved with Covey. We felt we needed him, because we are in transition and need help. We are moving from crime-control policing to a collaborative, responsive, and client-centred model of service, which we call community-based policing. What we hope to achieve is quality service delivery through the application of the principles of community-based policing. What makes Covey an attractive process is that his principles are common sense to you and me. You just put them into a process, build trust and concepts such as improved interpersonal relationships, managerial alignment, and stewardship. Those exposed to the training unanimously say everyone should experience Covey."

Covey's all-encompassing philosophy is basically a recipe for peace of mind for businessmen being tossed about in an unruly world where all the moral and ethical anchors have been lost. It is an easy-to-digest package of paradigms, illustrated with interlocking circles and triangles and charts, mixed in with aphorisms such as this one from Aristotle: "We are what we repeatedly do. Excellence, then, is not an act, but a habit." Or how about this one, from former U.S. president George Bush: "I take as my guide the hope of a saint; in crucial things, unity – in important things, diversity – in all things, generosity."[12]

Covey's ideas seem perfectly suited to a generation of business people whose serious reading might run the gamut from *Fortune* magazine to true crime, and who might get most of their ethical lessons from watching *Friends*, *NYPD Blue*, or *Seinfeld* reruns. Covey is the Costco of leadership-management gurus, packaging years of serious sociological, psychological, and philosophical theories in one convenient location. There is a little Émile Durkheim, a touch of Max Weber, a grain or two of Thomas Hobbes and Adam Smith, a dollop each of Aristotle, Cecil B. de Mille, T. S. Eliot, Albert Einstein, Erich Fromm, Johann Goethe, and God – the Golden Arches meets the Golden Rule, or is it the other way around?

Covey endorsers include the likes of Richard M. DeVos, the president of Amway, the cult-like multi-marketing program, entertainer Marie Osmond, astronaut Jake Garn, "the first senator in space," and ex-NFL quarterbacks Roger Staubach and Fran Tarkenton.[13]

Just reading the list of those who endorse Covey's work is enough to send a chill up the spine of most rank-and-file Mounties. Read Covey and it's immediately apparent that fattening his followers' bottom line is Covey's bottom line. Covey wants his followers to accomplish their goals, and to feel good about themselves afterward. The presumption at the heart of all of Covey's work is that his followers, to one degree or another, are concerned about the moral and ethical implications of their moneymaking activities. The RCMP is a guardian agency, empowered to enforce the law, which by its very definition demands moral and ethical behaviour.

One of the real concerns many have about the direction in which the force is headed is the result of the meaning and implications of one of the most popular words in the RCMP management lexicon – *empowerment*. As the RCMP downsizes and cuts out layers of checks and balances, more and more responsibility is being thrown onto the backs of the street-level police officer. They are being given more latitude and discretion in the execution of their duties. Personal empowerment is a business-world concept, which became fashionable during the eighties as business downsized and cut out middle layers of management. Personal empowerment for a police officer is a controversial idea, of course, but Commissioner Murray says the public shouldn't be worried: "The whole concept of empowerment to me means that you're empowering someone to fulfil the mandate of the organization, fulfil the objectives, the parameters, that you provided people to work towards. It doesn't mean that seventeen thousand people are running off doing their own thing, by any means. But what we have tried to do is provide our service to be much more client-focused, whether we're in a municipal role, a provincial role, or a federal role. . . . We're holding people accountable, very much so, and they know they are going to be held accountable for what they do. We're focusing our management, what's left of it, on the high-risk areas, the areas that are problematic. The routine stuff will be self-managed, by and large, and we still have an audit capability to go in and spot-check and make sure that people are directing their resources to the objectives. I think it's safe to say that we are much better informed today as a senior management than we ever were."[14]

As fervently as Murray and his administrators believe that they are headed in the right direction, somewhere along the line they all seem to have missed the debate in recent years about downsizing, and how it crippled so many organizations. Downsizing usually meant knowledge and institutional memory were the first assets to go out the door.

"The people at the top say they are trying to run the force like a business, but the RCMP is not a business. No police force is a business. It's a public trust," says former assistant commissioner Michel Thivierge, one of the most articulate critics of the force, whose observations echo those of many others. "Most of these people clearly don't know what they're doing. They fundamentally do not understand what it is that a police force is supposed to be doing in a democratic society. They all see themselves as technocrats, trying to manage away problems, but they're not addressing the deep, underlying problems. They're not getting to the roots. There is no real vision. They're just lurching from one thing to another, with no real long-term solutions and no deep understanding of the implications for both the force and society."

As Thivierge sees it, the government and its powerful bureaucracy wants to hear the RCMP's leaders say that they will operate the force like a business, even though that might not make much sense. The RCMP's leaders have no alternative but to go along with the government or they will lose their jobs. In the end everyone is playing a dangerous and important game in the most superficial manner possible, mainly because there are few within the RCMP capable of mounting a more sophisticated or courageous defence of the force.

"The police culture does not lend itself to open discussion or to intellectual development," says Thivierge. "The current leadership of the force talks about leadership and recommends books to be read by the members, but I'm not sure that all that many people read those books, anyway. I think the problems within the RCMP start right there. You don't have a culture that encourages or creates a climate where people develop themselves. This is a life-long thing."

What this means within the RCMP is that, while it strives to disassemble and move away from the paramilitary model, it really can't. Orders are orders. The RCMP might feed its members the latest business or leadership theories and tell them to be creative, but there is little or no room for contrarian ideas. Not one of the dust jackets on the bulletin board in the cafeteria at 1200 Vanier Parkway talks about any alternative ideas on business and leadership, and there are many. "I haven't seen a management theory that six months later is not refuted, discredited, or highly criticized," the well-read Thivierge says. "Virtually every theory the RCMP is using today to manage itself is based on business, the making of widgets and turning a profit. There are no management theories that I am aware of that deal with organizations in the public-security field, organizations that hold a public trust. You can't run the police like a business; they're not there to make a profit. In the end, the force just keeps building on past mistakes."

The other side of the argument, the side that says the business model is not the best solution, is well represented, Thivierge says. He thinks the leaders of the force should be reading thinkers such as John Ralston Saul, Jane Jacobs, and others who have given deep consideration to the problems at hand, because "they are badly in need of some perspective. They have no sense of history about what happens when guardians of the public interest take on the values and objectives of the corporate class."

Another who has written extensively on the subject is Seymour Melman, a professor of industrial engineering at Columbia University. In 1983, he published a seminal book, *Profits Without Production*, which focuses on an arcane subject, the decline of the machine tool industry in the United States. The book's dust jacket effectively describes Melman's thesis: "Why does American industry continue to deteriorate while company profits soar? A noted economist traces the decline to a generation of executives – corporate, government and academic – whose obsession with profits and power has made them incapable of organizing production effectively."

Melman's focus was the relationship between the U.S. government, the military, and private industry, which is analogous to the relationship between the Canadian government, the RCMP, and the privatization of policing services in Canada. In his book, Melman deals with a number of government procurement fiascos, and all but predicts – fourteen years ahead of his time – that the $2-billion Stealth bomber would be beleaguered by technical problems, such as its inability to fly in humid weather.

Melman made two observations particularly worth noting: "So powerful and extensive are the pressures for short-term gain that many corporate managers have moved outside the law. *Fortune* magazine reported in 1980 that of 1,043 major corporations included in a study of illegal activity, 117, or 11 per cent, have been found guilty of criminal charges or have pleaded no contest to such charges. . . . The *Fortune* report noted that 'The common practice of running a company through decentralized profit centres, giving each manager his head but holding him strictly accountable for the results, often provides a setting in which the rules can readily be bent. The temptation comes when heightened competition or a recession squeezes margins.'" Melman writes further:

The special intensity of short-term effects is associated with an ongoing decline in the value assigned to production work, of every sort. Money-making and the enhancement of decision-making power are seen as cardinal virtues in the managerial occupations and as yardsticks of achievement. They are displacing such other criteria as organizing people to work, or producing excellent goods, or enhancing the quality of life for a wider community. The development of management with a primary emphasis on short-term rates of profit has been further facilitated in the United States by strong ideological support from the schools of business."[15]

Apply these principles to today's decentralized, empowered RCMP and, critics such as Thivierge and Jensen fear, the inevitable will happen – poor policing, corruption, and a failure to serve the public interest.

John Ralston Saul put another spin on the argument in *Voltaire's Bastards*, where he too used the military as an example: "The swollen officer corps of the West have progressed from the myth of modern organization to the myth of modern manager. All the syndromes of bureaucratic life are to be found in their headquarters. A nine-to-five attitude. Group decisions to protect each individual. An inability to respond to information which indicates that the system is doing the wrong thing. Leadership rarely rewarded."

Saul goes on to quote Richard Gabriel, who writes that in "these entrepreneurial officer corps competition and careerism make every officer look out for himself. . . . Personnel managers are actually in charge of the system and they have redesigned the system of military promotion and rewards to reward managerial bureaucrats. Army promotion boards are controlled by staff officers who have little or no frontline experience. It isn't surprising that Western military organizations are unable to adapt themselves to doing battle with fast, light armies that fight outside the rational tradition."[16]

Substitute RCMP for army, and crime for the enemy, and one has a perfect picture of today's RCMP, right down to the fact that the last two commissioners were personnel managers, although Murray had somewhat more field experience than his predecessor, Inkster, who had virtually none.

Saul's most disturbing condemnation, however, might well be his alarming comparison of what is happening with the government in Canada, today, with aims of the corporatist movement in Germany, Italy, and France in the 1920s. These were: "shift power directly to economic and social interest groups; push entrepreneurial initiative in areas normally reserved for public bodies; obliterate the boundaries between public and private interest – that is, challenge the idea of the public interest."[17]

As the RCMP adopts a business model, it has become incapable of enforcing many of the most important laws in the country; that is, it is not able to defend the public interest and the national interest as well as it should.

What is happening to the RCMP is more than just a managerial process. The police force is being restructured as if it were a corporate body, making decisions out of economic expediency, not in a way that reinforces its functions and values. In fact, this is a transformation of values. When a business model is superimposed onto a guardian institution that has a mandate to defend the public interest, the inherent values of the institution are automatically changed. For example, the determination of what is a crime is no longer based so much on social or legal indicators, but on business and budget indicators.

It is a point not lost on Jane Jacobs – or on many rank-and-file Mounties, for that matter. "The police should never think of cost recovery as part of their purpose. The government is absolutely wrong to say the police should earn money. That is not the function of the police, and that should not be the function of the police," Jacobs says.

But making a profit from the RCMP is precisely what the government is trying to do these days.

Chapter Eight

·· ● ··

TAX COLLECTORS WITH AN ATTITUDE AND A GUN?

ON MOST DAYS IT can take up to an hour to drive from downtown Toronto north to the RCMP Toronto sub-division in Newmarket, halfway to Ontario's cottage country. The gleaming white building, located beside Highway 404, is a $16-million architectural delight, poking out of a predictably utilitarian industrial park, so unlikely in design that anyone familiar with most RCMP buildings across the country would find it easy to miss. Everywhere else, the RCMP is housed in standard, no-frills, modern buildings – red brick, compact, and utilitarian to a fault.

The Newmarket building is a statement, an exception to the rule of modern government buildings. Government buildings used to be grand and ostentatious, symbolizing the spirit, power, and good of government. But since government started thinking as if it were a business, with rare exceptions they have been designed to be basic and architecturally uninteresting. The subliminal message seems to be that government and business are equals, in many ways, one and the same. Modern government buildings are plain because the people – that is, the government – have no money. If there is to be any ostentation, it is to be reserved for businesses that can *afford* it. Perhaps that is why the Newmarket building is so special: it houses the fastest-growing RCMP unit in the country – a virtual business, whose success is measured by how much money it brings into government coffers every year.

This business is called the Integrated Proceeds of Crime Unit, or IPOC for short. It is the first and largest of what are now thirteen IPOC units across the country. In Newmarket, there are sixty-six members, comprising mostly Mounties and a smattering of Justice Department prosecutors, civil lawyers, and accountants – and the unit is growing. Every IPOC unit also has a few police officers seconded from local police forces. In Newmarket there are three outside officers – whose salaries are paid by the federal government. IPOC units are unlike any other RCMP or policing operation in Canada.

What has been happening in Newmarket in recent years is an accurate reflection of what happens when a police force begins to operate as if it were a business.

In Newmarket, pure federal law-enforcement functions such as commercial-crime investigation are so starved for funds that experienced officers have been leaving in droves, to the point at which, in October 1997, going-away parties were being held for groups, and, in the bustle, sometimes overlapped with each other. Federal investigations in Newmarket's jurisdiction, North Toronto to Northern Ontario, have been hampered by a lack of available resources and support – including lack of sufficient fuel for cars – particularly near the end of each fiscal year. Their offices look tattered and utilitarian.

At the same time, IPOC units are rolling in taxpayers' money. In their Newmarket offices, there is flashy new furniture, a virtually unlimited budget, and the support both of their leaders and the government. No matter how little they might be paid, IPOC unit members love coming to work, even for unpaid overtime.

IPOC units work on a project basis. Tips about people with unusual or unexplained amounts of cash are directed to the unit by police investigators or from groups such as the Canadian Bankers Association, with whom the IPOC program has a working agreement. IPOC units also depend heavily for information and leads from the network of ex-Mounties who run the security operations of most financial institutions across the country. The Mounties rarely initiate an investigation, but instead latch on to the investigations of others. That's one of the reasons the units include local police members, each of whom serves as a liaison between the RCMP and their own force, so that the Mounties can find appropriate and lucrative enough cases to pursue. While the police are investigating criminality, the IPOC team of police, lawyers, and accountants conduct a parallel investigation in order to identify assets, quietly build a case, and secure court orders to seize whatever they can. IPOC investigations are usually very technical and make use of much surveillance and high technology, such as the force's state-of-the-art CenCIS automated wiretap system.[1]

When criminal investigators are ready to make their arrests, the IPOC unit has usually already begun legal proceedings to seize all the criminals' assets. It is not unusual these days for the police to show up at a suspect's door in a convoy: the investigating officers, a tactical team to gain entry to the premises and effect the arrest of the suspect, uniformed cars for crowd control, and a moving van to cart away the physical assets of the suspect for the IPOC unit.

"Our primary function is to disrupt criminal organizations by taking away their motive – their profits. Nobody should be able to make money from crime," says Inspector Gary Nichols, one of the founding members and head of the Newmarket IPOC unit.

The history of such units within the RCMP dates back to the late seventies, when Canadian police became increasingly aware of the need for stronger laws and tactics to deal with organized crime. In the summer of 1981, the Enterprise Crime Task Force was set up to study the problem. The task force made a number of recommendations, including Criminal Code amendments to provide for:

- Judicial hearings with powers to compel testimony and disclosure of documents during investigations into organized-crime operations;
- Court orders to freeze the assets in an organized-crime investigation and, on conviction, seizure and forfeiture of the profits;
- The right of a trial judge during sentencing to consider evidence on enterprise-crime profits that the defendant has outside Canada and impose additional jail terms and stiff fines.[2]

While proposed legislation was before the House of Commons, then-deputy commissioner Henry Jensen authorized the creation of units whose task it would be to target and seize the ill-gotten gains of organized crime in the area of drug-trafficking only. In March 1982, then-superintendent Rod Stamler, senior officer in the drug-enforcement branch, announced what he called a new line of attack on drug traffickers. The Mounties no longer would be concentrating on seizing the drugs themselves, but the flow of money from their sale. To that end, Stamler announced the formation of what was called the Anti-Drug Profiteering Program. The RCMP was going to place in every major city in Canada two investigators whose sole function would be to identify those occupying the highest rungs in the drug-trafficking world, and hit them where it hurt most, in their pocketbooks. "I feel that's the key," Stamler said. "That's what motivates these individuals. If you take away the profits it will have a tremendous effect."[3]

From the outset Jensen and Stamler intended that the Anti-Drug Profiteering Program would help the force refocus its priorities and identify major drug dealers. Up until then, Mountie drug investigators were all too happy building statistics by arresting just about anyone who came into contact with illegal drugs, whether they were trafficking or not. While arrest rates were high, the drug problem would not go away – for the obvious reason that the large traffickers were still in business.

As high-minded as it all might have sounded in 1982, the Anti-Drug Profiteering units, as they were called, didn't make much of an impact. In 1983, the force reported that $10 million in illegal assets were seized, but that wasn't entirely true. The hyperbole clouded the fact that there was no legislation authorizing such seizures, and everything taken by the police eventually had to be given back. In many respects, the police used the media in an attempt to scare off the criminals. But the criminals weren't that easily frightened.

Recognizing their weaknesses, the force, as it always does, lobbied the government of the day for legislative changes. In the RCMP's view at that time, any new law must provide ways of identifying sophisticated laundering systems, identify offences and provide penalties to deal with secondary criminal acts associated with concealing cash flow, and be capable of being enforced outside of Canada. "Criminals will take full advantage of foreign international banking systems – especially those protected by bank secrecy laws. We can expect the use of tax-haven countries to launder money will increase," Stamler said, adding, "We will also use income-tax law to facilitate the recovery of a portion of the funds which can be identified as profits of illicit drug trade."[4]

Pierre Trudeau's Liberal government stalled on doing anything about the recommendations from both the task force and the RCMP, letting a proposed bill die on the order paper before the 1984 federal election. On December 2, 1985, the Mulroney government picked up some aspects of the previous bill, mainly pertaining to seizures, while dropping the methods of attacking the proceeds of crime. The new amendments to the Criminal Code were, from the RCMP's point of view, just a slice from the loaf, but it was better than nothing.

Perhaps the most important thing that the government had refused to give the police and the justice system was expanded and new coercive powers to pursue their anti-profiteering duties. The notion of coercive powers alarms most Canadians, who have become extremely and, one could argue, unreasonably sensitive about the prospects of the powers of police being increased. What has largely been lost in the hysteria is the fact that, among Western democratic countries, Canada has the fewest and weakest investigative mechanisms. In the United States, for example, the grand jury is an investigative tool. Congress and the Senate, among many other institutions, can conduct its own investigations. Each institution has the power to name special prosecutors, call hearings, and compel witnesses to testify under oath in the face of real penalties. Even municipal governments have the power to set up investigative commissions, as has been the case a number of times in New York City with regard to police corruption, the education system, and financial management, among other things.

Similar systems operate at the federal level in France and even Italy. From the Canadian perspective, the most interesting developments in this area may well be in Australia, where the government found that its justice system and police were incapable of dealing with the rapid and insidious growth of organized and white-collar crime.

A series of royal commissions in the late seventies and early eighties identified sophisticated criminal networks operating both within Australia and internationally. The royal commissions also identified a lack of co-operation amongst law-enforcement agencies. As a result of those revelations, the Commonwealth Parliament passed the National Crime Authority Act in 1984, establishing the National Crime Authority. Its mission is to counteract organized criminal activity and reduce its impact on the Australian community, working in partnership with other agencies.

The National Crime Authority is unique in the law-enforcement community, both in Australia and overseas, in having a national and multi-jurisdictional focus. The NCA has jurisdiction to investigate offences against federal, state, and territory laws. The enabling legislation reads:

> The NCA is not a police service. Multi-disciplinary teams of lawyers, police, financial investigators, intelligence analysts and support staff investigate organized crime. The Act gives the NCA coercive powers to compel people to produce documents and to give sworn evidence. These powers are not available to traditional police services. These characteristics enable the NCA to co-ordinate a national attack on major organized crime by complementing the efforts of other law enforcement agencies and working co-operatively with them. . . . In special investigations, the NCA is able to exercise the coercive powers under the Act, including the power to hold hearings and to require a person to appear before the Authority at such a hearing to give evidence and to produce documents.[5]

In Canada, meanwhile, over the past thirty years the justice system has been progressively softened, largely in the name of civil and individual rights and universal equality. This has largely removed from the law the necessary elements of respect, fear, and punishment, thereby inviting organized and white-collar criminals to penetrate society in an unprecedented and extremely detrimental manner. "In the United States a guy caught dealing cocaine can get a hundred years in jail. White-collar criminals can go to jail for a long, long time. Those kinds of penalty make it easy for police to get accomplices to roll over and become agents. It makes the police work easier," Inspector Nichols says. "Here, nothing's easy. Everything is cumbersome. There are no short cuts. It's almost impossible to be creative. Everything is by the book, and if we make a mistake, we're toast."

Without any effective or predictable inquisitorial process, criminal investigation in Canada has been reduced to a single approach: police officers working under strict and almost impossible guidelines. The last remnants of the grand-jury system were eliminated three decades ago. The concept of royal commissions and public inquiries as independent investigative bodies has been severely compromised. In Ontario, a 1990 inquiry into the so-called Patti Starr affair was blocked by the courts. At the federal level, a 1997 inquiry into the behaviour of the Canadian military in Somalia was stopped by the government just, as it seemed, testimony was beginning to turn towards the government's own policies and possible culpability.

So, with no special or coercive powers, the RCMP Anti-Drug Profiteering units trundled along, not making much impact on organized crime. One of the problems is the ingenuity and resourcefulness of criminals. "They study the laws and actually bring in people to give seminars to them," Nichols says. "Organized-crime groups will send observers to monitor trials to learn about the latest police methods and techniques."

Their field also widened. By the late eighties drug-trafficking was not the only source of fast cash for criminal organizations. The smuggling of cigarettes and alcohol across the border had become a booming business, and hundreds of thousands of Canadians across the country were willingly participating in this illegal industry because the criminals offered a better price on these commodities than did government.

This came at a time when the Mulroney government had stepped up the drive to rid the government of its guardian mentality. If the government were acting as a true guardian, logic would have dictated that the cigarette- and alcohol-smuggling businesses had been caused by excessive and unreasonable taxes on those products. But the government, thinking like a business, saw those taxes as revenues from a monopoly it owned, revenues which, if lost, could not be replaced. The right thing would have been to lower taxes – as Chrétien later did – and wean normally law-abiding citizens off the habit of cheap smuggled goods, a decision which would have served the public interest. Instead, the Mulroney government sought ways to protect its monopoly and revenue stream, even if that was not in the public interest, which it wasn't.

In 1989, Bill C-61 was passed, an Act which made money-laundering a criminal offence for certain crimes, mainly drug offences. The next year, armed with that law, and in response to Solicitor General Pierre Cadieux's "Police-Challenge 2000," the RCMP beefed up the Anti-Drug Profiteering Unit and created a similar unit within the Economic Crime Directorate, the former Commercial Crime Branch. This new unit was known as Enterprise Crime, and it was designed mainly to target cigarette smugglers and other organized violators who were depriving the government of tax and excise revenues. All monies seized by either unit were turned over to the federal government. In an incremental way, the RCMP was losing its purity of purpose; its guardian role as an agent of the law was being diminished as it was being transformed into an agent of the government.

In 1992, a report by the auditor general on the strengths and weaknesses of the two units led to their being merged and enhanced to their current format as Integrated Proceeds of Crime units. Between 1992 and 1997, Ottawa invested $33 million in a pilot IPOC program, with units located in Montreal, Toronto, and Vancouver. The government was so impressed by the early results that, by 1995, it expanded the legislation to include a wide range of offences that could be classified as proceeds offences under Section 462.3 of the Criminal Code. They were consensual – or "victimless" – crimes, mainly offences under the Customs and Excise Act, dealing with profiteering from the smuggling of alcohol and tobacco. But the profits from crimes such as gambling, prostitution, and immigrant-smuggling, among other things, were for some reason not covered under the legislation. In 1997, the government expanded the three original units and created ten new ones across the country, injecting another $18 million into the project, for an extended four-year "trial." There are currently 450 Mounties across the country involved in the IPOC project.

•   •   •

These days, no Mounties have hotter career prospects or sexier reputations than those members attached to IPOC units. As commercial-crime and other federal law-enforcement functions are allowed to wither on the vine, IPOCs are the *Miami Vice* of Canadian policing. Like the old Commercial Crime Branch in the late sixties and seventies, IPOC units are seen as launching pads to the top echelons of the RCMP. There is a swagger and cockiness to the IPOC investigators, which in police circles is usually reserved for homicide detectives. But unlike the fictional detectives in *Miami Vice*, or most of the real-life world of law enforcement in the United States for that matter, the Mounties don't get to keep the Ferraris, airplanes, and cigarette boats for their own use. The money the RCMP seizes goes directly to the Seized Property Management Directorate, a department of the federal government. The Mounties would have it no other way. As Superintendent Tim Killam, B.A., B.Comm., LL.B., the IPOC program director in Ottawa, puts it: "Murders don't make money for the police. Rapes don't make money, and this shouldn't. We have to be doing what's right. We don't want to be tied to the dollar. That's why we're quite a bit different from the United States, and we want to continue to be different from the United States and other countries that take this approach."

Since 1992, the RCMP has taken in virtually anything of value, from mountains of cash to a ski hill in Quebec, from herds of cattle to linens and silverware. In 1994, the RCMP valued the seizures at $48.5 million. In 1995, the force claimed $43.7 million. When the assets were liquidated, however, the government realized only $7.2 million and $14 million respectively. Then, in 1997, the Mounties made their biggest score – a plea bargain in one case alone in Vancouver resulted in a $15-million forfeiture to the government.

Along the way, Inspector Nichols says, the RCMP has learned a thing or two about the business, often the hard way. Each case takes years to go through the courts, meaning that the government and police must maintain the assets until a resolution is reached. In the case of the Quebec ski hill, for example, the government ended up having to operate it, which it didn't really know how to do, running down its value and losing some money in the process. Over the years, neighbours and municipal authorities have often complained about the weeds and high grass at properties taken over by the police, which are subsequently neglected. Maintenance people have had to be hired. The police also learned that herds of cattle not only have to be fed, but that, as a herd ages, it loses its value and marketability. All of which, Nichols says, has helped to change police thinking about what should be considered an asset: "Don't seize anything you can't restrain and never seize anything that eats, because then you have to feed it and take care of it for two or three years," he jokes.

There have been other embarrassing moments. In one case in Hamilton, Ontario, in early 1997, an RCMP-led joint-forces squad used a backhoe to smash through the front door of a suspected drug trafficker's house early one morning. The man, the leader of a motorcycle gang, was considered dangerous and was also a prime suspect in a bombing the previous year outside the headquarters of the local police in Sudbury, Ontario. What the raiding police didn't realize was that tanks containing rare fish were just inside the door of the suspect's house. The backhoe crushed the door, causing the tanks to explode. The fish flopped out onto the porch. Some of the police officers got down on their knees and tried to save the fish. "Fortunately," said one of those involved, "the guy was in the shower. The guys at the door could have got themselves killed in any other circumstance." The much-feared biker suspect was then led out of the house wrapped in a towel, crying over his fish. He was forced to stand on the sidewalk and watch the police remove everything from his residence, including the well-used stove and refrigerator, as if there were any resale value left in them for the government.

In Project Tome, which was an arm of the larger Project Amigo that saw the destruction of a Colombian drug cartel operating out of Toronto, the results were more typical. In that case, beginning in 1990 and 1991, the

Mounties seized seventeen residential and commercial properties with a total market value of $15 million, although, when they were finally liquidated in 1997, the government netted only $250,000 from the sales. "Most of the properties were purchased at the height of the market from 1987 to 1989, and a lot of them were mortgaged for more than they were worth," Inspector Nichols says. "Some went in powers of sale. The bad guys were able to draw on the equity in the properties to defend themselves, which is allowed under the law. And there was some poor management on our part. We ended up with nothing, but so did the bad guys."

In spite of such apparent setbacks, the IPOC unit seems to be perfectly suited to the times, a powerful tool for law enforcement. It is a police unit that pays for itself by taking away the profits from criminals – cost recovery with a social benefit, a perfect example of the fusion of commercial instincts and a guardian responsibility. Taxpayers couldn't ask for better. Or could they?

Even the Mounties in the IPOC units recognize the possible pitfalls. In interviews, Inspector Nichols and some of his cohorts, such as Inspector Rod Knecht, clearly have some doubts about both their own effectiveness and the efficacy of what they are doing. Their intention is to use legal objectives and not business ones to select cases to investigate, even though the pressures from government to produce revenues for the general coffers are growing. "It takes just as much time for us to seize $80,000 as it does $3 million," Nichols says. "When we as a unit measure what we do, we have a dozen criteria for success. Our first priority is the disruption of criminal organizations. That's the most important thing for us, by far, followed by convictions, the quality of our court briefs, the consistency of legal advice, charges laid, and so on. Way down near the bottom are things like dollar value forfeited, dollar value seized, cases generated, public perceptions, and speed of investigations. That's the way we see ourselves."

"We can stand on high moral ground doing this job," says Inspector Knecht, "but it's not as high as it used to be."

Knecht, like many Mounties, sees the IPOC units as a potential slippery slope for the RCMP, a force that prides itself in its commitment to integrity and ethics. From their point of view, the IPOC units, much like the current RCMP itself, was not a positive creation, but actually the result of a negative response to political and economic imperatives. In many ways, the IPOC units are a testament to the failings of politics, the justice system, and the way the police in general have become organized in Canada.

As they stand now, the IPOC units are a "business" unlike any other. They operate with the authority of government and in the name of and with the protection of the law. IPOC units are a vertically integrated, legally sanctioned government business – they have the ability to target suspects (raw material), use the power of the state to investigate them (manufacture product), arrest suspects and seize assets (bring product to market), and liquidate those assets (create revenues and profit).

As a result, there is a good argument to be made that the law is not being enforced in an equitable and disinterested fashion, because the government is using its influence through budgetary control to select, indirectly or otherwise, which cases will be pursued. Under the IPOC concept, the single measure of success is not necessarily effective law enforcement that makes society a safer place, but selective enforcement based mainly on monetary concerns. The richer the suspect and the more easily traced his assets, the more likely he or she will be targeted for investigation. Those who are better at hiding their assets have a better chance of being ignored by the police.

In effect, therefore, the intent of the IPOC units is far from pure. No matter how one cuts it, the IPOC units are little more than tax collectors with an attitude and a gun.

So why do we have them?

The answer is simple: IPOC units were created to solve a pressing problem that was created by other deeper and more fundamental problems that no one in government really wants to address.

Allow me to explain.

•　　•　　•

When ordinary people hear the phrase "organized crime," more often than not they think of the Mafia or a mafia – of whatever group. These criminal organizations have a long and colourful history, filled with characters such as Al Capone, John Gotti, and Canada's own John "Johnny Pops" Papalia. In movies like *The Godfather*, *Goodfellas*, and *Donnie Brasco*, the public is shown a world of organized crime that is ethnically based and filled with treachery, violence, and death. But this tends to mask the true nature of organized crime. As Marlon Brando's Don Corleone put it in *The Godfather*: "It's nothing personal, it's only business."

From Al Capone to the Colombian drug cartels to whatever group stole $12 million from the Canadian treasury in the 1987 Airbus deal, organized crime is merely a form of business that provides goods and services restricted or prohibited by government. Whether it be prostitution, cheap cigarettes, or secret payoffs to bureaucrats and politicians, all these transactions are conducted through a myriad of "storefronts," from secret couriers and street vendors to seemingly legitimate outlets. These fronts serve as money-laundering facilities; that is, a way to convert illegally gotten cash into electronic money and make it usable. With their access to easy, cheap cash, these fronts are sharks in the waters of free enterprise, often competing against truly legitimate businesses in a decidedly unfair fashion. The object of the business of organized crime is to make as much money as possible without paying taxes – which, when you think about it, makes organized crime sound like just about any other modern business.

To understand what organized crime really is, however, one must cut through its effects – the street drugs, prostitution, and thefts – and look at its intent. The engine of organized crime is fraud. No matter what its supposed illegal business line is, organized crime uses deception, trickery, and deceit either to rob individuals of their assets or to cheat the public treasury of taxes and duties. Organized crime is a business that is entirely immoral and unethical, and absolutely driven by the profit motive. It is a business in the purest and vilest sense, with no sense of guardianship or the public interest. As such, it never concerns itself about the damage it might be doing to the social, economic, or legal fabric of its host nation.

In Canada, one of the mandates of the RCMP has been the investigation of organized crime on a national and international level. In the sixties and seventies, conventional investigations were becoming successful in putting a dent in organized-crime operations around the country. A number of mob leaders were jailed: the Cotronis in Montreal, the Commissos in Toronto, and Johnny Papalia in Hamilton, among others. But the effectiveness of the police was overtaken by events.

The first problem the police had was the nature of fraud itself. Fraud is unlike any other crime. In a robbery or violent crime, the police investigation usually goes from the crime to the suspect. In fraud, it's the other way around. The pursuit is from the suspect to the crime. The police often know who committed the fraud, but they must prove that the suspect *intended* to commit a fraud. Among the best defences to fraud are ignorance or admitting to an error in judgement ("it was just a bad business deal"), which brings us to the second hurdle facing the police.

Organized crime conducts most of its affairs under the cover of business. The main reason for this is that Canada, perhaps more than any other Western country, has refused to invoke, with rare and limited exceptions, any legislation that might be used to control the excesses of business. Although each business is considered under tax law to be an individual, with the same rights and privileges as a human being, businesses, unlike humans, can't be put in jail. The difference between Canada and most other Western democracies is that the individuals who control the businesses enjoy the same privileges. It is rare for the controlling mind to be jailed for offences by a corporation, as is the case in the United States, for example. In fact, with the implementation of the Charter of Rights and Freedoms, businesses in Canada, legal or otherwise, have even more rights than in most other countries. As we have seen earlier, since the Charter, Canadian businesses operate today in the much more lenient climate that has always existed under the Quebec Civil Code.

In the post-Charter world, Canadian lawmakers have insisted on making a distinction between "true" crime – that is, violent crime and offences against property – and crimes committed by business, which are seen to be mostly regulatory offences, and therefore not as serious or worthy of police intervention.

True crime is easy to understand, business crime often isn't, even though the implications of crimes by business have been proven to have a much more devastating effect on societies than violent crime.[6] The ordinary citizen can rally against the notion of broken windows, the odd mugging, or a killer loose in the community. But a phony bankruptcy (that puts thousands out of work), money-laundering, or economic parasites aren't sexy enough for either the police or politicians to sell to the electorate, therefore they tend to fall off the public agenda. As Sergeant Gabe Marion of the RCMP's Newmarket IPOC unit says, "In a white-collar crime, somebody might steal eight or ten million dollars, but the judge looks at the case, says, 'I see no evidence of a weapon or violence,' and metes out a token sentence. Judges think these should be classified as civil cases – business disputes – and that white-collar crimes are victimless. They are usually anything but."

Over the years, every time law enforcement seems to have shown signs of effectiveness against white-collar criminals, roadblocks have been thrown in the face of the police and the justice system. Crimes by the business class, no matter how heinous, are not treated with the same degree of determination and outrage as are crimes by individuals. Osgoode Hall law professor Michael Mandel says the distinction between "true crime" and "business crime" gives business an unfair and unwarranted advantage. "The distinction between true crimes and regulatory offences is completely ideological. It is not based on the harmfulness of conduct but on the class of the criminals. The crimes characteristic of business are regulated with financial disincentives, even though they cost more in terms of lives and money than the 'street crimes' of the working class and the underclass. Historically, however, the most severe and intrusive punishments (death, imprisonment, probation, supervision) have been reserved for the latter. Thus the distinction between types of crime is of great benefit to business."[7]

This overt distinction, therefore, has caused the government to create a hybrid such as the IPOC units to deal with the problem. The key question is, how did the RCMP end up in this awkward and ill-fitting box?

The answer lies in Canada's nearly perverse obsession with secrecy and privacy, and in its income-tax laws.

In Canada there is a long tradition of keeping information private which isn't given that privilege in other countries, such as how much corporate leaders are paid, or whose secrecy defies the public and national interest, like the protracted fight in 1997 to name those who were responsible for the country's tainted-blood scandal.

In Canada, privacy laws make it almost impossible for an ordinary citizen to find out if someone has a criminal record or is under criminal charge, which is simply irrational. The concept of a criminal record was intended to serve as a public-safety measure – to warn citizens about a deviant or potentially dangerous individual. In Canada today, there is no mechanism for a citizen to find out this information. To distribute or publish such information is considered a violation of the country's privacy laws and the Charter of Rights and Freedoms. If ordinary people can't find out from the police or courts exactly who the convicted criminals are, what is the value of compiling criminal records? Why bother? The right-to-privacy movement has not only subverted the purpose of a criminal record, it has actually made life easier for anyone with such a record at the expense of the law-abiding public. What has been lost in the politics is the essence of what criminality means in a democratic society. That is, since a criminal has the right to commit crimes, society has the right to take away his freedom and punish him according to the laws and statutes of the land. By his very conduct, a criminal in a democracy eschews the right to privacy about his criminal past – that's one of the penalties society imposes and must be able to impose on a criminal if it is to continue to function properly and maintain public order.

However, where notions of secrecy and privacy have perhaps had their most detrimental effect on law enforcement is the manner in which they have been applied to the country's income-tax laws. What the Mounties in the IPOC units are being asked to do is to build cases against and collect taxes from people – criminals – who don't pay taxes. A logical question is, where is Revenue Canada in all this?

A missing link in Canadian legislation is the recognition and acceptance of the fact that organized crime is an illegal business, one of whose primary tools is tax evasion. Although Revenue Canada, which regulates the Income Tax Act, has investigative capabilities, it has shown over the years that it does not have the will or strength to mount criminal prosecutions, unlike its counterpart in the United States, the Internal Revenue Service. Since Revenue Canada is not feared by organized crime, and since the government is not willing to strengthen the powers of Revenue Canada investigators, and since the courts in Canada are not willing to treat tax evasion as a serious offence, the government has created the hybrid IPOC units to deal with the problem. Just as the Mounties in their entirety have evolved in a negative response to the opposition of Quebec and Ontario, the IPOC units are an ungainly protrusion within the policing function, a reaction to the Canadian tax system, its philosophy and regulations. "The Income Tax Act is a powerful act, if they'd only use the damn thing, but they don't," says RCMP Inspector Gary Nichols. "When you really think about it, organized crime is tax evasion, so why don't the laws reflect that reality? It's a criminal offence. The average police officer can't understand why it is that the government pussyfoots around the issue. Do what they do in the United States. Put the offenders in jail."

Tax policy in Canada, however, is extremely politicized. Numerous reputable works over the years have shown how Canadian governments have used income-tax policy to reward businesses and the wealthy.[8] That's indisputable. Authors such as Linda McQuaig have shown conclusively that much of the country's long-term debt was caused not by the expense of social-welfare programs, the justice system, or the $1.22 each Canadian pays annually for the RCMP's commercial-crime investigation. The debt was accumulated largely through grandiose tax concessions to the country's wealthiest citizens and largest businesses. Successive governments have always ensured that there were no teeth in the income-tax legislation or that the gaps in the bite were large enough for the astute and well-heeled to escape the revenuers. It is extremely rare that anyone is jailed for tax evasion in Canada. The contrast between the tax laws in Canada and the United States is instructive for understanding why the

RCMP has the responsibility for IPOC investigations, and what this duty really means in the overall scheme of things.

Conditioned by television dramas and casual study, most Canadians seem to believe that citizens of the United States enjoy stronger privacy laws and constitutional rights than we do in Canada. A convincing argument can be made to the contrary, especially when it comes to money. In the United States there are strict laws and records kept about the transfer of money in and out of the banking system and across borders. In Canada, the laws in this area are curiously lax, some would say almost criminal, although modest moves are now being made to tighten things up. Illegal money flows in and out of Canada as if the country had no borders. Some of the cash even takes up temporary residence in the form of buildings or enterprises, where it is laundered, then liquidated, and later removed. Canada's tax laws are, perhaps, one of the best indicators of the laissez faire attitude successive governments have had towards business crime.

In the United States, tax information is not viewed with the near-religious attitude that it is in Canada. The Internal Revenue Service has its own law-enforcement arm. IRS agents are federal police officers. They are armed and have the powers of arrest and search and seizure. In Canada, the RCMP is the only federal police force. Enforcing the Income Tax Act is one of the functions of the beleaguered and underfinanced Economic Crime Directorate, but far from a priority. A handful of officers in each federal detachment might be assigned to such duties.

Unlike in Canada, income-tax evasion is considered a serious crime in the United States, theft from the public treasury, and those convicted of tax evasion face up to one hundred years in prison. The IRS put Al Capone and many like him in jail, after other policing agencies failed to make their cases. In organized-crime investigations in the United States, the IRS works alongside other police forces. They co-operate and share information because they each see themselves working towards the same goal: taking a criminal off the street and relieving him and his organization of their profits.

In Canada, the tax system has been constructed not with the interests of the "people" in mind, but rather the protection and convenience of the individual taxpayer. Revenue Canada investigators are mere bureaucrats. The difference in attitude between revenue investigators in Canada and the United States is instructive. In late 1996, for example, a Toronto lawyer and a Vancouver man suspected of being involved in a massive fraud were charged instead with evading taxes of more than $18 million. After being charged, the lawyer joked to friends: "It's only a tax beef."

You may recall from a few pages ago that, in announcing the creation of the Anti-Drug Profiteering Program, Rod Stamler had talked about using the Income Tax Act to make inroads into the bank accounts of criminals. That was a short-lived idea, because it is impossible for the police and Revenue Canada to work on an equal footing on investigations. Because of secrecy laws and provisions of the Income Tax Act, in Canada there is a one-way flow of information. The police can pass information on to Revenue Canada, but Revenue Canada investigators can't tell the police anything, not even how they handled the investigation – or even if they conducted one at all.

The Income Tax Act also plays a role in the current relationship between the Canadian Bankers Association (CBA) and the IPOC units. The CBA, the lobby for the banking industry, has been somewhat sensitized over the years by stories about money-launderers and drug cartels using Canadian banks and taking advantage of the lax Canadian laws regarding the transportation of money across the border. In the Bahamas in 1985, a royal commission found that the Royal Bank, the Bank of Nova Scotia, the Canadian Imperial Bank of Commerce, and the Bank of Montreal Bahamas Ltd. accounted for 80 per cent of all foreign deposits and loans in the Bahamas. The banks were laundering money for criminals, which didn't surprise the police in Canada.[9] Here, the banks have always been reluctant to co-operate with law enforcement. When they finally agreed to do so in the mid-nineties with the IPOC units, it was on one key condition: the banks would tell the police who they thought might be involved in criminal activity, but they didn't want that information going any further. "In the memorandum of understanding we had to guarantee that we wouldn't pass on any of the information we get from the banks to Revenue Canada," says Inspector Nichols. "The banks are very sensitive about that."

A further complication is that Revenue Canada can be political, and make some rather bizarre decisions which might not be in the national interest. The best example occurred in 1996 when a prominent Montreal family, believed to be the Bronfmans, moved $2 billion from a trust fund out of the country to the United States, without paying the government any withholding taxes. The family had received "a favourable ruling" from Revenue Canada bureaucrats, which was later defended by the Chrétien government.

Law professor and author Michael Mandel summed up the difference between the intentions of the Canadian Income Tax Act and its true effects. According to Mandel, businesses, again, be they legal or illegal, have a leg up on the ordinary taxpayer: "The Income Tax Act applies to working people as well as to businesses, but the primary source of violation is businesses, because of the lack of opportunities for wage earners to cheat. Probably for this reason Canadian governments and the courts have never taken violations that seriously. Prison sentences are rare."[10] You can't put a business in jail.

• • •

As mentioned, most organized or white-collar criminal operations *are* or, at the very least, *call* themselves businesses. Historically, it has always been in their interests to fight their cases under the Income Tax Act, where everything is done out of public view, in private, and nobody, not even the police, can legally find out what has taken place.

The core argument government has used in invoking strong privacy legislation is the protection of the individual from Big Brother and his friends, but of what use is such a law if Big Brother and his friends have their hands in the till? The law effectively prevents little people from defending their own interests or the national interest, which, in closing out this chapter, brings us to the recent decisions of the Supreme Court of Canada.

Since the Charter of Rights and Freedoms, the Supreme Court in its decisions has tended to favour the rights of individuals, private interests, and defendants over those of the collective rights of all Canadians, public interests, and victims. Many of these controversial decisions have given Canadians a potentially inappropriate sense of confidence that their rights are protected, while the collectivity is not. Only certain rights are protected, making it difficult for people to feel truly safe.

From the police perspective, the effect of some of the Supreme Court decisions undoubtedly has been beneficial: it has forced the police to be more professional in their work. However, no amount of professionalism can overcome some of the seemingly inexplicable decisions made by the Supreme Court, which, unlike the police, is unaccountable to the public in any way. As the police see it, the Supreme Court appears to be determined to create for defendants rights which most Canadians not only feel are unnecessary, but counter to their own experience, *not just the police experience.* That being the case, the police feel they have been knocked off balance because the courts have in many cases left them with only two alternatives: bend the rules to be successful or do nothing. When they do bend the rules and get caught, the result is more restrictions on their activities, reinforcing the old police adage: "bad policing creates bad law." When the police do nothing – which is increasingly the case – they create the need for alternative, private investigations.

At the end of the day, what the Supreme Court has done while protecting individual rights to an apparently unreasonable degree is create the need for even more private investigation, which is almost entirely unregulated and conducted outside the rule of law.

In their determination to bring "equality" to the application of the law, the Supreme Court has made rulings in the area of business crime which have served to further confound and impede police investigations that are legitimate, warranted, and important to the public interest.

For example, in the opening chapter Anton Piller orders – private search warrants – were discussed. The test for a corporation to get an Anton Piller order is about as flimsy as it used to be for the police, prior to the implementation of the Charter. On the other hand, says Inspector Gary Nichols, "today it's not unusual for a police search warrant or a wiretap authorization to run one thousand pages or more. People think that the police can just waltz in and get a search warrant or wiretap. It's not like that at all. The courts are demanding that we have to virtually prove our case before we can even get such an order. It makes criminal investigations very, very difficult."

In 1987, the Supreme Court, "outraged" by a "reverse sting," ruled that such operations were illegal. A typical reverse sting occurs when the police set up a sting operation, and perhaps sell illegal goods to criminals, as a way of gaining their confidence. "The government quickly closed that loophole with new legislation," said Nichols. "We're often dealing with large, sophisticated criminal organizations. We couldn't lay a glove on them without undercover work and reverse stings."

Finally, there is the 1991 Stinchcombe decision in which the Supreme Court ruled that the Crown must make "full disclosure" to the defendants in a trial. The intention of the majority of judges, led by the late John Sopinka, was that such disclosure would expedite the process and encourage more and quicker guilty pleas. The effect has been somewhat different. "We have had cases," says Inspector Nichols, "where we had to use a flatbed truck to present our disclosures to the defence. In another case, we had to copy 750,000 pages of evidence – five cube vans full of paper – to make full disclosure. The real effect of Stinchcombe is that instead of encouraging plea-bargaining, what often happens is that the defence pores over the mountain of evidence looking for one mistake, one opening to taint the case or to extend it. That's not how the justice system should work, is it? But that's how the Supreme Court says it should work." The only saving grace for the IPOC unit is that technological advances have helped ease some of the pressure. In particular, a high-speed scanning system called Super Gravity allows the Mounties to put their entire case on computer, but all the technology in the world can't alleviate the legal and ethical problems at the core of the operation.

While the RCMP defends the intent and integrity of IPOC units, dismissing suggestions that the units have been created to raise revenues for the federal government, the government by its own actions clearly sees the IPOC units as a profit centre, as it were.

Last year, the government issued tenders for private accountants and consultants to evaluate the IPOC units, instead of government auditors, as had been the case in the past. "Our concern," says Inspector Nichols, "is that the government's view of what might be considered a success might be more focused on the dollar values than the law-enforcement benefits gained, and that would be rather unfortunate."

The members of the IPOC units seem determined to fight hard to stay near the top of the highest moral hill, but as long as it can be construed that the police are acting as revenue agents, their purity of purpose is clouded. "I won't lie about it, it's a problem for us, a serious problem of perception," says Nichols. "I think a solution might be that any money that is realized from our seizures be donated to medical research. That would help clean our hands." Nichols knows full well that his suggestion won't get much of a hearing in Ottawa, and might only muddy the waters more, because, as noble as the above suggestion might be, there would still be no purity of purpose.

In the final analysis, the major problem facing the Mounties, and Canada, is that much of what is being done doesn't make sense. The government says it wants the Mounties to be a better police force, but then it uses budget restrictions to prevent it from doing its job as well as it can. Then policies are implemented which seem to be at cross-purposes with both the rule of law and the greater good. Yet there is no real debate about what is going on and why.

Part of the problem is that, since the Glassco Commission reforms in 1965, it has been all but impossible to hold the government, its ministers, and its bureaucrats accountable for their decisions and policies. Since Glassco, Ottawa has become artful at manipulating revenues and expenditures. For example, every year the federal government collects $5 billion in gasoline taxes, revenues which were originally earmarked for highway improvement across the country. Today, the nation's highways are falling apart, but the government says it has no money. Manitoba premier Gary Filmon believes that a well-maintained highway system is essential to Canadian unity,[11] yet his complaints have fallen upon deaf ears in Ottawa. The same story goes for the Canada Pension Plan, Unemployment Insurance, and so many other government programs. It has long been government policy that all contributions to these programs be diverted into general revenues and dispensed as the government saw fit – that is, for political purposes. It seems that no matter how detrimental the results of Ottawa's actions might well be – poor highways, a depleted pension plan, or a threat to the integrity of the rule of law – the government's position has always been the same: dedicated taxes reduce the government's policy-making flexibility. In other words, the politicians who are ostensibly accountable for spending insist that they be trusted to have good intentions, even if they won't take any blame for negative effects of their decisions. In the process, it seems that Canada is losing its sense of the greater good, and is being undermined, weakened, and dismantled, piece by piece. As this happens, blame shifts from the politicians to the bureaucrats and back, rarely sticking to anyone, which brings us back to the state of the RCMP itself.

Commissioner Philip Murray sees the IPOC units as the wave of the future, one of his greatest achievements, along with the implementation of community-based policing. However, the fit isn't as smooth as Murray likes to pretend. In rushing to implement these and other policies, the RCMP seems to be working against the long-term success of IPOC units. For example, as we shall see, the RCMP is headed on a deliberate course which will lead to the devaluation of specialization and knowledge, the effective dismantling of federal policing, and an almost universal focus on community-based policing. "The trend right now in all of policing is to drive resources from federal policing down to the street level," says Inspector Nichols. "The same thing is happening with the municipal forces. Organized crime is at the root of most policing problems, but police managers are being forced to fight fires on the street. We are only as strong as the investigators under us, the guys who make the initial cases. If they're not making good cases, there's not much room for us."

Sgt. Gabe Marion picks up the thread. Marion has been involved in some of the Mounties' biggest drug-trafficking investigations over the years. He thinks the force is putting so much emphasis on drug traffickers that it's going to compel many in that line of work to change their specialty, into the precise area the RCMP is abandoning. "Put yourself in the shoes of a drug trafficker. He has to make the contacts, come up with the money, and make sure everything goes right. He might even have to do some of the heavy lifting himself. He has to deal with sales people, distribution people, collections, laundering the money, and all the while the police are breathing down his neck, ready take every last thing he owns. Meanwhile, some white-collar criminal rips off $8 million and gets away with it because the police ranks are depleted and the justice system isn't interested in prosecutions because they don't think that kind of crime is really a crime. Criminals aren't stupid. Guess what they're going to be doing."

The observations and opinions of Mounties such as inspectors Nichols, Knecht, and Marion are commonplace throughout the ranks of the RCMP. Mounties from Bonavista to Vancouver Island are scratching their heads over what the long-term strategic plan really is. The general perception is that the force is eliminating specialization (and knowledge), while empowering those on the front lines, many of whom are not trained or at all interested in sophisticated criminal investigation. Community-based policing – marketing the human face of policing – is seen to be the remedy for all that ails the police, but many of those on the street are suspicious and extremely wary of what Ottawa may really be trying to do. At a time when IPOC units require solid investigation by other officers in order to make their cases, the RCMP is moving away from investigation.

Assistant Commissioner Cleve Cooper, in charge of implementing community-based policing, can't understand why some Mounties don't believe in the grand plan. As Cooper puts it: "We're getting some resistance, especially from some of the older members who are set in their ways. We can't get them to buy into the program." The brass in Ottawa can't seem to understand how any one Mountie would wish to quarrel with their leaders' stated objectives, yet at every turn the contradictions are apparent to all and cause for considerable concern. The confusion extends right down to the very bottom of the force – cadet school in Regina.

Chapter Nine

•

REGINA: THE SCHOOL OF CONTRADICTIONS

WITH HER SCOTTISH lilt, fair features, and university degrees, twenty-nine-year-old Diane Cockle might well be the perfect cadet, the personification of everything Commissioner Philip Murray means when he says he intends to re-engineer the Royal Canadian Mounted Police. When she applied to join the RCMP in December 1995, Cockle already had a job – chief archeologist for the Province of Saskatchewan. She had held that job since she was twenty-five, having won it before receiving her master's in archeology. She was also a lecturer at the University of Regina.

In the good old uncomplicated world of policing, recruiting police officers out of high school, giving them a few weeks' training, and then throwing them out on the streets might once have been enough to fight crime. In the main, that's what crime-fighting was – more fight than it is today. Mounties were hired for their brawn and their ability to ride horses. They were the New Centurions, the Thin Blue Line, urban warriors in an ever-violent world. If some happened to have brains, all the more power to them. The RCMP would take them, groom and polish them by sending them to university, and turn them into detectives and officers in the force.

That was then, this is now. In what has been called the Age of Information, knowledge is power – supposedly. Brawn is deemed to have become less important, but the federal government has set aside less money for the RCMP, meaning that the force can no longer afford to pay for the higher education of its members on the same scale that it used to do. Meanwhile, the knowledge gap between criminals and police has widened. The criminals often have all the intelligence money can buy. The practical and efficient solution for the RCMP seems apparent: recruit older cadets who already come equipped with a higher education. To that end in recent years the force has brought in a number of professionals – lawyers, a few doctors, and accountants – who have taken their training and started out as constables performing general policing duties, usually in the towns and cities of British Columbia. To the public this may seem like a waste of skills, but that is where most young Mounties end up these days; the demand is so high for Mounties in the province that the force can't keep up.

Diane Cockle got the police bug working with bodies and bones. Part of her duties included working with Bob Blair, who was the RCMP's forensic anthropologist in Regina. "Any time human bones were found it was treated as a crime scene. Bob and I would go out together. Bones younger than fifty years were Bob's jurisdiction. Anything older than fifty years fell under the jurisdiction of the provincial archeologist," Cockle says. "The more I worked with Bob, the more interested I became in the forensic work being done by the RCMP. It looked like a challenge, more than just working with human bones and corpses. So I thought it was time to diversify."

In December 1995, Cockle filled out an application to join the RCMP as a cadet. "I'm definitely not the normal one in my family, but it was just something I felt that I had to do." She had a wonderful job with a bright future, and now she seemed ready to throw it all away. Her parents couldn't believe it. "We were absolutely shocked," her father, Derek, says. "But we'll get over it. She may have been born in Kilmarnock, near Glasgow, but she just has this overwhelming sense of commitment to Canada." In August 1996, Cockle's application was accepted, and she headed off to Regina for almost seven months of training.

•   •   •

The RCMP calls it Depot (Depp-oh). It is the original headquarters of the Mounties, situated on the western edge of Regina, the gateway to the western prairies. Its southern boundary is the Canadian Pacific Railway line which, like the Mounties themselves, was created in the late 1800s to help define Canada and link its people from sea to sea.

Depot is everything that the Mounties were, are, and will be. If the head of the RCMP resides in Ottawa, the heart is in Regina. Commissioner Murray says the RCMP is moving away from the military model, but at Depot the cannon on the parade square reminds everyone of the force's history. The RCMP museum catalogues every moment from the founding of the force as the North-West Mounted Police in 1873 to today. It is a world of discipline, decorum, and tradition. It is the place where all new Mounties are trained. New cadets run everywhere on the interior roads, being denied the dual privileges of walking and sidewalks. Those must be earned in time. The air is filled with the sound of marching feet, drill sergeants shouting, and troops singing. At Depot old Mounties come to train new Mounties in a seamless passing-on of wisdom, knowledge, and tradition. Depot is where Mounties go to become what they think they should be. Mounties are extraordinarily proud of their own force.

Depot is also the place where any confusion about the RCMP's primary and ultimate purposes begins these days.

The contradictions between theory and practice abound. Headquarters says the RCMP is moving away from being a paramilitary force, yet cadets live in a barracks and their training regime is very much based on the paramilitary model. Cadets are graded for their bed-making abilities. Each spends endless hours marching around a drill hall, forming fighting formations that were already obsolete when the force was founded. It's all done in the name of instilling discipline and a sense of detail into each and every one of them. As one might well expect, each Mountie is taught to shoot and how to fight, using the latest in self-defence and combat techniques. Until 1968 the force still required that every Mountie be an expert horseman as well, though horseback riding is now reserved for special squads and the world-famous Musical Ride. But also gone is the old-style teaching method, whereby experienced RCMP instructors dictated ideas while the cadets took notes, followed orders, and wrote exams.

Today the instructors are not so much teachers as facilitators. The new style of teaching, created by consultants and driven from headquarters, is rooted in notions of problem-solving promoted by Stephen Covey. The commissioner believes that the style of teaching dovetails with the life and education experience of the more mature recruits. The assumption is that such people will immediately be able to take on more responsibilities than cadets in the past, who were only high-school educated. Instead of being lectured to, the cadets are given scenarios and then asked to work in teams to find solutions to the problems. A premium is placed on innovation, creativity, and sensitivity. The ultimate goal is to "empower" each constable to make his or her own decisions, as often as possible. In that way, it is hoped that the force will become more efficient – that is, less costly to the taxpayers. For that is the bottom line: the police are trying to address the concerns of politicians, pressure groups, and the media that they should be less authoritarian, more willing to defuse situations and avoid the arrest option – as a way of saving money and court time.

This is made more complicated by the fact that police are both agents of the law and captives of the law, they enforce the law and their work is circumscribed by the law. When the law changes, they must change with it, but, as we saw earlier, the law seems to be changing so quickly these days that the police can barely keep up. The ongoing tussle since 1982 between Parliament and the Supreme Court over individual rights has served almost to paralyse the police on the streets.

One of those at Depot charged with keeping up with the changes is Corporal Norm Gaumont, a legal analyst. For example, on May 21, 1997, Gaumont issued a bulletin he drafted for trainers about recent amendments to the Criminal Code contained in Bill C-17. In all there were about sixty areas of change, covering almost every aspect of the law from general policing to search warrants to the proper way to question suspects. "From our perspective many of these changes are positive. They make our job easier," Gaumont says. "But for every change the government might make to help the police, the Supreme Court seems to find a way to make it more difficult. Everything is changing so fast that we have to constantly keep amending the curriculum. As a result, cadets from the same graduating year are going out to detachments with distinctly different levels of knowledge about the law. The last cadet out of Depot usually is the legal expert in any RCMP detachment across the country."

At the time he issued the May 1997 bulletin Gaumont was getting ready to deal with the outcomes of yet another Supreme Court decision, which had come down days earlier. In *Regina v. Feeney*, the Supreme Court made a ruling that had virtually every police officer in Canada scratching his head about what the court in its wisdom might be thinking. Since 1987, the court has expanded the rights of defendants to what many believe is a preposterous extent, but few of those decisions were clear-cut, giving the police and everyone else a decidedly mixed message.[1] In the Feeney case the Court ruled in a narrow 5–4 decision that suspects cannot be arrested at any home unless police have a warrant, except in cases of hot pursuit and possibly exigent circumstances. The majority of the court ruled that the police had wrongfully pursued a murder suspect into a house trailer, while the minority ruled that the police had done nothing wrong.

"What that means in practical terms," Gaumont says, "is that if a person suspects the police are looking for him, all he has to do is go to the next house or the next apartment and wait for the police to leave and go get a new search warrant. It makes policing in a small town almost impossible. Many arrests are made on tips, just tips. Who's going to give you information that is good enough to put into a search warrant? How can you justify it as reliable? A tip is not good enough for a search warrant. The federal government is going to have to come up with something for us, but I'm not sure what that might be." (It took six months, but Parliament did respond to the police concerns about the impact of the Feeney decision, passing new legislation which effectively negated the Supreme Court's decision and returned things to the status quo.)

The vagaries of the law are only part of the problem facing the trainers at Depot; the vagaries of the RCMP, in many ways, are just as confounding. The legal experts back east at headquarters in Ottawa may come up with bright ideas to please their political masters, but in Depot each order is weighed and assessed, probably a bit like a criminal suspect is assessed by members of the force. At Depot the suspicions about Ottawa's intentions – in both the government and at headquarters – run deep.

From the commissioner's point of view in Ottawa, the cadets being produced at Depot today are better prepared for life on the streets than ever. The average RCMP recruit today is almost twenty-eight years old, and the force boasts that most recruits have some post-secondary education. The master plan involves the recruitment in equal proportions of white males, visible minorities, and women. "We are trying to get rid of that paramilitary attitude," says Assistant Commissioner Cleve Cooper, one of the key players involved in reshaping the RCMP.

The new thinking is based on what the force calls the CAPRA problem-solving model, an acronym for Clients, Analysis, Partnerships, Response, and Assessment. To that end the force has issued to detachments across the country quaint posters in delicate watercolour shades, depicting the history of the RCMP – according to CAPRA. In one poster, "The Evolution of Policing in the RCMP," a Mountie on horseback is seen riding through history, a friendly, personable peacemaker – the perfect model for community-based policing.

In another poster, "Quality Service Through Community Policing," the transition from the old Professional Crime Control model of policing to the new Quality Police Services is mapped out. In this new vision, based on Stephen Covey's leadership theories, there are thirteen areas of concern on which members are to focus, including "restructuring," "risk management," "restorative justice," "demonstration projects," and "client consultation." Not one directly mentions law enforcement. Each poster is filled with little people having little conversations, such as, "I would like your input on selecting high-risk activities," "Thanks for helping me with Quality Assurance," and "Any deficiencies?"

The last question may best suggest how things are really going in Regina, where it seems that even the most eager Mountie trainees are having trouble digesting the latest dogma. As high-minded as Ottawa's intentions might be, Mounties at Depot complain that the meritocracy has been gradually and deliberately eroded, which, in their view, isn't serving the public interest. They worry that being the best and doing the best job for the public is no longer the criterion for recruitment or advancement. The force is being reshaped to meet the new and currently fashionable theory of community-based policing, whether it makes sense or not. Standards, both physical and intellectual, have been lowered – despite the existence of the occasional Diane Cockle – to the point where cadets, who might not have made the grade only a few years ago, are today being allowed to sail through Depot.

The RCMP allots $37 million annually to the Depot operation. The force calls Depot the premier police-training facility in the country, and one of the best in the world. But inside the walls of Depot, this is a view that's not shared unanimously, not even by many of the trainers themselves. The teachers at Regina are the same as they ever were – experienced RCMP constables, corporals, and sergeants who have spent some time on the streets and have won promotion back to Regina as instructors for three to five years or so. "We are a supposedly world-class operation preparing members for the twenty-first century, but we don't have one sergeant on the training staff who has a university degree. We've still got a long way to go," says trainer Corporal Gary Morin, expressing the widely held views of many Mounties at Depot. As much as the executives at RCMP headquarters in Ottawa talk about the value of higher education, there is an unshakeable belief elsewhere in the force that formal education is not so important or relevant in the scheme of things. Many middle managers within the RCMP continue to believe that schooling comes behind training and instinct. In other words, any police officer experienced in general policing duties – that is, street patrols and investigations – knows as much or more about the law and policing than almost anyone else.

As one cuts through the layers upon layers of marketing hype and myth about the RCMP, another apparently glaring anomaly about the force presents itself. The lasting impression many Canadians have of the RCMP is that it has become a thoroughly bilingual force, with a solid mix of women and visible minorities. At Depot in the summer of 1997, the reality is otherwise. While one-fifth of the RCMP is officially bilingual, the number of French Canadians at Depot seems well below that ratio. Every year about six hundred cadets are trained, but only one troop – twenty-four recruits – is taught in French. In the other troops, it is normal for one, or perhaps two, of the new recruits to come from French Canada. From the late sixties to the early nineties, there was a flood of French Canadians coming into the force, most of whom eventually settled in jobs in Central Canada, and at headquarters. But that's not the case today; the dearth of French Canadians training for the RCMP is more visible evidence of the deep divisions within the force.

The fact is, there's not much room for them in the RCMP these days. British Columbia, Alberta, and Saskatchewan want more of their own policing their provinces in RCMP uniforms. Commissioner Murray's 1995 ruling prohibiting cadets going directly to federal policing without first spending at least five years in contract work eliminated even more openings for French Canadians who didn't fit well into anglophone communities. With positions at headquarters in Ottawa – and in federal policing jobs in Ontario and Quebec – out of the picture for new Mounties, there are precious few positions for French-Canadian recruits. That is the primary reason for the RCMP's desperate fight for a municipal policing contract in Moncton, New Brunswick, which it won in mid-1997. The RCMP drastically underbid for the job against the Moncton, Dieppe, and Riverview police services, saying it could perform the task with 127 officers, compared to the 177 or so who already were policing Greater Moncton; this would create a potential annual saving of almost $5 million for the community.

The Moncton decision poignantly reflects the changing dynamics and values – few of them for the better – within the Mounties, says RCMP Superintendent Gary McPherson, who heads up the Parklands subdivision in Dauphin, Manitoba. "When Bob Simmonds was the commissioner he had a plan to make the RCMP a truly federal force, like the FBI, rather than what it has become today, a hodgepodge of duties spread out across the country. Ten or twenty years ago, the force would never have taken on a contract like Moncton. That's not what the RCMP was supposed to be all about."

Eventually, the RCMP hopes, Moncton will provide a location where French-Canadian recruits can learn general policing principles. At Depot, the all-French-language troop receives an education that is similar but not precisely the same as the English-language troops. The stacks of books in the library tell the tale: there appears to be five to six times the number of English-language books as there are French. Most of the English books, especially the secondary reading material, have not been translated into French. French and English recruits come away from Regina with a slightly different view of the RCMP, which in and of itself does not seem appropriate for a national police force.

The underwhelming French-Canadian presence at Depot these days is disappointing to French-Canadian members such as Corporal J. J. Gaétan Roussel, a Montreal-born RCMP trainer. Roussel says he joined the Mounties in 1979 because he didn't like the way the Quebec police treated citizens. Today, like many of his colleagues, Roussel says he doesn't know why the RCMP continues to recruit French Canadians. "Every year we have one French-speaking troop, but we don't have anywhere to put them. It looks like it's all political to me. The force feels that it has to have at least one French troop because it looks good."

In a nutshell that seems to be the problem with today's RCMP: little is as it seems. By the time cadets finish their seven months of training, there is no question that each and every one of them is well schooled in all the hot points of the day, whether they be cultural, racial, gender-based, or political. The RCMP intends that each new Mountie will be the perfect fit for the times – parent, teacher, confessor, and friend – as sensitive as a nurse, as single-minded and proficient about law enforcement as Robocop, yet as warm and personable as a Wal-Mart greeter. The RCMP brass say that brawn is no longer a prerequisite for policing because smarter police officers to deal with smarter criminals are needed.

Yet all the new Mounties at Depot, no matter how intelligent and schooled each one of them might be, are being trained to spend years in patrol cars, far from where the smartest and most dangerous criminals are found. Every one of the new constables is headed to contract work in provinces and cities. The federal government subsidizes these contracts, picking up 30 per cent of the tab for provincial police contracts and 10 per cent of municipal contracts. The reason for this, Ottawa says, is that the contract police officers devote about that percentage of their time to federal law enforcement, which most Mounties say is not true. In fact, at Depot, even though between 10 and 30 per cent of their work might be federal work, not one minute of class time these days is spent on federal law enforcement, such as white-collar-crime investigation. "They're supposed to pick it all up by osmosis, I guess," said one veteran Mountie. The other explanation, of course, is that the dearth of such training is likely further evidence of the agenda laid out in 1990 in "Police-Challenge 2000," which advocated the demise of federal law enforcement.

Whatever the case, confusion reigns. For example, Diane Cockle, the star cadet who left her job as chief archeologist of Saskatchewan to become a Mountie, went through Depot in Troop 22. The members of the troop chose as their motto the phrase "With Your Shield or on It," which they had emblazoned on T-shirts they wore. After spending seven months in training, learning the supposedly new sensitive ways of community-based policing and alternative-resolution skills, they decided to adopt a war cry that would have suited a Roman centurion.

"That's the strength of the RCMP culture speaking," former assistant commissioner Michel Thivierge said knowingly, when told about Troop 22's motto. "You can't change it just by saying you're going to change it. It's not that easy. It's the same with any military or paramilitary system. Go to a Marine school, walk through those gates and past the monuments of the heroes, the trumpets, the parade square, the legends; it's all part of the myth and history of the organization. That all goes with the territory when you get into a police force. I don't think you can find a company in the world that has a stronger, more powerful influence on human beings than a paramilitary or military organization."

•   •   •

It's graduation time and the family and friends of the members of 1997's Troop 22 have come at their own expense to spend a weekend in Regina, because it takes three days for Mounties to graduate. On Sunday afternoon, everyone gathers in a lecture hall where a chaplain and other senior officers tell them what to expect and answer their questions. Monday morning, to the unlikely strains of heavy-metal band AC/DC, the troop struts their physical stuff, running, jumping, and climbing. Later, they show all their moms and dads and husbands and wives the tricks they learned about defusing potentially dangerous confrontations and arresting suspects, willingly or otherwise.

Troop 22 is representative of the Mounties' current recruiting targets. Eight of the twenty-four are married, including Steve Holmes from Kelowna, B.C., who is the oldest, at thirty-four. Almost all of them are white. Thirteen of the twenty-four come from Manitoba or west, with four from Ontario. There is one each from every other province and the Northwest Territories. Most have some post-secondary education, but few have degrees. There is not the high number of visible minorities that one might expect. The Mounties are still having trouble recruiting some minorities, especially Chinese. One of the so-called minorities is Peter Tewfik, twenty-six, a former waiter and ambulance driver from Kingston, Ontario, who happens to have Egyptian ancestry, but who could pass for a Smith or Jones. There are two aboriginals, Debra Richard-Church from Cartier, Manitoba, and Grant Thom from Gift Lake, B.C., but Thom is not a Mountie. He's being trained under a federal program by the Mounties for the Gift Lake Police Department, an aboriginal force. Four of the men have armed-forces experience or training, including Alfonso Benavente, a bull-necked Argentinian, who came to Canada in 1992. Benavente speaks English with a heavy Spanish accent and appears destined for drug undercover work in the not-too-distant future. When approached for an interview, he makes it clear that he doesn't like reporters.

There are nine women. Andrienne LaPlante, at twenty-two, is the youngest member of the troop and comes from a policing family. Her father is Montreal police detective Roger LaPlante, who, at the time of her graduation, was in training to take over command of the city's detective squad. Her brother Patrick is a member of the St-Lazare, Quebec, police force. LaPlante is the only French Canadian in the troop, which is not untypical these days. LaPlante says she chose to study in English because she wanted to see the rest of Canada.

By almost every measure, Cockle is the star of the class, the kind of Mountie the force likes to showcase. Not only is she blessed with intelligence, but also stamina. At one of the graduation ceremonies, she received her runner's certificate for accumulating the most kilometres during her stay – 894 – three times that of the lowest qualifier for the certificate.

For all of these cadets, however, the seven months have finally come to an end in the drill hall at a formal swearing-in ceremony. They are assembled for one last time. All but one are in scarlet tunics and stetson hat, the exception being Thom of the Gift Lake Police, who wears dress blue. The ceremony is performed as it always has been, with much military pomp and circumstance. One by one each cadet is called forward to receive his or her badge. LaPlante's father, looking entirely out of place in his Montreal police blues, swears in his daughter, making for a teary-eyed moment. When Cockle's turn comes, she gets badge 46053, providing a perfect count of the number of Mounties who preceded her in the force.

Afterwards there is one final series of marches around the mirrored hall. The new Mounties march in single file, by twos, fours, and eight abreast, in straight lines, at diagonals, and in squares, before ending up in a circle facing outward. Then one by one they shout out the detachment to which they are headed: Surrey, Courtenay, Portage La Prairie, Port Alberni, Inuvik, Yellowknife, Surrey, Nanaimo . . . Fully eighteen of the twenty-four are headed to British Columbia, including Cockle, who's going to Quesnel, a logging town with four native reserves in the area. "It's quite the rock-and-roll kind of place," Cockle says. "They've issued me two sets of handcuffs and a can of pepper spray. I'm sure I'll be terrified the first few times out there, but I'll get used to it."

Cockle will be paid about $33,000 a year, the same as LaPlante and everyone else in her troop. The RCMP's plan is that, like all the others, Cockle will spend the next five years in general policing, learning her trade from the ground up. After that her performance will be evaluated. Then, a few years later, if there is a suitable job opening and she qualifies, she might make it into forensics – that is, if she is still interested and is still on the force, which is not entirely guaranteed. This is the best Cockle can hope for, because in Commissioner Murray's plan to take back the centre of the force gradually from the grasp of Quebeckers, there is no room for a quality cadet like her to jump the promotion cue and move immediately to Ottawa. She may well be the Renaissance Cop, but all her education, sophistication, and charm won't buy her – or the public who might be able to benefit immediately from her talents – a break. In spite of Ottawa's intentions, the Mounties have rules that are unbending and devastating to anyone with a career plan. "The force tends to wear down overachievers like her," says Sergeant Mike Seliske, the public-relations chief at Depot. "It doesn't take long for them to become disillusioned."

Former assistant commissioner Thivierge echoes Seliske's observation, wondering why an elite cadet such as Cockle is being forced into the same mould as everyone else. "With her educational background and drive, she's a bona fide asset to the force. You have to wonder why she would want to become a cop. But, now that she has, the force should be trying to take advantage of her skills immediately. God knows they need the help. But by placing her in general policing duties, the real danger is that she will quickly lose that edge and her interests. Anything can go wrong for her, and it wouldn't necessarily be her fault. In the end it would be the force's loss, but it's a loss that can't be quantified, so nobody really is too concerned about it."

One indication of how true that observation might well be is that the RCMP's success at keeping their women recruits has not been great. About one-quarter of all cadets are female, but only 11 per cent of Mounties today are women. The force has the same problem with some of the lawyers, doctors, and accountants who signed up, flattered by the interest the RCMP showed in their skills. Many feel unfulfilled and have given up any hope of using their professional experience and interests within the force.

The case of three Vancouver-based lawyer-Mounties is a prime example. One of them, Stephen Thatcher, is tall, thin, and wears glasses. His rail-like arms dangle out of his striped T-shirt. If one had to guess what Thatcher did for a living, professional student might leap to mind – and it wouldn't be far off the mark. He studied English and German languages and literature at the University of Victoria and the University of Toronto. Then he attended the University of British Columbia, where he earned a law degree. He spent a few months working in a Vancouver law firm, and now, at age thirty-three, he's been a Mountie for six years. "I'm not the kind of cop who's going to put fear into the heart of anyone," Constable Thatcher jokes.

If Thatcher were a U.S. citizen, he would have all the credentials needed to be an FBI agent. He would be investigating federal crimes and making more than twice what he's being paid by the RCMP today – which is a little more than $50,000 a year. His duty today is identifying inter-provincial cigarette smugglers. "My job is to collect unpaid duties. It's not exactly a crime about which there has been much of a social outcry," he says sarcastically.

How Thatcher ended up where he is speaks eloquently about the real attitudinal problems and penny-pinching that exist within the RCMP. For two years, Thatcher and two other lawyer-Mounties had been working in the operational-policy section of "E" division in Vancouver. Eventually, they came to see that they had a conflict. They were acting as lawyers giving legal advice to the force, but they were not members of the British Columbia Bar Association. "We tried to advance the view within the force that a handful of legally trained members in critical positions could advise the force on how to avoid bad press, bad prosecutions, and bad calls in general. We thought that would serve everyone's interests. That's not being done now by the Department of Justice. We took the position that we, as lawyers, should be in compliance with the regulations, so we requested that the RCMP pay the $1,500-a-year annual fee for each of us. Commissioner Murray personally denied the request. He was quite emphatic about it. 'The Department of Justice are our lawyers,'" Thatcher quoted the commissioner as saying.

Thatcher and the other two lawyers were soon back on the streets conducting relatively minor investigations. "Our leaders are so caught up in the traditions and mystique of the Mounties that they have lost sight of what really is important," says Thatcher. "At some levels, it is a whitewash organization. The image of that serge coat comes first. There's not the level of maturity and sophistication one might expect in this day and age. I see that as a sign of weakness. We should be opening ourselves up to criticism, then see what we can do about it. Let's try to fix things, not endlessly cover up our mistakes."

So many of the best and brightest – from young enthusiastic members like Thatcher to old warhorses like Henry Jensen and Michel Thivierge – leave before the force and the public can benefit fully from their intellect and instincts. In many respects today's RCMP is merely a revolving door for the well-educated. It doesn't take long for them to learn that there is no real long-term plan for them.

In fact, in her own words, Cockle seems to know what the real game is. After all her formal education, seven months at Depot, and the hours upon hours of sensitivity training, her view of the world seems unchanged from that of her less-educated, mostly white, male predecessors: down on the streets a cop is a cop is a cop. The one thing a street police officer knows is that, if he or she is doing the job properly, arrests are going to have to be made, and there are going to be violent situations.

That being the case, what is disturbing and potentially dangerous is that the force relaxed physical requirements for women in the fall of 1997 so that more could make the grade, to satisfy political imperatives. The rationale given at the time was that police work these days was not all about chasing down suspects and wrestling with them. There was more brainwork to the job. Yet every one of the new recruits that Depot turns out today is being sent into street situations where his or her brawn is inevitably going to be tested. The real fear, and it clearly is not unwarranted, is that someone who can't make the physical grade and defend themselves properly is going to either fire their weapon out of fear or be overpowered, injured, and possibly killed.

Throughout their training each new Mountie is fully instructed on the laws of the land, but then are told that it would be best if they take a more entrepreneurial approach to justice, as it were. That is, once on the streets the Mounties should take a few calculated risks from time to time, and find ways not to enforce the letter of the law, not to lay charges, and not to bring suspects to justice – in order to save the taxpayers money. The inevitable result of such a mixed message is a troop of potentially distressed soldiers of the law.

In that context, a motto such as "With Your Shield or on It" is an anchor, something that gives the new cadets a sense of purpose. It is perhaps an outdated slogan, but it conveys a clarity of vision nonetheless. It is the spirit of all Mounties: doing the right thing and defending the laws of Canada – to their own death, if need be. Every history of the force and every conversation with a Mountie indicates that this has always been the standard by which good Mounties have measured themselves. Many members today feel that the force has lost that focus and, with it, much of its moral power. Some Mounties feel threatened, even neutralized. Their anger is palpable because, as Commissioner Philip Murray promises to lead them into the twenty-first century, they seem to think they're headed back to the nineteenth and the vision of Robert Peel. For these Mounties, Commissioner Murray, with his business-minded plans and bottom-line attitude, has made a pact with the corporatist devil. To understand why they think this way, let's visit in the next few chapters the world in which cadets like Diane Cockle will be spending their first five years, or more, in the RCMP.

Chapter Ten

.... ● ....

NIGHT PATROL IN DUCK BAY

EARLY ONE EVENING in late June, I joined Constable Ken Aspen, seven years a Mountie, as he got himself ready to head out on patrol from the RCMP detachment in Winnipegosis, Manitoba, a three-and-a-half-hour drive northwest of Winnipeg. In one hand he held a box of nine-millimetre hollow-point shells for his sidearm, in the other a 12-gauge Remington Wingmaster Model 870 pump-action shotgun. The door of the white one-storey police building locked behind him, Aspen headed me out to the four-wheel-drive Yukon that he would be using that night, and we climbed in. He locked the shotgun into place between us. We drove out onto Constable Della Beyak Road, a short street that runs beside the defunct grain elevator near the detachment. Beyak, a native of Winnipegosis, was the first female Mountie to die in the line of duty, in an horrific highway accident near Assiniboia, Saskatchewan, on March 15, 1989. She was only twenty-one, and had graduated from Depot just three months earlier.[1]

Winnipegosis is a provincial contract for the RCMP, which means Manitoba pays 70 per cent of the cost of operations, while Ottawa subsidizes the rest. It is considered a sergeant's detachment, pure working class, with no white-shirted officers. It is also a limited-duration posting, which means anyone can transfer out after four years' service there.

Before leaving the quiet little town, Aspen steered the big, white Yukon into an alley, to the rear of a series of white frame government-owned houses. This is where the ten Mounties and their families in Winnipegosis live. Before he headed out into the wilderness, Aspen stopped to say goodbye one more time to his pregnant wife, Rebecca, and their year-old son. For the three years since he was transferred to Winnipegosis from Dauphin, an hour's drive to the south, Aspen has been following this routine. When he leaves town anything can happen. He has been in melees, threatened, and even shot at. Even so, on this night he sported short sleeves and wore no bulletproof vest. "It's too hot. I usually wear it on the weekends and band paydays."

Soon we were driving north on Highway 20, up the west side of Lake Winnipegosis. Constable Tom Wallach had left Winnipegosis at the same time as Aspen, and he was patrolling the east side of the lake, up as far as the Waterhen Indian Reserve. The two Mounties served as backup for each other. At best, they would be about one hundred kilometres from town throughout the evening, often farther, enforcing the law on trails that the Mounties have been riding since the Great March West from Dufferin, Manitoba, in 1874.

In Constable Aspen's vehicle, the CBC news and information show *As It Happens* was playing on the radio, creating a strange fusion of national institutions, not all that far from the geographical centre of Canada. "It's the only station we can get out here," Aspen said. "It's interesting. You can learn a lot from it." Over the next eight hours, Aspen would go about his job while being educated by some of the great writers, artists, and musicians of modern times, not what one would expect a prairie cop to be doing during his working hours.

Born in Porcupine Plains, Saskatchewan, a little more than an hour's drive west from his patrol area, Aspen is the youngest of six children of a Ukrainian mother and Norwegian father. His father died when he was a baby. Aspen attended the University of Saskatchewan for a couple of years, studying agriculture, then went to work for the Sask B grain pool, before joining the RCMP.

As we whipped along the nearly deserted highway, Aspen painted a picture of the communities we would be visiting. There were three impoverished villages along Highway 272, from the beautiful old residential-school church at Camperville through the Pine Creek Indian Reserve to the Métis settlement at Duck Bay, the end of the road. In between there were mostly empty stretches with maybe a shack or two here and there. "It's a rough place," Aspen said, "It's pretty hard to tell the people here to get a job where there are no jobs. Their job is social assistance. There's second- and third-generation welfare families. One sixteen-year-old girl in Duck Bay has three kids. Life starts young here."

A few minutes later, at about 7:30 p.m., we passed slowly by the Pine Creek Recreational Complex on Highway 272, where there were maybe forty, mostly beat-up cars in the parking lot. The dual entertainment attractions inside are bingo and video lottery terminals. On Highway 272, the Pine Creek Recreational Complex is a Quonset hut of simple and pathetic dreams. As social workers Susan Nurse and Barb St. Goddard put it, "They go because they think they can turn their five dollars into food for the kids or a graduation dress for their daughter, or maybe, if they hit the jackpot, a beat-up car."

Constable Aspen realizes this, but he still can barely contain his anger at the government for allowing and encouraging gambling. Every time he passed the complex – at least ten times throughout his patrol – he couldn't resist saying something. "From 7:00 p.m. to 9:00 p.m., it's hard to find people, because they are all here at the bingo. People talk about child poverty. These people don't have a lot of money, but from what I can see they have enough to feed their children. But then the government sets up gambling businesses and takes all the money away. The money goes to the government and not to the children. . . . Most of the parents are drunk. Nobody gives a damn. . . . At 5:00 in the morning you'll find nine- and ten-year-olds wandering around in the dark. . . . Nothing in this society works right."

On this evening, it soon became clear that Constable Aspen was the sole guardian, looking out for all the people who lived along Highway 272. In a community without hope, Aspen spends his working hours being a parent, teacher, peacemaker, and priest, plugging his finger time after time into the leaking dikes of despair. There's nothing easy about the job.

Outside the variety store at McKay's Service Centre, a group of children, the oldest of which might be twelve, taunted him: "Hey, can you buy us a case of beer?" Aspen ignored them. A teenaged girl rode by on a bicycle, awkwardly covering her face so that Aspen couldn't identify her. He just let her go; if he stopped everyone who behaved like her, that's all he'd be doing. Later, two young teenaged girls, wearing the black-and-white uniform of the notorious Indian Posse gang, scowled at him when he tried to interview them about a complaint about misbehaviour on the school ground. The I.P., as it is known, is a prison-based criminal gang that has moved into the outlying native communities along with the Manitoba Warriors. The attitude of the girls got to him a little, mainly because he could see the terrible future their criminal associates were creating for them.

As American writer Calvin Trillin spoke to Eleanor Wachtel on CBC about his latest book, *Messages from My Father*, Aspen half-listened and half-concentrated on everything going on around him. The previous night he had gone off patrol around 2:00 a.m., but was called back around 5:00 a.m., because three children had been brought to the hospital by taxi. They were suffering from convulsions after a drug overdose. In a community where few have cars or money, the only available public transit is often a taxi for trips that can range up to 125 kilometres to the hospital in Dauphin.

Everyone in the community knows who the drug supplier was; he all but flaunts his wares in front of the police. But to investigate him, Aspen needs someone to talk, to give him a lead. It's all so futile. "He is a danger to the community. He'll sell to anyone. He doesn't care how old they are. Speed. Cocaine. Marijuana. You name it. The people are afraid to say anything, because they know just as well that the courts won't do much about it. He'll be back in no time, and there will be no one there to protect them."

Dealing drugs is a federal offence, and, technically, Aspen should be spending 30 per cent of his time on federal duties, to reflect the federal government's share of his salary. That's the theory, at least; in practice, that's not what happens. For a serious drug investigation in his area, Aspen must depend upon full-time federal investigators in Winnipeg, who are so busy there that they rarely even bother to try to penetrate outlying communities like these.

These are places where all the best intentions of the Supreme Court about individual rights and Charter freedoms are lost on victims, suspects, and innocent bystanders alike. To make the point, Aspen pulled out a card on which is printed the warning he must read to every suspect before he arrests them. Like most police officers, he is soon propelled into a critique of the justice system itself. "When I started seven years ago, all you had to say was: 'You have the right to contact legal counsel. Do you understand?' Now case law dictates that I have to give this *speech* when I go to place someone under arrest for, say, assault causing bodily harm." As he drove, he read:

> You have the right to retain and instruct counsel in private without delay. This means that before we proceed with our investigation you may call any lawyer you wish or get free legal advice from duty counsel immediately. If you want to call duty counsel we will provide you with a telephone and telephone numbers. If you wish to contact any other lawyer, a telephone and telephone book will be provided. If you are charged with an offence, you may also apply to legal aid for assistance. Do you understand? Do you want to call duty counsel or any other lawyer? Do you understand? Do you want to call now?[2]

"More often than not, when I read that the guy will have this puzzled look on his face. So I tell him, 'You can call a lawyer.' And they say, 'Oh, yeah, right,'" Aspen said, shaking his head. He continued with his train of thought. "To be effective the law must be simple and easy to understand. Many of these people have grade-three educations, *at best*. The justice system shouldn't always be making things more complicated. In my opinion, the Supreme Court makes decisions that just don't make sense. They don't live in places like Duck Bay. They don't see the anguish and the poverty and the reason for crime. For the most part, judges are from large cities and communities, live in nice houses, and they have nothing in common with the people who they pass sentence on."

Finally, he segued to the problem – as he perceives it – that legal aid has created. "With legal aid there is no incentive for anyone to plead out, no matter how guilty they might be. They stall and stall and try to grind the police down. That's not the way the justice system should work."

A few minutes later, Aspen broke off his analysis and flicked on the Yukon's flashing roof-lights to pull over a car. You never think about the courage it takes for a police officer to do his job until you are sitting in the passenger seat beside him when he pulls over an overloaded Delta 88, dragging its rear end along an empty stretch of highway.

"Do we have to do this?" I asked weakly.

"If it looks like we're going to die," Aspen said calmly, "hit this button. It will release the shotgun. Pump it once to push the shell into the breach and come out firing."

"If that's the case, we're dead," I told him.

He pointed to his mouth. "This is my best weapon," he says before heading off cautiously towards the driver's side of the car. The six or seven occupants were sitting ramrod straight. Aspen poked his head inside the car and I fingered the shotgun. After a minute or so he returned to the Yukon. "Nobody wants to talk." At least about the drug dealer.

Before we went too far into the shift, the residents realized Constable Aspen was on patrol that night. Calls for his service began to flood into the dispatch centre in Dauphin. During the night, it seemed that we ended up visiting every second house in the three communities, some of them a number of times. "We like Kenny, he listens to us," said one man. "When the people see he's on, they call. That's the way the Mounties and the Indians have always got along. The Mounties are trusted. We have our disagreements sometimes, but most Indians prefer the Mounties over anyone else, even Indian police. They're our peacemakers."

The complaints were mostly sorry excuses to chat with the blond Mountie. They were the kind of calls to which the Metro Toronto Police, for example, wouldn't even respond. In Toronto two police officers, who usually live in the deep suburbs, patrol the downtown streets at night, glued to their seats. In Duck Bay, Aspen was in and out of his vehicle every few minutes, alone, in unfriendly territory, but absolutely committed to his duties and responsibilities. Every house he visited, whether there was a disturbance or not, he approached the same way, parking the vehicle at the side, out of sight of open windows. He then hurried to the back door, his demeanour at all times firm, polite, and irresistibly friendly.

One complaint came from a woman who said a teacher slapped her autistic child on the side of the head at school that day. After an hour of Aspen's time, she said tiredly, "You know, I don't want to have her charged. I just want someone to talk to her. I know my son acts up, but she shouldn't have hit him like that. It wasn't right."

In another ongoing situation, Aspen visited one tiny street four times, trying to resolve a dispute between two neighbouring families over the behaviour of a teenaged boy. Both sides seemed to know a little bit about the law, and less about civility. Aspen ended up passing messages between them, like an armed carrier pigeon flitting between two socially handicapped combatants.

"The people up here are difficult to deal with, but if you treat them the way you would like to be treated, everything will be fine. You can't go out and start throwing your weight around," Aspen said, "The biggest assholes I've met by far are white people in Dauphin. They're rude and racist – just a bunch of bullies."

"Is this community-based policing?" I asked.

"This is what the Mounties have always done in these communities," Aspen replied. "That's what I call community-based policing. The chiefs back in Ottawa are a little more formal about it. They want us to fill out forms and sit on community consultative groups. That takes up a lot of time, time that is lost from investigations. Maybe the need for investigations might decline if these groups work, but I don't know about that."

In Camperville, Pine Creek, and Duck Bay, the breakdown and degree of dysfunction in the community seemed potent enough to challenge even the most strongwilled do-gooder. While Aspen was on patrol, everything remained rather quiet. That's the way it usually goes. "We're supposed to be providing twenty-four-hour service, but we don't have the manpower. On weekdays I try to quit around 2:00 a.m., and maybe 4:00 a.m. on weekends. After I go home, that's when the criminals come out. They start carrying stolen goods around and the place often goes wild. It's completely unprotected. They know we're not likely to come back, unless there's something really serious. Every so often we change our shifts and catch someone, but then they just lie low again until we revert back to our normal routine."

That night in Duck Bay there was a rather comedic incident which shows the variety of skills a Mountie has to display. It is worth a short digression.

As we headed out of Duck Bay for about the fifth time, we came across a middle-aged man carrying a grocery bag, walking towards us on the shoulder of the road.

"I think this is the guy I was telling you about," Aspen said, bringing the Yukon to a stop.

I rolled down the window, and the man poked his bright red face through a lace of mosquitoes into the vehicle. His name was Louie. He was a handsome fifty-eight-year-old, with a wonderful shock of grey hair. He wore wire-rim glasses, a soiled jacket, gum boots, and an election campaign button: "Revive Riel's Métis Vision: Vote Billy Jo."

"Hop in," Aspen ordered him. "Let's go investigate that thing right now, then I'll drive you home."

Louie got into the back seat of the Yukon and, on the ride back to Duck Bay, told us his woeful story. For more than a year he had been receiving a series of crank and obscene calls from a heavy breather at all hours of the day and night. For a man his age, and a devout Catholic, it was an extremely disturbing turn of events. Eventually he stopped answering his phone. "Then my brother-in-law died, and my sister kept trying to call me for the whole weekend, but I wouldn't answer the telephone," Louie said in a matter-of-fact tone of voice. "So she sent someone over to see me. She thought I'd died, too. Boy, did she give me hell."

Louie's sister told him about the *69 phone function which identifies the most recent caller, so he had the service added to his line. The first time the heavy breather called, Louie hit *69. A number came up, but he thought it must have been wrong. By the third time this had happened, however, he knew the technology wasn't lying, so he set out to confront the woman. "I asked her if it was her, and she said it was. I told her if she didn't stop, I was going to tell the RCMP. Well, she didn't call for a while, but then she did."

As we reached the women's driveway on a property overlooking the mauve waters of Duck Bay, a young Métis boy by the side of the road pretended to dial a telephone and started laughing. Everyone in town obviously knew what had been going on.

Constable Aspen stopped near the front door, got out of the Yukon, and took the long and embarrassing walk up the steps of the nun's residence to have a little chat with the suspect sister . . .

• • •

By the fall of that year, Constable Aspen was ready to leave Winnipegosis. As good as he was at handling people, he had done his tour. It was time to move on. In Commissioner Murray's grand plan, cadets like Ken Aspen are supposed to hone their skills in detachments like Winnipegosis, before moving into more important and sophisticated duties, such as federal policing. For the next three years, however, Aspen wouldn't be building on his experiences patrolling around Lake Winnipegosis. The RCMP is a big, complex national organization with thousands of opportunities that have little or nothing do with "real" policing. Aspen's next assignment was one of those: he was promoted to the Musical Ride to be an entertainer. Such is the perverse logic of the RCMP, which doesn't surprise anyone close to the force. For the deeper one gets inside the RCMP, the more illogical the RCMP becomes.

Commissioner Philip Murray's plan for the future of the RCMP envisions a force that is run like a business: lean, flexible, and innovative. The Mounties of the near-future are to be even less agents of federal law enforcement than they are today. Instead, each and every new and improved Mountie will be trained to focus on and deal with micro-problems in their respective jurisdictions, much as Constable Aspen did in Duck Bay, spending hour after hour tending to the specific, and often non-criminal, problems of Canadians and their communities.

As we shall see in the next chapter, those whom the commissioner tends to recognize and reward within the RCMP today are the ones who subscribe to, or at least appear to subscribe to, his vision. These police officers, like Ken Aspen, are being marketed by the force as the new, sensitive, twenty-first-century-model Mounties, proof that the force is progressive and in touch with the times. But even some of these star employees are suspicious about what's going on. A lot makes no sense to some of them, especially the total emphasis on local policing as opposed to federal law enforcement. The great and growing fear within the ranks, even in small and remote municipal detachments, is that the new business-minded RCMP is fast losing sight of its true mandate and duty, which is the big picture – defending the national interest and the greater good.

Chapter Eleven

.... ● ....

COMMUNITY-BASED POLICING: LAW ENFORCEMENT AND POLITICS

UNDER PRIME MINISTER Pierre Trudeau, the federal government began the process of decentralizing many of its powers and responsibilities to the provinces, but this didn't affect the Royal Canadian Mounted Police much – if at all – during Trudeau's term in office. Prime Minister Brian Mulroney moved the ball of decentralization further down the field, when, among other things, his solicitor general, Pierre Cadieux, published his 1990 white paper, "Police-Challenge 2000," which recommended that federal law enforcement by the RCMP be de-emphasized in favour of community-based policing. Jean Chrétien took these recommendations and, in 1993, adapted them to fit into his Red Book of campaign promises.

"Safe Homes, Safe Streets," was one of Chrétien's rallying cries in the October 1993 federal election. Chrétien promised that Canadians would once again feel safe in their own communities, as if Canada, one of the safest countries in the world, were a place where people couldn't go outside anymore because of all the criminals lurking in the shadows.

Then-RCMP Commissioner Norman Inkster says that, a few weeks after Chrétien assumed office, he decided to retire, and he was succeeded in June 1994 by Philip Murray. Murray took up Jean Chrétien's message from the Red Book and ran with it, altering the message a little. "Safe Homes, Safe Communities" became the early theme of Commissioner Murray's time in office. The RCMP was now going to be focused on individuals and their problems and their communities, rather than on the nation as a whole. Decentralization was no longer going to be an abstract theory to the Mounties.

The common thread linking the Trudeau, Mulroney, and Chrétien governments is that all three were driven by the notion that government should operate more like a business. As we have already seen, Commissioner Murray has applied this same line of business-like thinking to his management of the RCMP, right down to the way the force describes its law-enforcement duties.

When Commissioner Philip Murray waxes eloquent about the RCMP these days, it is easy for the undiscriminating listener to get lost in the vision, the grand images, and the rhetoric. Murray likes to talk about "re-engineering the RCMP," or about the "New Service Delivery Model," or "partnerships with the community." He is high on new programs such as the Integrated Proceeds of Crime units and aboriginal self-policing, and especially proud of the intelligence and education of new recruits like Diane Cockle, the former chief archeologist of Saskatchewan, whom we met in Chapter Nine.

However, what may be most revealing about Murray, and the conflicted mandate of the RCMP that he must manage, are found in the small community-based projects across the country and the grass-roots personnel Murray seems to hold closest to his heart. At a time when organized crime, fraud, and corruption are costing the economy billions of dollars a year, the RCMP, pushed by the government, is focusing more and more on the little things.

In the tiny hamlet of Faust, Alberta, three hundred kilometres north of Edmonton on Lesser Slave Lake, the only pavement in the community of three hundred people is the highway running through it and the RCMP detachment compound. Three years ago, the sergeant in charge came up with the idea of purchasing two portable basketball hoops, which he placed in the compound for the use of local youth, giving them a way to entertain themselves and lose their fear of the police at the same time. "That was a wonderful initiative, the kind of thing we'd like to see more of," Murray says.

Other projects that capture the commissioner's imagination include what is known as a restorative-justice program at Lennox Island, P.E.I., where alternatives to the criminal-justice system are used to deal with offenders. The commissioner also champions the community-policing initiatives at Cole Harbour, Nova Scotia, which suffered a considerable setback with racially motivated student riots in October 1997. He is proud of the work of the RCMP in its municipal detachment in Burnaby, B.C. "You should go there, and see for yourself," he told me, which I did, during a trip that is the focus of the next chapter.

In a police force with more than twenty thousand employees, Murray can't be expected to remember everyone's name, but among his clear favourites are two sergeants in obscure locations – Ronald J. Marlin in Dauphin, Manitoba, and Jake Bouwman in Sparwood, B.C. We met Bouwman briefly back in Chapter Two speaking critically of former commissioner Norman Inkster. Murray considers Marlin and Bouwman to be two police officers who are "thinking out of the box," as the modern business vernacular puts it. That is, they are finding solutions to problems, other than resorting to pure policing and law enforcement. "You should go and see what they're doing," Murray urged. So I visited them, too.

•   •   •

Staff Sergeant Ron Marlin may have been born and raised in Bridgewater, Nova Scotia, but he has spent his entire career in the West – twenty-six years in Manitoba. Now he would sooner retire than leave Dauphin, an agricultural-service town of nine thousand residents. The town lies on the northern edge of Riding Mountain National Park, and there are nine native communities in the area. In most other RCMP postings, a staff sergeant like Marlin would be a middle-ranking supervisor with no profile. In the world of RCMP municipal policing, however, Marlin is a somebody. He is effectively the police chief of Dauphin.

The Mounties have been in Dauphin since December 11, 1941 – four days after the bombing of Pearl Harbor, an event which brought them to the town. Dauphin was the site of a Royal Canadian Air Force training centre, which meant three to four thousand men were in town at any one time, more than the local police could handle. The RCMP were ordered in by the federal government, and they never left. The town of Dauphin currently pays $1 million a year for the thirteen Mounties who police Dauphin, with Ottawa picking up 10 per cent of the cost. But they are not the only Mounties in Dauphin. Their municipal detachment occupies the first floor of the new police building on Hedderly Street; the second floor is home to the regional headquarters – the Parklands sub-division, commanded by Superintendent Gary McPherson. He watches over Marlin and the wider area for the RCMP.

In Dauphin, though, Marlin has the public profile. Since October 1995, when the town was selected as a community-based policing demonstration project, Marlin has spent almost every waking hour knitting together the community and the police. The intention of community-based policing is ostensibly to get residents more involved in their own security and safety and to rely less on police response. The theory is that, by encouraging such an attitude, the society will make itself more orderly. Problems will be solved before incidents occur, thereby leaving the police, with their ever-decreasing resources, more time to investigate serious matters.

To educate residents about this new policing model, Marlin, like the well-trained Mountie that he is, has seemingly boundless energy and is a master of detail. He has forged links with every political, educational, and social group in the community. He sits on committees, attends meetings, and knows everyone by his or her first name.

Marlin has his own vision of how Dauphin should be policed, and his actions make it clear what that is. When young skateboarders began to use the parking lot and front steps of the RCMP building as a ramp, politicians and Mounties alike protested. But Marlin and McPherson encouraged the children to play around the police station as a way of making them feel more comfortable with the police. There was only one proviso. Marlin warned the thirty or so kids, who assemble each night from April to October, not to use one set of stairs for a launching pad: "Don't end up as a hood ornament when you're heading towards the north wall, or I'm going to end up in doo-doo, and then there will be no more skateboarding here." To the kids and many of their parents, Marlin is a hero.

When some in town government complained that traffic-ticket revenue was down, Marlin argued that raising revenues shouldn't be the police mandate. "The reason we patrol and use radar is to prevent speeding and bad driving habits. A perfect day for us is one where no one is ticketed, because every one is obeying the law," he says.

Friendly to his core, he seems to confront every issue head-on, firmly but with compassion, no matter how small or how explosive each situation may be. When a reporter and cameraman from the local television station showed up unannounced at the scene of a fight between two women, one of them with a knife, Marlin threw a bit of a fit. He didn't like the idea of the media charging into situations where, he believed, they did not belong. He called an urgent lunch meeting at Irving's Family Restaurant on First Avenue, bringing along two of his underlings (and me) to meet with the station manager, reporter, cameraman, and the sports reporter, who had tagged along for the meal. After the niceties, Marlin opened the discussion: "I'd like to chat with you folks about the use of the police scanner in your office and what calls you respond to. We're used to you coming out to fires and accidents, but this last call involving the two women, well, that's something we haven't experienced here before. I just want to make sure we're working from the same page."

Then, Marlin led the group through a discussion of the kinds of stories the television station might be interested in covering. He pointed out that the Mounties normally would have used telephones when talking between themselves about such an incident. But in the case of the knife-wielding woman, there was no one in the station manning the telephones, so the report went out over the radio system and could be picked up by scanner, one of which is constantly monitored at the television-station newsroom. Marlin said he sympathized with the television station's dilemma: "You are a visual medium, we realize you need pictures."

While station general manager Sue Schlingerman sat with her arms folded, and doe-eyed reporter Keri Ferguson munched on her salad, news director Sean Irvine tried to lead the negotiations. "The first thing we need in television is immediacy," Irvine says. "We can affect every sense by smell or touch. When we pull up to a scene, all we need from you is to send an officer over to say something like: 'Sean, we have two females in custody involving a knife. We have no further information.' That's all we need. We don't need the full details."

"So," Marlin says, "how about we work out an arrangement where we'll call you and let you know about stories that you might be interested in?"

Schlingerman, gently rocking in her seat, looked suspiciously for the catch, but there seemed not to be one. She didn't really have any negotiating power, anyway. Marlin had gently made it clear to her that, if the television station insisted on showing up at situations "uninvited," somebody might get charged with obstructing police. A handshake agreement was struck. The police would inform the station about what it believed to be newsworthy events and would provide Mounties to speak on camera as much as possible. "I'm trying to teach the other guys to do more television. My ugly mug doesn't have to be out there all the time."

Marlin may have been a life-long policeman, but along the way he has learned a thing or two about managing.

That May, a teenaged girl was killed when she was run over by a car at a bush party outside of town. Rumours soon began sweeping through Dauphin that the girl had been tortured and sexually assaulted by the Indian Posse and then deliberately run over. Community outrage began to build.

As soon as the autopsy report was done, Marlin called two meetings – one with staff at school and a second one with the student body. When that wasn't enough, he called a public meeting, brought his investigation file, and laid out the details for all to see, proving that the dead girl had been the victim of an accident. "She had not been beaten or raped, and there was no connection to the Indian Posse," Marlin said. "With all the rumours, there was a real danger that things were going to get a little out of hand, so I made public all the evidence to cool things off. Unsubstantiated rumours take on a life of their own. They can cause a lot of problems. What better way to hear the truth than directly from the Horseman's mouth?" he said with a chuckle.

In the old, more traditional style of policing – the "professional" or "reform" model – the police both jealously guarded their right to enforce the law and kept their distance – and information – from civilians. In the RCMP's community-based concept, everyone shares in crime prevention and law enforcement. Marlin oversaw the development of Neighbourhood Watch programs in town to go along with Range Patrol, the rural version of Neighbourhood Watch. Forty-eight citizens, whose identities are kept as anonymous as possible, were enlisted for another program known as Citizens on Patrol, or COP. The citizens, mostly retirees and businesspeople, use their private vehicles. For a while, their gas was donated by a local business, but that support was withdrawn. Each COP volunteer is given a log sheet, a flashlight, and a portable radio so that he or she can stay in contact with the RCMP dispatcher. "They're our eyes and ears," says Marlin. "If they see anything suspicious they jot it down on a log sheet. When they actually see something happening, which is quite rare, they're supposed to call us. We've made it quite clear to them that they haven't been deputized. Three break-and-enters have been discovered by them."

When Ron Marlin drives through town in his unmarked car, he is met with a constant barrage of waves and tooting horns, mostly from senior citizens, who dominate the demographic of the community. You can't help but get the feeling that he's a real-life Andy of Mayberry, cheery, happy, and effective at his job, and the Mounties who work for him are much the same.

For example, one morning in September, Corporal Brent Penner was patrolling the highway through Dauphin when he came across a fifteen-year-old girl he didn't recognize. Penner stopped and soon found out that she was a runaway from Kapuskasing, Ontario, and was a ward of family services there. The Mountie brought her into the station, and then he and Marlin spent the day dealing with local social services, trying to arrange transportation for the girl back to her home town. Because she was a runner, however, social services didn't want to take responsibility for her while she was in town.

"It was obvious in our minds that the kid had had a rough go in her life," said Marlin afterwards. "I didn't think she was the kind of kid who belonged in a cell. So I made her a deal. If she behaved, she could travel around with us for the day. She gave me her word, and that was good enough. So she went with me to a community-policing meeting in Gilbert Plains, to the west of us. During the afternoon she fiddled around on the computer in the office. We gave her a job to take out all the recycling in the station to the depot. The plane to Winnipeg wasn't going to be leaving until 7:00 p.m. When I finished my shift I took her home and my wife made dinner for her."

The girl was carrying a diary with her. Cpl. Penner wrote a poem in it. "There once was a girl / From Kapuskasing / Whom the police were always chasing / Can she live with her past / And stop the police time she's wasting."

A few weeks later, the girl wrote the police officer a letter from the detention centre where she was confined:

Dear Ron: I'm in jail because I always runaway. I'm suposto be out on October 4, but I am getting charged for taking my mom and dad's car. . . . So I am writing every body I said I'd write so now you know I'm not a lier, I may be a criminal as Officer Penner says but I'm not a lier. . . . Please don't think I'm rued . . . I don't even want to be close in getting cops on my back anymore but I *might* keep in touch. I'll sign off for now until the nexed time I write.

There is no doubt that most everyone in Dauphin loves Marlin and the Mounties. There's talk of placing a sign at each entrance to city which would read: "This community is policed by the citizens of Dauphin with the assistance of the RCMP." Some think that Marlin should run for mayor in the next election, an idea that brings a twinkle to his eye. "That wouldn't be a bad job to retire to," he says.

"Ron could be the poster boy for the entire community-policing concept," says town administrator Jim Puffalt. "Every problem he has been thrown, he has come up with a solution."

Having said that, even the Mounties themselves concede that the problems in Dauphin are and never have been all that huge. As Superintendent MacPherson puts it, succinctly, "This is a low-crime area."

In April, for example, this is what the RCMP had to contend with in Dauphin: fifteen assaults, seven break-and-enters, seventeen thefts, twenty-seven complaints of vandalism, thirty-seven general offences such as disturbing the peace, twenty motor-vehicle accidents, sixty-one highway-traffic violations, and six drunk drivers.

In the town of nine thousand, there was only one man considered potentially dangerous – and he is believed to have been involved in a suspicious death in another jurisdiction.

Now let's head to Sparwood, another of Commissioner Murray's pet projects.

•   •   •

It's the Sunday afternoon after the Mike Tyson–Evander Holyfield boxing match in which Tyson bit off a chunk of Holyfield's ear. For Sergeant Jake Bouwman, it had been a long night. The fight had been shown in the bar at the Black Nugget, "East Kootenay's Finest Full Service Motor Hotel." The crowd was a mix of seismologists, who had been living in the motel for weeks while they worked in the abundant coalfields around the town, and a group of local men who felt the seismologists were stealing all the town's single women. For a couple of nights, a number of the women had been dancing with and enjoying the company of the out-of-towners. Some of the seismologists were considered by the locals to have been "smart mouths." A beer bottle was thrown. A brawl broke out. Mountie Jake Bouwman was called out of bed. Every few months this same script is played out, but this time there was a bit of a difference. When it was all over, one of the local boys had imitated Tyson and taken a rather large chunk of flesh out of the upper arm of one of the seismologists. The victim went to the hospital for a tetanus shot, and a bunch of the combatants got doused with pepper spray. One of the seismologists, angered by the experience, threatened to shoot one of the Mounties, but that didn't happen. Eventually, the local boys scattered, the seismologist apologized, and no charges were laid. It was just another Saturday night in Sparwood.

Sparwood came into existence in 1976, after three old coal-mining towns – Michel, Natal, and Middletown – were torn down and the residents relocated to the new town, which was built a few miles to the west. Today, anyone driving through the Crowsnest Pass, fifteen minutes west of the Alberta border, can't miss Sparwood's feature attraction – the world's largest truck. The enormous green Titan was shipped on eight rail cars to Sparwood in 1978 to be used in the coalfields. It weighed 260 tons empty and 610 tons loaded. Its box could hold two Greyhound buses and two pickup trucks or two million golf balls. But as large as it was, like the Mounties themselves it wasn't entirely effective. The Titan suffered constant mechanical breakdowns and was eventually taken out of service to be replaced by smaller mobile units that were more practical. It now sits by the side of Highway 3, a monument to monstrous hybrids.

Born in Holland, Jake Bouwman came to Canada as a child in 1953. After completing grade eleven, he joined the Mounties in 1969. His entire RCMP career has been spent in town policing in British Columbia, in Gold River, Nanaimo, Duncan, Prince George, Lytton, Sidney, and finally Sparwood, where he took over command of the six-man detachment in 1994. With its huge and profitable coal fields, Sparwood has some wealth, but, with a little more than four thousand residents, it is not considered large enough to pay for its own policing. That's covered by the province and by Ottawa, which picks up 30 per cent of the tab. Still, there's not much money for policing. "If one of our cars is damaged in an accident, we'll have to live without it. There's no money in the budget to even repair them."

Six months after coming to Sparwood, Bouwman was invited to lunch by Glen Purdy, a local lawyer. Purdy didn't expect much from the Mountie. The force had always been distant and unapproachable, but Bouwman seemed a little different. Purdy launched into his concerns about the way the youth-justice system was working in Canada, using as his foundation a report by Heino Lilles, a judge in the Yukon Territorial Court in Whitehorse. Lilles had written the report while on sabbatical at the University of New South Wales in Australia. While in Australia, he had become fascinated with changes and innovations being implemented there and in New Zealand in the way young offenders were being treated under the law. In New Zealand, it was determined that the courts were ill-suited to deal with social and family problems, and that the "justice model" was ineffective in preventing delinquency. There was a tendency to confuse welfare and justice issues, and this resulted in interventions which were inappropriate and perhaps too soft. Further, Lilles wrote, victims wanted more say about reparation and restitution. "In addition, the adversarial court proceedings were considered inappropriate to the culture of the indigenous Maori population, who were over-represented in the criminal system."

Lilles wrote that Canada has one of the most punitive criminal-justice systems in the Western world, with a rate of adult incarceration of 129.6 per 100,000 population. This compared to 90 for the United Kingdom, Spain, and Austria, 80 for France, Portugal, and Australia, and 60 or lower for Finland, Belgium, Italy, and Sweden. Only the United States was higher with 330 per 100,000 population. What concerned Lilles is that young people aged twelve to eighteen were being incarcerated at an extrapolated rate four times that of the adult population.[1]

Conditions similar to those in New Zealand and Australia existed in Canada, Purdy told Bouwman. "In Sparwood, kids were going to court and coming out heroes to their peers. Nothing was getting done. I suggested to Jake that we need to look at ways to reform youth justice and that we couldn't wait for the system to do it. I expected that he would get his back up, but his reaction was precisely the opposite."

Like Ron Marlin in Dauphin, Bouwman seized the opportunity to become a leader in the community – Sparwood's Andy of Mayberry. In January 1995, the first Family Group Conference was arranged. Its advocates consider it to be the perfect fusion of the native notion of restorative justice and modern community policing. It is based on an Australian model. In it, everyone who has an interest in a particular crime attends a meeting. In Sparwood, two cases are cited as examples of how successful the process might be.

The first conference involved a case where a local clothing-store owner noticed a boy walking down the street wearing a unique sweater. The clothier recognized the sweater as one that had disappeared from his store. He confronted the youth, called the police, and wished to lay charges. A Family Group Conference was held, which brought together the youth, his parents, his teacher, the store owner, and the police. Everyone expressed their views, and, in the end, the store owner hired the youth to work off his debt. The experiment went so well that, at the end of the "probation," the youth applied for and received full-time work at the store.

The other case involved a ring of young shoplifters. In this case, peers from their school sat in on the conference, because they were affected by the crimes; store owners were treating them like thieves because of the actions of their classmates. Eventually everyone, including the suspects, came to an agreement and the shoplifting spree ended.

Over the next two years, fifty-seven Family Group conferences were held in Sparwood, transforming the youth-justice system dramatically. In 1994, sixty-four youths were handled by the court system. In 1995, after the system was in place, no youths were before the courts and forty-eight were in the program. In 1996, no youths were before the courts and twenty-one were in the program. In 1997, one repeat offender ended up in court on a serious offence, while three were involved with Family Group Conferencing.

"I'm still surprised that the conferences work," says Bouwman, a father of four. "If somebody had told me this would happen, I wouldn't have believed it was possible."

Soon, the RCMP was flying Bouwman and Purdy around the country as guest speakers and trainers to set up similar programs. "I'm a lawyer in a small town in the Rockies, and now it appears we're getting some national respect, and that's quite gratifying," Purdy says.

Family Group Conferencing in Sparwood and many isolated communities is considered by Commissioner Murray and his followers to be an important and efficient addition to the justice system, something which might be expanded across the nation. But in spite of these apparent successes and the opinion of its advocates, everything is not as rosy as it might first seem. Bouwman's right-hand man, Constable Dave Wilks, describes Sparwood as "the quietest place I've ever been. It's almost boring." In many respects Sparwood is far from the perfect test centre for such a project. It's just not dysfunctional enough. The pump-handle on the Remington Wingmaster in Bouwman's Yukon patrol vehicle is worn thin from use – from shooting injured wild animals, and the occasional bear that might wander down the main street.

On the streets of Sparwood, the self-described "bad" teenagers – Dave Peck, Tanya Dodge, Dale Fedorek, and Jon Fraser – aren't all that impressed with the work of the Mounties. "The big shoplifting ring was a bunch of little kids stealing bubble gum," says Fraser. "Another time, some thirteen- and fourteen-year-olds broke into the golf course and stole some golf carts and destroyed them. They just got 120 hours of community service. You know what they did? They were supposed to be cutting the grass, but they spent all day in the woods smoking weed. What did they learn?"

Dave Peck, of "no fixed address," says the problem with Family Group Conferencing is that it will only work on good kids who live in a stable family atmosphere. "They all seem to think that kids are going to be embarrassed by having their parents know they stole something or did something wrong. The reason the kids are on the street in the first place is that they don't like or respect their parents. They don't give a damn what they think. That's not punishment enough."

In the end all four agree on one thing: as Fedorek puts it, "We're the bad kids in town. Every time the Mounties drive by us, they slow down to see what we're doing. All we're doing is hanging out, but they treat us like we're the Crips and the Bloods. There's lots of money in this town but no facilities for people our age. The town thinks we all should be playing basketball. I'm sorry, I hate basketball. What are they trying to tell us? If we don't play basketball we're criminals? It's sick, really sick."

The four teenagers hit upon the inherent weakness of Family Group Conferencing. It's only as strong as the faith of the defendant in his peers and the community. Bouwman had one successful Family Group

Conferencing with an adult, over an automobile collision, but otherwise adults have generally refused to participate. "They prefer to go to court," says Bouwman. "They're not much interested in the prospect of being publicly humiliated by everyone they know."

While that may well be the message coming out of Sparwood about how Family Group Conferencing is really viewed, such mixed reviews don't have much effect on Commissioner Murray. The force is desperate for innovators and eager to reward those who are "thinking out of the box."

Bouwman came up for promotion in 1997. All he wanted was a pay raise for his good work, and the opportunity to stay in Sparwood, but the RCMP wanted to move him to a staff sergeant's position in the Economic Crime Unit in Vancouver. "That's how poor the promotion system is," says Bouwman. "I've been a town cop all my life. I'm pretty good at being a town cop. I only have grade eleven; heck, I can't even add. But by the force's standards, I'm the kind of guy who might benefit from a couple of years in commercial crime. I couldn't help them one bit. All I want to be is a town cop, but to move up I have to move out of Sparwood. I don't think I want to do that at this stage of my career."

In fact, Bouwman says, when and if he leaves, the man who should replace him is Constable Wilks, who has served for seventeen years in the force. "Dave can run this place like a sergeant. He knows what he's doing, but the way the system works, he doesn't have a chance of moving up. Somebody looking to move out of Vancouver and relax a little can bump him at any time."

•   •   •

So, you might ask, what is community-based policing and why is it so popular with politicians and police executives?

The genesis of the community-based policing movement was an *Atlantic Monthly* article, published in 1982, entitled "Police and Neighbourhood Safety: Broken Windows," by James Q. Wilson and George R. Kelling, two well-known students of police behaviour. The theory behind "Broken Windows," which later was expanded and published as a book, was that "police departments that focus solely or even primarily on serious crime – as virtually all do – will not be of much help to a community struggling to keep its head above water. There are often clear signals that marginal neighbourhoods are going downhill, signals like broken windows, trash, street prostitution, and drug dealing. Such disorder, while often too minor to warrant much attention from police, attracts miscreants and breeds fear in communities; fearful people avoid one another, and the deterioration accelerates. Alienation and hopelessness eat away at security and civility. Fighting crime is important. Fighting fear and disorder is essential."[2]

The trick to the broken-windows theory of policing is constant and visible policing, with unrelenting and strict law enforcement. There is a purity of vision in broken windows, which is absolutely consistent with the rule of law. The theory was used to clean up the New York City subway: the transit authority began enforcing laws against fare jumpers and scrubbing clean graffiti-covered cars.

Before too long, variations on the broken-windows philosophy began to emerge in Canada, with police officers moving out of cars and doing foot and bicycle patrols. Mini-police stations were being opened in malls, storefronts, and trailers. That's the public-relations side of the equation. Community-based policing has been sold as an antidote to the professional or reform models of policing, whereby police are seen to be always reacting to situations, racing from scene to scene. Community-based policing is seen as way of integrating the police with the community and its politics – breaking down the long-held attitude that the police must be independent and aloof to be effective. In the dance of life that is society, the police traditionally have been the monitors, stepping onto the waxed floor every so often to cart away in handcuffs those participants who are out of step. In community-based policing, the role of the police is dramatically changed; they participate in the dance, get to know the dancers, the steps, and sometimes coach the dancers into following their lead. In other words, the primary consideration behind community-based policing is not so much law enforcement *per se*, but order.

But Canada is already an orderly society, isn't it? Canadians live in one of the wealthiest and safest countries in the world. The country's worst neighbourhoods, whether North Preston, Nova Scotia, Jean Talon in Montreal, Regent Park or Jane–Finch in Metro Toronto, North Main in Winnipeg, or East Hastings Street in Vancouver, are relatively crime-free compared to their miserable U.S. counterparts: Roxbury in Boston, the South Bronx in New York, Camden, New Jersey, Washington, D.C., the east side of Detroit, Cabrini Green in Chicago, most of downtown Memphis, or South Central Los Angeles, to name just a few of the most dangerous urban areas in the United States and, for that matter, the world. There is a great difference between Canada and the United States, so why is Canada importing notions of policing that are best applied to the U.S. experience and U.S situations?

Perhaps because there's another agenda at work here.

Let us return to "Police-Challenge 2000: A Vision of the Future of Policing in Canada," the 1990 discussion paper by former solicitor general Pierre Cadieux, which has provided the framework for police policy in Canada ever since. In this "vision," Cadieux passionately stressed the need for dramatic change. The central thesis of "Police-Challenge 2000" is that each community must take "ownership" of its problems, which, at first blush, seems to make sense. People must feel a sense of responsibility for their own security. However, within the concept of "ownership" lies another intention – each citizen must be his own guardian. The government was easing out of the guardian "business," even though, in a democracy, government is by definition both the manifestation of the power of the people and its guardian.

As you shall soon see, the flaws and inconsistencies in the case Cadieux made are so obvious, one has to wonder how anyone could have taken his prescription at all seriously. While the entire work is based largely on U.S. police theory, the application of the ideas contained within "Police-Challenge 2000" was largely intended for the Royal Canadian Mounted

Police, and as an attack on federal law enforcement. Here are some excerpts, and some of the obvious contradictions between what the government said it intended to do and the true effects of its policies.

> With the stress on accountability and cost effectiveness, police agencies will be competitive organizations. If not, the trend toward increasing privatization will continue. . . .

Why the quid pro quo, that increasing privatization was the natural outcome if the police didn't meet government budgetary dicta? When Cadieux made his recommendations, he based his assumptions on 1988 figures. The total cost of all policing to Canadians then was $169 per person per year. The major part of that – 53 per cent – went to municipal policing, 30 per cent to provincial policing, and just 9 per cent to federal law enforcement. Yet, Cadieux argued that it was federal law enforcement which needed to be more "efficient"; that is, have its budgets reduced. Why?

> The excellent organization delegates authority and responsibility to its members; it does not operate in a militaristic fashion.

What was Cadieux talking about here? A business, obviously, and not a guardian organization. RCMP leaders took Cadieux's recommendation and ran with it, all too willing to ignore the experience and history of policing in democratic societies, particularly that the police are not, could not, and should not ever be considered a business. They are agents of the law. They have blatant power. One of the reasons police developed along paramilitaristic lines was to ensure that this power was effectively controlled.

> The police of the future will view themselves as one part of a community-wide effort to not only deal with crime but to improve community life in general. Police work involves more than technical enforcement of laws: a more fundamental goal is to promote safer and more harmonious communities.

In the absence of effective social policy by government, what Cadieux suggested was that the police *never* saw themselves as part of the community. That may have been true in the United States, but the record is quite clear on this: Canadian police, warts and all, have always shown an interest in the community. This is especially true of the RCMP, as we've seen with the likes of Constable Ken Aspen in Winnipegosis, Manitoba. The effect of Cadieux's pronouncement and subsequent budget restrictions was to force the RCMP planners into a survival mode of thinking. The RCMP began to implement policies and programs to please the government – such as community-based policing over federal law enforcement – which were not entirely necessary or justified, and in the process weakened the RCMP as a federal institution.

> There is growing emphasis today on developing healthy communities. A healthy community is one which contains equity, social justice, properly fed and housed citizens, resources of various kinds, educational opportunities, and a stable economy. A community seriously deficient in these areas will experience many social problems, only one of which is crime. As a result, playing a role in fostering a healthy community is in the interests of many community agencies, including the police. Thus, partnership is the name of the game.

Isn't developing a *healthy* community the government's responsibility? By lumping the police in with other social agencies, and pretending in this way that he was enhancing their status, Cadieux effectively diminished their importance within society. The police, as the last true guardian in society, have in the past chosen to remain aloof, because they must at the end of the day be neutral in enforcing the law. To force the police into partnerships – especially with private industry – not only puts the police officer in an awkward moral and ethical position. The closer police get to the community, the more their mystique and power is diminished. As my grandmother used to say: "Familiarity breeds contempt." The partnerships between police and private citizens are also a threat to the rule of law. Remember the old adage about justice: it must not only be done but seen to be done.

> The idea of the solitary police officer, single-handedly stemming the tide of crime, with villains on one side and citizens on the other, is an image from the past. The police can no longer be viewed as commandos, parachuted into a community to rescue it from the forces of evil. The police are the community and the community are the police. Police officers come from the community and reflect its values. They carry an obligation to the community they serve. At the same time, the community must support the police if its goals are to be achieved.

In the view of Cadieux, the only police worth discussing are those who wear uniforms, the most visible and most inexperienced police. Conveniently ignored in the debate is the role of major-crime and federal investigations, and the real hidden costs – social, economic, and political – of diminishing their roles. These areas are treated as if they were one and the same as the Boys in Blue.

•   •   •

RCMP Inspector Gary Nichols, whom we met in previous chapters, sums up the concerns of many police this way: "The biggest policing problem in Canada today is the influx and sophistication of organized crime. It's causing problems at all levels of society, but where it is most seen is on the street. The political response to this problem has been community-based policing. Community-based policing is an effective way of policing in times of good budgets. In times of bad budgets, it isn't. To put bodies on the street, in the malls, and walking the beat takes specialized skills out of investigative units. There isn't enough money to maintain investigative units. Community-based policing is a Band-Aid. It's an example of government playing 'hide the pea.'

"Let me give you one example. Metro Toronto Police recently closed down their Two District drug squad in the Parkdale area and replaced it with a community-based policing effort. Soon afterwards, drug charges went down in the area. Everyone proclaimed this as a success in community policing. The only reason charges went down was because no one was laying them. The problem hadn't gone away. In fact, in many ways it had gotten worse."

The same kind of situation happened in North Vancouver; there, the RCMP gave credit for a decrease in residential break-ins to its community-based policing program, though the extent of the program's involvement was to advise residents to lock their windows and take precautions. "What nobody mentioned was that regular policing put away the two biggest B-and-E artists in the city, which is the main reason why the number of incidents dropped," says one North Vancouver Mountie familiar with the situation.

The community-based policing propaganda aside, the recommendations for downsizing and eliminating specialized policing units is where the most destructive and misleading arguments were made in "Police-Challenge 2000." Cadieux effectively took arguments specific to U.S. concerns about public safety and security at the local level and transformed them into a general thesis on policing which could be applied universally across Canada. For example, Cadieux recommended that specialization be eliminated, and all police become generalists, an idea popular in U.S. municipal-policing services. After all, why have an elite homicide squad, when most homicides are committed by people who know the victim? Most of the stranger-stranger cases are rarely solved, so it makes sense that general detective bureaus could do the job. In today's RCMP, however, de-specialization has been directed not at the municipal policing function, where there is little specialization, but to the federal investigative ranks, such as economic-crime investigation, which clearly requires specialization. Remember Jake Bouwman's comments a few pages ago about his own experience as a town cop and how the RCMP saw nothing wrong with putting him in charge of a commercial-crime unit in Vancouver.

The inconsistencies in what Cadieux was saying were largely lost as government simply torqued up the public-relations machine so that any dissent over community-based policing was drowned out. Within a few years just about every politician, police officer, and community activist in Canada has been parroting the community-based policing mantra. Community-based policing has become an all-or-nothing proposition. There is no balance.

What has been lost in the propaganda and hysteria is that there is no simple formula for policing. Small towns and villages in Canada, for instance, *want* to police themselves. Everyone knows everyone else. The police station is usually only a short walk or drive away. Community-based policing is a success in such locales, because they've always had community-based policing, it just didn't have a name. In the major metropolitan areas, however, there is a much different attitude about community-based policing. In most cities, despite protestations to the contrary by local politicians, the inadequacies of community-based policing are most apparent. On the one hand, people don't have the time or energy to become involved in their own security, and no amount of prodding will change their minds. Many urban victims of crime have already come to see underfunded, undermanned community-based policing programs as anything but community-based. Their early experience with it has only served to sour many of them on the police themselves.

As soon as city police officers started riding bicycles on the streets and through the parks in the mid-nineties, citizens began to notice something else about the police: they stopped responding to calls. In downtown Toronto, for example, the number of car break-ins in the spring of 1997 was so great that the *Toronto Sun*'s Gary Dunford wrote about being tired of hearing the crunch of broken automobile glass under his feet any time he went for a walk. The police wouldn't even come to search the area, where as many as twenty cars might have been vandalized. Every day victims would line up at the 51 Division police station to file their reports, because the police would not visit the scene, unless an officer saw a car being broken into before his own eyes. Even then, there was no guarantee that they would respond to such a "minor" crime. At the station, all the police could give the victims were "incident numbers" for their insurance claims.

In the name of efficiency, the police aren't interested in investigating minor crimes. At the same time, aside from the bicycle cops, the visibility of police on the streets has declined in most centres. Short of a major personal injury or fire, it is almost impossible to get a police officer to come to your house. Victims must go to the police.

There are a number of reasons for this change in philosophy to community-based from rapid-response, again each grounded almost entirely in U.S. studies. In coming to his conclusions, Cadieux noted in "Police-Challenge 2000":

> Rapid response to all calls for service was an inappropriate basis for organizing an entire police force, when life-threatening incidents or events in progress are routinely less than four per cent of calls for service.

Cadieux, like many politicians and citizen activists, attacked the police for organizing themselves in such an inefficient fashion. Since the sixties, however, the entire notion of rapid response has not been the idea of Canadian police, but of their political masters, at all levels. The politicians believed that reaction time could be used as a measure of performance, something the bureaucrats and politicians could quantify. Everyone from the RCMP commissioner down to police chiefs in small towns eventually went along with the idea, many of them against their will, because the police have always known that rapid response in and of itself does little to solve crime. So the police, horsewhipped by the politicians, started racing around, but still found they couldn't go fast enough to curb crime. Then in the eighties, along came another idea – 911 service – whereby citizens could dial directly into the police-communications system. Politicians and, most importantly, the corporations marketing the service, pushed for its implementation on the grounds of convenience and improved public safety. It was seen to be a noble use of technology, but it has proven to be a disaster for policing at the local level. The rapid-response mentality, combined with the volume of 911 calls, began to render the police almost entirely ineffective. They found themselves devoting almost all their time responding to telephone complaints, as citizens became comfortable with the notion that a police officer was just a call away – no matter how small the problem might be.

In describing how investigations might work in the community-based policing model, Cadieux wrote:

> Most crimes are solved on the basis of information provided by the victim to the officer who first responds to the call. Crimes are seldom solved by subsequent investigation, with perhaps less than three per cent of all cases cleared or solved by this means. However, integrated teams of patrol and investigative functions have the highest rate of success in clearing reported crimes.

While true on the surface, there was much more to the argument than the bald statistics indicated. The notion of integrated patrol and investigative units founders on the shoals of one reality: such units are virtually impossible to keep functioning and current. What happens in real life is that such units became elitist in their approach, taking on only the largest crimes – in terms of outrage, publicity, or dollars. Meanwhile, the small crimes are ignored, leaving the victims – the vast majority of victims – with the sense that the police aren't doing their job. This effectively creates the will and need for private security and private policing.

In offering his opinion on the value of officers patrolling neighbourhoods in cars, Cadieux offered the following observation.

> Random motorized patrol has not been found to deter potential criminals, reduce crime, provide a greater likelihood of apprehending offenders or reduce the fear of crime. Moreover, random or preventive patrol intercepts only a small fraction of crimes in progress. Increasing patrol numbers has little or no impact on their effectiveness. However, while the impact of foot patrols on the level of crime is not yet clear, they decrease the level of fear by the public and increase public satisfaction with the police.

Cadieux has framed the entire argument in terms of policemen patrolling in cars versus patrolling by foot. But while each has its value, aren't both limited in what they can achieve? What Cadieux was really doing was trying to use a fake argument – that foot patrols are more desirable – to mask his real intention: reducing the budgets for car patrols to justify planned budget cuts. Law enforcement itself is not the main consideration.

The entire theme of "Police-Challenge 2000" was that the police must be made more accountable and more efficient; that is, operate more like a business. The intent of this business would be to save money – generate a negative profit – while the effect would be to cut back in investigations.

The attack on federal law enforcement aside, there is little about the community-based policing ideas embodied in "Police-Challenge 2000" that makes much sense. In fact, the more Canadians examine the notion of community-based policing, the more suspicious and nervous they may become about what the federal government and the provinces have really been doing over the past thirty-five years or so. What seems clear is that the political and economic imperatives of successive governments have begun to shape the policing function at all levels in a way that is not necessarily in the best long-term interests of Canada.

•   •   •

Canada is a wealthy country that should be able to pay for and enjoy a formidable public service, yet it has somehow been manoeuvred into believing that it is actually impoverished. Because of this, it has been deemed that everything must be run in an efficient, business-like manner. In this tyranny of efficiency the argument often put forward is that the public should not be worried about the overlapping of interests between government, the justice system, and the private sector. In a democracy the police are considered agents of the law and answerable to the courts. The government has no role in law enforcement. But in this new, "efficient" world, government has begun, at the behest of corporate lobbies, to deliberately blur the boundaries.

The public police have clearly been placed in an extraordinarily difficult position. As agents of the law they are empowered to enforce the law, which, individually, they desperately want to do. That is the intent of their job, and being able to do their job gives each police officer satisfaction. But the police and the law itself are a reflection of the society in which they each exist. If the society is confused, so are the laws. This is not a new concept. In *A History of Police in England and Wales* (1972), T. A. Critchley wrote:

> Total freedom is anarchy, total order tyranny. The police, who represent the collective interests of the community, are the agency which holds a balance somewhere between. Their standing is a rough index of society's own attitude towards the regulation of civilized living: regard for the police, which should not of course be uncritical, is regard for law and order. Patrick Colquhoun did not exaggerate when, writing at the end of the eighteenth century, at a time when the English were resisting the idea of paid professional police as being incompatible with liberty, he declared: 'Everything that can heighten in any degree the respectability of the office of constable, adds to the security of the state, and the safety of the life and property of every individual.'[3]

That's not what we're getting in Canada. The police, especially the RCMP, have been under constant attack and their role as guardian has diminished. In fact, the more one dissects the ideas expressed in "Police-Challenge-2000" – ideas which have come to drive the public police agenda ever since – the more one wonders how such a questionable document could ever have been taken seriously as a public-policy measure, never mind one that has become so influential.

In "Police-Challenge 2000," Pierre Cadieux made a revealing and important observation. In discussing the differences between U.S. and Canadian police he wrote: "Unfortunately, the reasons for exerting tighter control over police officers in the U.S. were not as applicable to their Canadian counterparts. In the present century at least there has been a general absence of routine political influence over the police and a lack of widespread corruption within Canadian police forces. Consequently, the means for exerting tighter control over the routine of street policing were, in the Canadian context, largely misplaced."

Having said that, Cadieux – surprisingly – argued that the way to improve policing in Canada was for politicians to exert more control over the police, as has always been the case in his home province of Quebec, and that the private sector should become more involved in policing.[4] Cadieux seems deliberately oblivious to the fact that as politics corrupts policing, business corrupts politics: it's a neat and well-established circle. In his own words, and this can't be disputed, Cadieux clearly implies that he and Canadians should be willing to live with the police corruption that would likely result from such a close relationship between the politicians and the police, although, to be fair, he does pray for some distance between the parties:

> Local community "ownership" of their crime and disorder problems will become expressed in new ways, particularly through new partnerships with the police. Police officers will become more integrated into the social and political life of local communities, as members of the community. Restrictions on police officer participation in local activities will only be in force where there is a direct conflict of interest with police work.[5]

Since the clear and primary intent of "Police-Challenge 2000" was to reform and restructure the Royal Canadian Mounted Police – especially its capability to enforce federal law – the true implications of Cadieux's ideas being implemented are profound and serious for Canada. Community-based policing, as envisioned by Cadieux, and as it is currently being implemented across Canada, therefore, has the potential to destroy the integrity of Canadian institutions and, along with them, the country itself.

While there might be some advantages to community-based policing in limited applications, the downside and the real and potential dangers have been carelessly or deliberately overlooked in Canada – to a considerable degree. Malcolm K. Sparrow, Mark Moore, and David M.

Kennedy address the issue in their well-regarded book, *Beyond 911: A New Era for Policing*:

> There is a clear risk in moving in this direction [towards community-based policing]. To many, both in policing and outside it, any steps toward enhancing police responsiveness to communities or political overseers risks opening police departments once again to inappropriate political influences. Neither politicians nor police have a sufficiently unblemished record to ignore the hazard in bringing together what was once, for very good reason, pulled asunder. The danger today, however, is probably not electioneering or simple corruption; these abuses may blemish any new style of policing from time to time, as they occasionally still do reform policing, but they will never again be considered the norm or fail to be fought when they surface. The danger in a less isolated modern policing is more subtle: that groups who win the police's ear will try to use their influence, with questionable propriety, to their own advantage. It is a problem that will arise, probably often, and – given the racial, ethnic, economic and other tensions that pervade cities and their communities – the prospect of the police opening itself to it is enough to give real pause.[6]

Philosopher Jane Jacobs concurs. She warns that the mixing of the private sector and the police creates fertile ground for the growth of not only police corruption, but potentially more disastrous consequences. In an interview, Jacobs elaborated on the thoughts she expressed in *Systems of Survival* – and that we have touched on earlier.

> Commerce and guardians have distinctly different mandates within society. It is entirely disingenuous for anyone to suggest that the two syndromes can work well together. They can't. Mixing the two can produce monstrous hybrids. For example, when government intrudes too far into the realm of commerce, the bureaucratic instincts serve to paralyze the commercial instincts. There are many examples of this depicting varying degrees of problems, but the best example was in the former

Soviet Union where industry became so bureaucratized that it was entirely unresponsive to the marketplace. On the other hand, when business intrudes too far into government, the worst possible example of what can happen is the Nazis in Germany.

The most ironic thing about community-based policing is that, while Commissioner Philip Murray says he's pushing the force forward into the next century, every advocate of community-based policing bases his or her argument on the ideas of Sir Robert Peel, expressed in *The Principles of Law Enforcement* in 1829. But while Peel's theories might be riveting to some, all was not so rosy with Peel's Metropolitan Police, says former RCMP assistant commissioner Michel Thivierge. "I hear people talk about how great Robert Peel was, but has anyone ever looked at the horrendous corruption problem they had in London? The bobbies were too close to the population."

But Michel Thivierge's concern about the impact of community-based policing on the integrity of the police and the efficacy of law enforcement goes well beyond Robert Peel's problems in 1829. "The system being implemented by the RCMP today is an invitation to corruption," Thivierge says. "The checks and balances are being removed from the structure. The police officer on the street is being 'empowered' to do his job, often with 'random' supervision. Finally, the police officer is encouraged to use his discretion to *not* enforce the law, because enforcing the law is seen to cost time and money. The police should be enforcing the law without fear, favour, or affection. The Mounties are the most honest and incorruptible police force I know. But the way things are going, the real danger is that a breakdown will come. This is inevitable if the police go about their business motivated by fear, favour, and affection."

The essence of community-based policing is that the police should work in partnership with the private sector and the general public. This is not the new model of policing for the RCMP, but an old one. In Chapter Four, we talked about how the modern RCMP came into being in 1920. At the time, corporations employed their own private investigators, who were also being used by the police for surveillance and other duties. It was a treacherous world with no regulation. The rule of law largely did not apply. The public police were created in part to take responsibility for all law enforcement, for good and practical reasons. Today, in the name of business-like efficiency, the police are being forced by government to cede some law-enforcement and investigative duties to private investigators and security companies. No matter how much this practice is being dressed up as an improvement in law enforcement, it is merely an old, very conservative way of thinking, a way of policing that has long been discredited.

Secondly, the notion of community-based policing has gone as far as it has in Canada with all police forces mainly because of the lead being taken by the RCMP. In the minds of most Canadians, the RCMP has garnered an image of being the country's premier police force – Canada's FBI. But as we've seen, it's not. Within the RCMP there is an inherent bias towards community-based policing, because it fits in with the experiences and the small-town mentality of the majority of RCMP administrators, most of whom rose through the ranks as small-town cops. It wasn't much of a stretch for them to accept the views of Pierre Cadieux and his Liberal successors that every community should have ownership of its criminal problems. The majority of RCMP leaders implicitly agreed with their political masters that the Mounties should not primarily be a *federal* police force, linking Canada from one end to another in an overarching fashion as a defender of the greater good. Instead, as has always been the case, the RCMP has been shaped in a negative way, in response to the parochial politics of Central Canada.

At the federal level, the trend is towards the police being reduced to tax collectors with an attitude and a gun – the IPOC units – not a guardian of all Canadians. What the rest of the RCMP is destined to become is a *national* police force linking one Andy of Mayberry after another in a chain from the Atlantic to the Pacific and from the U.S. border to the Arctic, with a big gap in the middle – Ontario and Quebec. This is the perfect extrapolation of Trudeau's federalism. Meanwhile, no configuration of the RCMP could better serve Quebec's separatist interest – other than to have no RCMP at all.

In his 1993 Red Book, Jean Chrétien talked about "Safe Homes, Safe Streets." Let's now travel to Burnaby, B.C., to see how this vision has been interpreted by the RCMP. In Burnaby, one of the wealthiest and most densely populated municipalities in the country, the RCMP is the local police force.

Chapter Twelve

·· ● ··

LOWER MAINLAND BLUES:
THE MOUNTIES AS CITY COPS

IN THE PREVIOUS chapters, I have attempted to show how various political, social, and economic imperatives have transformed the federal government and its institutions. In brief, two related forces have driven the agenda of the country over the past four decades: the notions that, first, the federal government should operate in a more business-like fashion, and, second, that Quebec nationalists must be appeased. Along the way, various policies and programs have been implemented which tended to meet both objectives. These included concepts such as official bilingualism, the francization of the federal bureaucracy, the Charter of Rights and Freedoms of 1982, the decentralization of the federal government, and the devolution of powers to the provinces. Among federal institutions, the RCMP had largely resisted much of the impact of these changes until the late eighties and early nineties. The RCMP has never thought more like a business than it does today, and one of the best places to see the impact of this bottom-line brand of thinking is in the Lower Mainland of British Columbia.

One-quarter of all Mounties in Canada are stationed in British Columbia, most of them in the Lower Mainland, in and around the Greater Vancouver area. Providing police services to British Columbia communities is a growth business for the RCMP. For example, the cities of Vancouver, West Vancouver, New Westminster, and Delta have their own police forces, but the Mounties serve as the contract municipal police in North Vancouver, Burnaby, Richmond, Surrey, Langley, Coquitlam, and Ridge Meadows.

To understand what this means, a hypothetical equivalent comparison in the new Greater Toronto Area would have the Toronto police serving only the old city of Toronto, while the RCMP provides municipal policing in what used to be Scarborough, North York, and Etobicoke, as well as the suburban communities of Mississauga, Halton Region, and York Region. In terms of Montreal, the same equivalent would have the Montreal police restricted to patrolling downtown Montreal, while the RCMP patrols Westmount, the Town of Mount Royal, Longueuil, the West Island, the South Shore, and the North Shore.

Every new cadet that the RCMP's Regina training centre – Depot – turns out for the next five years could be sent to British Columbia, and there would still be room for more. The cadets – bright, well-trained, and eager – are merely "cannon fodder," because the RCMP can't keep up with the demand for municipal police officers to fill its detachments in the Lower Mainland; as soon as an opening comes up anywhere else, officers with any experience at all tend to transfer out to less expensive and more idyllic locales.

Although the RCMP is an institution that prides itself in its commitment to serving Canada, the situation in the Lower Mainland, one of the most expensive areas in the country in which to live, is nearly disastrous for individual Mounties. They are forced to accept extremely unusual living arrangements. Cadets assigned to the area often end up living five and six to a house, an hour or more from their detachments, because that's the only housing they can afford on salaries that begin at around $32,000 per year. As quaint and efficient as that might sound, the problem is exacerbated by the fact that cadets in today's RCMP aren't all that young – remember, the average age is twenty-eight. "I know of a married couple, both members, who are living in a basement apartment, because that's all they can afford," says former assistant commissioner Michel Thivierge. "That's not good, not at all. It's not a good thing in a democracy to have your police living hand-to-mouth."

The potential danger that Thivierge is referring to is that hungry, desperate police officers are more likely to be corrupted.

In the Lower Mainland, many Mounties have taken on second jobs to survive, some with the official approval of the force, others without. Constable Stephen Thatcher, the lawyer we met earlier, who is the father of a four-year-old daughter, spent most of 1997 desperately struggling to make ends meet after his wife was bedridden with a serious illness. Taking advantage of his education, Thatcher regularly did part-time legal work. Other Mounties run their own businesses on the side, usually in construction and lawn maintenance. Some are long-distance truck drivers, others are contract bus drivers, and so on. As in Toronto, where operations were moved to cheaper, virtually rural areas, the hours of duty in the Lower Mainland have been redistributed over the years, largely to accommodate the personal needs of members, particularly their need to work at second jobs. During this period, the needs of law enforcement have clearly come second for many financially insecure Mounties. It seems as if every Mountie is living on the edge financially, and sometimes emotionally.

Monique Graziano, wife of Surrey RCMP constable John Graziano, is the mother of four children under the age of eight, with a fifth expected any day. Her husband has been in Vancouver for ten years and has been trying to transfer back to his native Manitoba, but can't find an opening. "We are struggling," Monique says. "We live in Abbotsford, because it's the only place we can afford. It's tough making ends meet. I worry all the time. Money is at the root of all our arguments. John has considered taking on a second job like a lot of the guys, but hasn't yet."

Mountie families like the Grazianos want to move, but can't. The RCMP won't let them, although moving, in and of itself, is no panacea. Inspector Dennis Schlecker, fifty, his wife, Barbara, and their four children endured sixteen transfers. All they wish for is a chance to settle down, even if it means a large mortgage hanging over their heads in their present home in North Delta. Over the years, they say they've lost "$73,000 in after-tax money" on real-estate transactions caused by the transfers. "I remember when I got married, a Mountie told me: 'Remember, your husband is married to us first.' I never forgot those words, even though I thought they were the strangest words I'd ever heard," says Barbara Schlecker. "Until you're on the inside, you can't see what that means. Then you realize that the RCMP is like a mistress to your husband that you can't get rid of, no matter how hard you try. The force is everything to a Mountie, but the force doesn't return the affection. It really doesn't care about a member's family. It doesn't care about what the wives and husbands of members go through. When the RCMP wants to move you, it doesn't matter when, it doesn't matter where. They have a spot that has to be filled and they fill it. The needs of the force always comes first."

The Schleckers have so far survived the ordeal, but things today are in many ways even more difficult for young Mounties than anything Schlecker, or his twin brother, Don, who is also a RCMP inspector, might have faced coming up through the force. The stress to survive, both individually and as a force, is beginning to take its toll. As enthusiastic about serving the public as any cadet might be right out of Regina, many soon lose their sense of commitment. Many are demoralized by their relatively low wages and living conditions, and many are uncertain and confused about what government, the courts, and society in general expects them to do as law-enforcement officers. In the Lower Mainland, one can clearly see how all the politics and policies have caused the Mounties to lose their own clarity of vision and purity of purpose. "There's not the passion for the job that there used to be," says Inspector Schlecker, who has his hands full trying to police Burnaby.

In 1997, there were 240 Mounties stationed in the Burnaby municipal detachment, next to City Hall. Burnaby is the second-largest RCMP municipal detachment in the country, next to the one in Surrey, southeast of Burnaby, where there are 325 Mounties contracted to patrol the local streets. Burnaby pays $22 million for its RCMP service, which is dirt-cheap for two reasons. First, the non-unionized RCMP works harder than a unionized force, does more with less, and has among the lowest salaries of any police force in Canada (since they were frozen in 1992). Normally, in a city such as Burnaby with a population of 300,000, the police force would be closer to 300 members, not the 240 on the RCMP payroll. Second, Burnaby also gets the 10 per cent federal subsidy, which even some RCMP members think is ridiculous, even outrageous, because they know the RCMP in municipal detachments like Burnaby rarely if ever do any federal policing, "This is one of the richest cities in the country, and it's getting a discount on its police," says Burnaby staff sergeant Jim Westman, who was born and raised near Toronto. "You'd think the people back east would be screaming blue murder. I don't get it. Why doesn't anyone complain about this? Burnaby should be paying its own way. It can afford it."

Burnaby is such a well-to-do place that just two of the 240 Burnaby Mounties can actually afford to live in the community which they police. Almost one-quarter of the people who do reside in Burnaby are East Asian. Many more are East Indian. But the language capabilities of the Mounties who must serve their needs are dramatically skewed. According to a list on a wall in the squad room, three Mounties speak Spanish, two Cantonese, one Gujarati, one Katchi, one even speaks Gaelic. Eleven Burnaby Mounties can speak French, but only they, among all the multilingual members, receive $800 a year in bonus bilingual pay, which is mandated by the federal government. It is a sore point with many of the other Mounties. "In all the years I've been here, I've never had a request for French," says Inspector Schlecker. "All our material is written in English and French. I usually tear the French side off and throw it in the garbage. Storage space is at a premium."

The outward face of the Mounties is always calm and professional, but that barely conceals the inner turmoil and tension. These are the by-products of the tyranny of efficiency that is the federal budgeting process, combined with the desperation of the Mounties to survive as a national police force in just about any form or fashion. "When it comes to policing, you can't look just at the bottom line," says Schlecker. "In Burnaby, we're trying to be as efficient as we can be. We're putting together a business plan and asking for resources over the next five years to make this operation truly functional, because I really believe that, where we're at now, we can't do a good level of policing. We have just barely enough resources to satisfy the public. The average guy out on the street has zero to two years' experience. We've got cadets, who have just been trained, training new cadets on the streets. It's far from an ideal situation. We're cost-efficient, but we're not effective. We need a balance. We're trying to give Cadillac service for 75 per cent of the cost of other police forces."

Despite all these internal tensions, Commissioner Murray is proud that, since January 1, 1995, Burnaby has been a test site for a community-based policing program. Murray's hope is that the force's experience in Burnaby will satisfy both his critics and his political masters that the RCMP is innovative and business-like as it heads into the next century, while at the same time appeasing sceptical RCMP members, many of whom believe that the entire concept of community-based policing is wrongheaded and potentially dangerous for the integrity of the force.

Let's consider how the RCMP reorganized itself in Burnaby to set up community-based policing, then we'll go out on patrol to see what law enforcement really looks like on the streets.

First, the RCMP divided the city into four quadrants, each led by a staff sergeant, who, like Ron Marlin back in Dauphin, Manitoba, serves as chief of police of his own quadrant. Each staff sergeant reports to Inspector Schlecker. One of them is Paul Willms, who, as a sergeant, was considered a top investigator within the Economic Crime Unit in Vancouver. To get to the next rank, however, Willms couldn't stay in federal policing, because there were no job openings. So he jumped to Burnaby for the extra stripe and the raise. He was now just one step away from a white shirt.

Everything about the community-based policing program is business-like and scientific. The police no longer talk about law enforcement but about problem-solving, as if the police can solve all that ails society. Each quadrant in Burnaby is further divided into "atoms," so that every event or incident can be pinpointed accurately and quickly. Community-based policing is extremely labour intensive. For example, each staff sergeant sits on a variety of committees within the community. Satellite offices have been set up in some of the high schools, and are occupied full-time by a constable or, in some cases, two. To meet the demand for resources, the number of traffic units on the road has been scaled back. Most nights the force has difficulty scrambling together enough cruisers to patrol the city and answer emergency calls. At every turn the Mounties are enlisting residents to help them police Burnaby.

Nevertheless, most business and community leaders are absolutely pleased, even ecstatic, about the program, although Mayor Doug Drummond seems to have spotted some illogic that concerns him. "Community-based policing was sold to us as being an improvement over what we were getting, but there were no major criticisms of the police or their performance before we implemented this thing," Mayor Drummond says. "I am concerned about the cutbacks in patrols by the police. In this new system, a lot of the security issues are being left up to the residents. That might have been fine when I was growing up in the east end of Vancouver. Back then, every mother or someone in the family was home all day. There were plenty of eyes on the street. Today, we have communities where both parents are wage-earners and are not at home all day. There are whole streets that are empty during the day. The police say they can't afford to patrol the neighbourhood, and they're leaving it up to the neighbours, who aren't there. It's a difficult problem to solve."

As we have seen, the entire theory of community-based policing is centred on citizen involvement, at the expense of routine patrols and other functions. At night, especially on weekends, a group calling itself Burnaby Citizens' Crime Watch, like Dauphin's COP program, does surveillance and odd jobs for the police. There are sixty-two volunteers in the group, some of whom – and this is no joke – exhibit one of the characteristics of some serial killers: they're police buffs who get a kick out of surveillance. These are the kind of people who, in the more vigilant past, were never allowed close to the police or what they were doing. But in the efficient, business-like world of new law enforcement, just about everyone is welcomed into the fold, with the public police giving them their imprimatur and lending them their good name.

At one level, all this might be a good thing – having the community involved in its own security. At another, the entire nature of community-based policing raises spectres of a burgeoning totalitarianism – police in schools, in the malls, working with social groups and businesses, while private citizens act as agents of the police, conducting surveillance and other duties.

On one level, there is a world of difference between community-based policing in Canada and policing in a totalitarian state, but those differences are narrowing. In a totalitarian state, the police are not bound by the rule of law, but are agents of the government, which inevitably results in their being political when it comes to enforcing the law. In community-based policing, the police are being asked to serve both the law and the agenda of government, to rub shoulders with citizens, politicians, and businesspeople in the name of the law. Traditionally, police in Canada in the British tradition have been servants only of the law, and, in theory at least, enforced the law in a disinterested fashion, blind to politics and economy. But in community-based policing programs, the police are asked not to be entirely disinterested, which is defended by its advocates as a necessary evil. But being not entirely disinterested is like being a little pregnant. One is either disinterested or one is not; there is no in-between.

Under community-based policing programs, the lines between pure policing and doing the government's bidding are, therefore, deliberately blurred. The police are asked to do two things: to be servants of the law and to enforce the law in a way that suits the political agenda of the day; that is, to make law enforcement more economically efficient or politically responsive. In Burnaby, as in many jurisdictions, the police are ordered to lay charges in all cases of spousal abuse: "You will arrest, you will prosecute," is the word from the provincial attorney general. But the Criminal Code says that charges should be laid "except for these circumstances." In charging in all cases, the police are told not to use their legal discretion, to ignore the Criminal Code and serve the agenda of government, which ironically leads to inconsistent application of the spirit of the law.

The same attitude has been brought to the rest of the justice system. While the government orders the police to lay charges in spousal-abuse cases, the police can no longer go before a justice of a peace and swear a complaint in British Columbia – and most other provinces – unless the complaint is pre-approved by a Crown attorney. The Crown attorney will not proceed with a case "unless there is a substantial likelihood of conviction," thereby leaving judges and juries out of the equation, and subverting the legal process further. Once again, police don't get to exercise their discretionary judgement, as the law contemplates that they should, and instead try to view every situation or witness as if they, the police, were a Crown attorney, judge, or jury. With such a mindset, the police find themselves always looking for ways not to lay charges, and are often reduced to giving legal opinions to frustrated complainants rather than just doing their job, which is to enforce the law.

With this aligning of the police and justice system within the orbit of government, rather than within the orbit of the law, the difference between community-based policing and policing in a totalitarian state becomes a matter of intent, doesn't it? In Canada, we are safe now because the intent seems pure. However, over time the police are being conditioned to be less vigilant, and within a few years, with the turnover in police personnel, the only system of policing that people will know is community-based policing. Once that is the case, the entire structure of policing in Canada could easily become perverted if the good intentions of government should ever change.

But none of that enters into the equation these days. As far as RCMP headquarters is concerned, the Burnaby municipal detachment is a model of what a modern police force should be and will be in the future. There is little or no room for dissent. Dissenters are just, as one of Commissioner Murray's assistants put it, "not modern thinkers. They don't get the picture."

So let's go out on the streets of Burnaby for a snapshot of what community-based policing means to the people in the community. With so many officers gobbled up communing with the community, there are not many left to do what the Canadian public thinks police should do – protect the population and investigate crime. In Burnaby, once you get past the public relations of community-based policing, you soon find out that it doesn't quite live up to the advance billing. For the Mounties in Burnaby, and elsewhere in the Lower Mainland for that matter, the everyday world of routine police work is a nightmare of conflicting priorities and agendas. "In so many ways," one Mountie said, "they've made my job easy for me. There's nothing I can do."

In Burnaby, there seem to be two kinds of Mounties: those who are scared out of their wits and those who have come not to give a damn any more.

·   ·   ·

It was the beginning of a long weekend. School was out and staffing was typically short. In normal circumstances Corporal Rod Booth would be on the road supervising one of Burnaby's southern quadrants, while Corporal Greg Stevenson would do the other. On this night, because of personnel shortages, Booth was to do both southern quadrants, while Stevenson supervised the office.

As he got ready to take me out on patrol with him, Corporal Booth stretched out in a doorway and uttered the following sentiments: "You know what? I care about where I live, not about what goes on here." Born in Montreal, Booth, thirty-seven, is married, with two young children. He was in his third year of university when he joined the Mounties, thirteen years earlier. Since then he has served in North Vancouver, the Yukon, and two and a half years in a Shangri-la setting, one of two constables who were the law on one of the Gulf Islands. This night was to be his last as a road corporal in Burnaby, babysitting new cadets. When he returned from vacation in a month, Booth would be moving to the bicycle squad in Burnaby, something he was looking forward to. As we got into the white cruiser, Corporal Booth said he expected it to be a quiet, uneventful evening. It turned out to be anything but – and, as I was to discover, Booth's job as a road corporal is like being a hamster on a wheel, constantly running but never seeming to get anywhere, which goes a long way to explaining his attitude.

To be a good police officer, Booth said, one needs what he calls "spider sense," the ability to pick up on the slightest vibrations. As the evening begins, spider sense made him pull over a beat-up old van because something wasn't right about it. As it turned out, one of the passengers was on charge for assault and was the subject of a restraining order. He was not entirely co-operative with Booth, but there wasn't much that Booth could do about that. We moved on.

On the border between Burnaby and New Westminster, the force has been working with a neighbourhood group to deal with prostitutes plying their trade in the area. "In the past, all we've done is play hooker tennis in the area," said Booth. "We'd push them down the street and across the intersection into New Westminster and the New Westminster police would return them to us. It wasn't really dealing with the problem."

An undercover constable in a Ford Explorer flagged Booth down. He'd picked up a prostitute who had an outstanding warrant against her, but the prostitute was disputing the warrant. As she stood there, she self-consciously struggled to keep herself covered with her flimsy dress (which was alternately falling off her shoulders and riding above her bare butt). The constable asked Booth to take the prostitute back to the station for processing.

Her name was Renée Sheri-dee L. She was almost twenty-eight years old, a heroin addict, and showed a glimmer of prettiness. On the inboard car computer, there was another notation. Renée also carried the HIV virus. On the way back to the RCMP detachment, Corporal Booth talked to her about her drug problem, her past life, and her future prospects. Her plan was to get off the streets and go to work in a hotel making beds instead of using them. She said she had sympathy for the plight of the neighbours, but that she didn't think she was part of the problem. "I don't do anything outside, and I pick up all my condoms and put them in the garbage," she said. As we drove across the city, she realized where we were headed, and her big concern was about how she was going to get home from the RCMP detachment. Although it is in the municipal complex near City Hall on Deer Lake Drive off Canada Way, it is a far-from-central location; in fact, it is rather isolated. "I haven't got any money," Renée said. "How am I supposed to get home?"

"You'll have to figure that one out yourself," Booth answered. "The rules are the rules. We can't be giving people rides. We're not a taxi service."

A few minutes later, Renée was left to sort out her problems at the Burnaby detachment, as Booth headed back for the streets. Meanwhile, Renée, half-dressed, broke, and infected with the AIDS virus, would have to hitchhike out of the place – a ticking bomb about to be set back on the public. The Burnaby detachment's motto is "Partners for a Safe Community," but this seemed to be anything but safe.

A little while later, a call came in about a noisy party on Hurst Street. It's in the southwest corner of Burnaby, two blocks east of Boundary Road, the Vancouver city limit. As Booth headed to the call, going west on the Kingsway, a four-lane business artery, he pulled in behind a parked RCMP cruiser. Neither Mountie knew the area and both were studying their maps. Even after they thought they knew where they were going, this lost Mountie patrol still had difficulty finding the street and house.

In the old days, long before the Charter of Rights and Freedoms, the police used to go to noisy house parties and, if need be, throw their weight around and shut things down. Not any more. On Hurst Street, the parents of two teenagers had gone away to a Whistler resort for the weekend. The nineteen-year-old boy told Corporal Booth that the party was his idea, a surprise for his sixteen-year-old sister's birthday. They both promised to keep the noise down, but, as they did so, a beer bottle smashed on some pavement nearby, almost punctuating the boy's sentence. There were three police units on the scene, all very visible. They couldn't have been missed. The broken bottle seemed like a challenge, but the Mounties accepted the word of the teenagers that they would put a lid on the party, and then moved on. There were too many outstanding calls for the number of officers on the road, and they couldn't spend any more time on Hurst Street.

Forty-five minutes later, the Burnaby dispatcher raised a second alarm about Hurst. This time the sixteen-year-old girl herself had called the police. She was on a portable telephone and was trapped in the second-floor bathroom with her brother and some friends. A gang of armed youths had crashed the party and threatened them. Nobody had any idea what they might be armed with, which served to slow the police response down considerably. The panic in the dispatcher's voice angered Booth. "She's got to be calm. The panic gets the adrenaline pumping. That causes mistakes to be made."

In Toronto, the police ride around at night in two-officer cars, but

Mounties travel alone, so Booth ordered no one to approach the house without backup. The Mounties, who by now had been scattered all over south Burnaby, headed back to Hurst Street – but not too quickly. They got lost again, and by the time they reached the house, the intruders had left. Booth politely but firmly asked the two teenagers to send everyone home. Constable Jonathan Ko, who, with two and a half years' experience is the senior constable on the road, stood by for a while as people left (Ko had twice as much experience as the other two constables combined who were on patrol with him). Soon, Ko left Hurst Street to answer radio calls, none of which, we learned later, proved to be that important.

At 1:37 a.m., a third complaint came in from Hurst Street. Now, the house was under attack by a gang of about ten young men. By the time the Mounties arrived, a long piece of two-by-four had been propelled through the front picture window. Every window on the house had been shattered. As on the two previous visits, the Mounties were exceedingly polite, but they conducted no investigation – in fact, they failed to notice the extent of the damage until it was pointed out to them by a neighbour.

"Did you see who did this?"

"No," said the nineteen-year-old boy.

"Do you know who they are?"

"I've never seen them before."

"They might be from Vancouver," one of the police officers suggested. "Maybe."

Vancouver is two blocks away and out of bounds for the Mounties. There was nothing they felt that they could do. The reality of modern policing strikes home. The police, hemmed in by social and political directives, all well-intentioned, are ever so careful not to make mistakes. The effect, however, is that they are reduced to constantly looking for ways not to enforce laws, anticipating what a Crown attorney or a judge might say, though the cost of justice or what a judge might think or say shouldn't be their concern.

A few minutes later, near Hurst Street, Booth pulled over a vehicle with four passengers who he thinks might be related to the house destruction. As it turned out, however, they were friends of the teenagers who lived in the house and were out seeking revenge on the attackers. As Booth stood on the dark street alone with them, another car pulled up with four more youths in it, obviously part of the same group. Booth, concentrating on the first car, didn't see them arrive. So I puffed myself up, pretended to be a police officer, and ordered them to turn off their engine. If this was community-based policing – ordinary citizens being involved with the police – I didn't like it one bit. If these fellows had been armed and had evil intentions, Booth could have been a dead man. No police force should be that understaffed.

But then we cut to the chase – the high-speed chase, that is.

It had begun at 2:10 a.m. when Constable Rafael Hsu, four months out of Regina, noticed two cars drag-racing away from the traffic lights at the Kingsway and Gilley Avenue. Hsu made a U-turn, and raced to catch up to one of the vehicles, a beat-up twenty-year-old beige Ford Granada. Hsu activated his overhead flashing lights. He could see two occupants in the car, a man and a young woman. As it approached Royal Oak Avenue, the Granada slowed down. Hsu gave a short blast from his siren. The car turned the corner to head north on Royal Oak, almost coming to a stop.

"They're stopping," I could hear Hsu tell the dispatcher, but a few seconds later, he shouted, "They're not stopping." The Granada headed down Royal Oak Avenue, reaching a speed of well over one hundred kilometres an hour. There is a line of thinking current these days that the police shouldn't chase vehicles, because the danger of a crash is too high. The thinking is well-intentioned, but the effect is something entirely different. When a driver who has done something wrong or has something to hide knows that the police won't give chase, there is an incentive for him or her to use speed to escape. In other words, placing a blanket prohibition on the police chasing suspect vehicles can do exactly the opposite of what is intended: it can encourage suspects to run. For the police, it is a terrible dilemma, because they know that, if someone is running they have something to hide, and every so often that something to hide has proved to be a kidnapped child or some other victim in danger.

For Constable Hsu, it wasn't much of a chase. Royal Oak Avenue is a narrow, rutted, and potholed road that makes a long, steep descent into a dark, unpopulated valley. It had not been repaired for years, because a new interchange was being planned for the intersection at Deer Lake Drive. As the Granada sped down the hill, Constable Hsu frantically described to the dispatcher what was happening. "There are cars coming the other way. I'm backing off." Then, he moaned, "Oh, no . . ."

The Granada had slammed into the rear of a northbound Altima, spun counter-clockwise, then slid between two other southbound cars, before ramming a brand new Subaru Outback almost head-on, demolishing the front end of both cars and driving the Subaru into the ditch. The two occupants got out of the Granada, checked on the female driver of the Subaru, then hobbled off into the bush, injured and drunk. Before even coming to a stop, Hsu called for backup and emergency vehicles. After making sure that the female driver of the Subaru was all right – she had suffered some fractures and a slight concussion – Hsu headed off in pursuit of the suspects, up to his knees in water. The two would eventually be tracked down a couple of hours later by a police dog.

I first saw Constable Hsu within five minutes of the crash. He was standing by the roadside, ashen-faced and on the verge of tears, after having received a blast from Corporal Stevenson, who arrived on the scene just after the crash. In recent weeks, high-speed chases have become a political football in the Vancouver area. Even though Constable Hsu had done nothing wrong, he now had a blemish on his record, something that could be used against him in the future. Seeing Constable Hsu's agitated state, Corporal Booth tried to console him. Minutes later, Booth chastised Corporal Stevenson for being heavy-handed towards Hsu. Everyone was on edge.

At about 4:00 a.m. I was standing alone on the road when I noticed that the point car at the top of the hill was no longer there. Suddenly three vehicles were moving down the hill towards the crash site, where the four cars remained scattered across the road, hidden in pitch-darkness. I screamed to one of the Mounties, who frantically came running up the road, using his flashlight to slow down the cars – just in time. It was at this moment that the entire issue of what the RCMP has become hit me.

The Mounties are the symbol of Canada – not of the individual provinces, but of Canada – from sea to sea to sea. They are the country's premier police force. Most Canadians think of the Mounties as a federal police force. Once it may well have been that way, but it is far from that, now. They are the Everypolice, trying to be everything to everybody. Through administrative procedures, regulations, and self-interest, politicians have subtly transformed the RCMP into a police-services business, selling its personnel, talents, and patriotism on the cheap to satisfy the wishes and needs of shortsighted provincial governments.

The force is divided by the French–English question, sabotaged by an internal promotion system that rewards longevity and mobility over promise and intellect, and seems to be just too big and unfocused. The RCMP has been designed to carry so much social, political, and historical baggage that it can't get up the hills it needs to climb to serve either the law or the public interest. Like the world's biggest truck parked beside the road in Sparwood, B.C., the RCMP is a wonder to behold, but has it been rendered dysfunctional by all its encumbrances and commitments.

Most Mounties are shuffled through detachment after detachment, avoiding corruption, yes, but never staying in one place long enough to really get to know the local history and the players. Meanwhile, economic crime is rampant across the country. It is the kind of criminality that tends to undermine the efficacy and integrity of a country. Yet successive federal governments have argued that there is no money left in the public kitty to increase the efforts to fight such crime or to keep federal institutions such as the RCMP vibrant. Government has convinced RCMP Commissioner Philip Murray and his predecessor, Norman Inkster, to cut back on federal law enforcement, which runs entirely against what should be the instincts of the force. Government has made the case that it is inevitable that the private sector handle some policing duties and investigations, even though the private sector doesn't play by the same rules – and the commissioners have bought into the scenario.

Meanwhile, in Burnaby, distressed and confused junior Mounties – the policemen of the present and future – play hooker tennis, try to break up house parties, and chase cars down the Kingsway in Burnaby, while governments pretend they are doing some federal policing on the side.

Can Canada ever hope to stay united when the ideal member of the RCMP – its proud national police force – is considered to be a town cop rather than a top-flight investigator? Any well-trained department can police highways, towns, or cities, but no police force in the country can do what Canadians think the Mounties are supposed to do – properly enforce federal laws and regulations.

From the Glassco Commission, through Trudeau, Mulroney, and Chrétien, there has been pressure by Quebec separatists, the United States, and corporate interests, who have placed their self-interest above the interests of Canada. They all have the same motive. All three prime ministers have either charmed us, promised to protect sacred trusts, or wrapped themselves in the flag to prove how Canadian they really are, Their protestations to the contrary, the records of all three show that their actions have weakened Canada's federal institutions. That may not have been the stated intention of their policies and actions, but it certainly is the effect, and that is the measure by which they must be judged.

So, the question remains, how important is federal law enforcement to the average Canadian? For an answer to that question, let's begin in Hamilton, Ontario.

Chapter Thirteen

······································ ● ····································

HAMILTON: A CITY WITHOUT GUARDIANS

IN THE INTRODUCTION to this book, I indicated that my initial intention was to show how the RCMP, as a federal police force, was in many
ways failing to fulfil its primary duty: defending the public good. What
I was going to show was how the RCMP had largely abandoned the
investigation of white-collar crime – serious fraud committed by those
hiding behind commercial entities. As was pointed out earlier,
Commissioner Philip Murray agreed with this supposition, explaining
that the RCMP no longer had the financial resources needed to combat
commercial crime.

The usual way to illustrate this point would be to take a case in which
the RCMP was heavily involved and show how they were defeated. But I
believe there is another, possibly more effective, way to illustrate my
point. What is the danger to society, if the RCMP withdraws entirely from
enforcing federal laws – a negative exposition of the point, as it were.

Such a situation effectively exists in a city with which I am extremely
familiar: Hamilton, Ontario.

On the evening of July 9, 1997, a series of unexplained fires broke out in
the mountains of plastic waste stored in a decrepit warehouse on
Wellington Street, in the north end of Hamilton, Ontario. The company
was called Plastimet, and had been in business for less than three years. It
was located in the middle of a working-class neighbourhood, a one-
minute walk away from the largest hospital in the city. At the time the
fire started, the owners of Plastimet were facing an order by the Hamilton

Fire Department to install a million-dollar sprinkler system, without which action would be taken to shut the company's operations down.

The Plastimet fire burned for four days. Thousands of tons of waste plastic and God knows what else went up in flames. The effects of the disaster may well be felt for decades. From the outset, federal and provincial politicians didn't want to get involved. Dithering local politicians on site didn't call for an evacuation of the residential area north of the site for two days. The city's fire department did not know how to fight the blaze, which, experts say, prolonged it and increased the health hazards for everyone in the area. About 250 firefighters breathed in the toxic fumes. The fear that many of them will be stricken with cancer is real, based upon the experiences of firefighters who have been involved in similar fires in other jurisdictions. The health of the firefighters is to be studied over the next twenty-five years in a $1.3-million project.

The cost of the cleanup alone exceeded $2 million, but at the end of the day, the provincial and federal governments were disinclined to launch an inquiry into the blaze and its after-effects. The Ontario government said that, if the City of Hamilton wished to conduct its own inquiry and pay for it, it could do so. This all made perfect sense in a world where responsibility is being pushed down to the lowest levels of government. Hamilton's politicians refused to dig any deeper into what had happened, but if they had, they would eventually have come across an RCMP federal investigation, which, if it had been successful, could well have changed the course of history.

For decades the site of the horrific 1997 fire on Wellington Street was the home of the United Steel and Refining Corporation (USARCO), one of the oldest and most profitable privately held companies in Hamilton history. The origins of the company can be traced back to before the First World War when Moses Levy began a small scrap-metal business. Later, his son, David, founded David Levy and Sons, which eventually grew to become USARCO. David's son, Frank, succeeded his father in running the company.

Over the years the Levys built a huge fortune and became part of the Hamilton elite, living in the upper-middle-class Westdale neighbourhood, next to McMaster University. Their prominent social status belied the fact that their companies were among the largest polluters in the region, if not the country. As solid as they seemed to be, their companies were chronically in arrears for municipal taxes.

By the late eighties, Frank's son, Monte, had taken over the business, but he wasn't all that interested in the day-to-day operations, and the company began to founder. Just when USARCO needed it, saviours within the scrap industry offered "help." To that end, in 1988, USARCO entered into a series of agreements with other companies to become a broker of copper scrap. Copper was soon flowing into Hamilton from around the continent, to the point at which at least one scrap-industry accountant, Malcolm Elliott, who worked for Morris Lax Scrap Metals, one of the companies that was funnelling copper through USARCO, began to wonder what was going on. In Elliott's considerable experience, the entire process seemed to defy any natural economy of scale. Elliott, who wears his long grey hair in a ponytail which he often tucks under a tam, recalls a conversation he had with his boss, Morris Lax: "I couldn't understand how we could make any money bringing in copper from Nova Scotia. When I asked Morris about it, he told me not to worry: 'Just keep buying all you can get.' So that's what we kept on doing."

Lax, a Holocaust survivor, was one of the financial godfathers of the scrap community in Hamilton. Over the years he had made tens of millions of dollars for himself in the business, operating on the edge of the law. Along the way he had been convicted of criminal offences involving possession of stolen property, but that went with the territory in the scrap business in Hamilton.

Back at USARCO, Monte Levy saw the new copper business as a bonanza. He thought he was making fast, easy money, mainly because, improbable as it was, there seemed to be a ready market for all his company's copper. In fact, however, there had never been all that much copper coming through USARCO's doors. What Monte Levy didn't seem to realize was that the company was being subverted from inside by an agent who was working for its enemies by selling off the inventory, a fact confirmed by numerous sources within the industry and the police.

The copper scam progressed for more than a year, draining between $10 million and $13 million of inventory from USARCO. Everything seemed to be going well, until Morris Lax tried to collect the $3 million he was owed by USARCO for copper he had sold to them. When Monte Levy checked on Lax's claims, he found that there was no money from the copper sales in USARCO's bank accounts. The secret agent in his own company then said that the copper had been traded away on a contra basis for red brass, telling Levy that the red brass was in the company's inventory – packed in barrels piled high inside the company's warehouses. There were even invoices to prove the deal had been made. In fact, there was no red brass. The invoices were phony, too.

A further complication was that phantom inventory of copper – that Lax thought he had sold to USARCO – had been used as collateral on an $22-million mortgage obtained by USARCO in early 1989 from the Toronto-Dominion Bank. By mid-1989, as USARCO began to falter, the bank realized it had a serious problem. Sources close to USARCO say that the mortgage proceeds had been quickly moved to an offshore bank account. By the fall the bank moved in and forced the company into receivership, putting 240 people out of work, but not before relatives and friends associated with the company were taken care of. The rest of the staff were owed $1.4 million in severance, termination, and vacation pay. Although the provincial government said it would pick up some of the difference, it never did, USARCO employees say.[1]

A portion of USARCO's operations was quickly sold off by receivers, with the Levys maintaining ownership of the property on Wellington Street. Then, as the copper débâcle was coming to light, Frank and Monte Levy, the company's secretary, were charged with ten counts under the Environmental Protection Act involving air pollution. The charges were resolved in 1991, when the Levys were fined $10,000 each for allowing chronic smoke emissions from USARCO.

Meanwhile, during the receivership period, the company was stripped of its remaining and still-considerable scrap assets by a group of businessmen from the Hamilton and Montreal areas, who were sent in by the bank's receivers "to save USARCO" and generate income. Precisely the opposite happened. Over a six-month period, a daily convoy of between five and ten twenty-five-ton trucks, as well as train carloads of scrap, were moved out of Hamilton in a massive raid on USARCO's assets. USARCO employees themselves were stealing inventory and stockpiling it at a warehouse in Stoney Creek, immediately east of Hamilton.

Then, early one Saturday morning in December 1992, Morris Lax was bludgeoned to death in his scrapyard. At the time he was demanding the last $600,000 he was owed from the $3 million in copper he had sold to USARCO. Lax's accountant, Malcolm Elliott, said Lax had been partially reimbursed, not by USARCO, oddly enough, but by a Montreal company and another Hamilton company. Two itinerant scrap dealers, who appeared to have no connections to the USARCO deal, were eventually charged in October 1997 with the Lax murder.

Members of the RCMP Economic Crime Unit in Hamilton were assigned to investigate the USARCO matter after the bank moved in. Allegations were made that USARCO was a phony bankruptcy. Bankruptcy is a federal matter and, therefore, a tiny corner of the Economic Crime Unit's responsibilities. Members of the Hamilton–Wentworth Regional Police were also investigating the Lax murder and other aspects of the case.

The USARCO case should have been a natural for the Mounties. Over the years, the force had investigated and prosecuted many phony bankruptcy cases, one of the most significant being the collapse of the trucking company Route Canada in the late eighties, which put almost two thousand people out of work. In that case, the Mounties eventually laid criminal charges against the founders of the company and won a conviction, which is still under appeal.

As the RCMP investigators in Hamilton began to poke away at the USARCO file, however, they soon found themselves deep in the world of an extremely corrupt city. Through USARCO, the Mounties found a number of threads leading to other criminal acts. In effect, they were retracing some of the steps taken almost two decades earlier in Hamilton by Rod Stamler, who is still viewed as one of the RCMP's great investigative heroes from the old Commercial Crime Branch days.

Back in 1973, Stamler, then an inspector, initiated what appeared to be an arcane investigation into dredging practices in Hamilton Harbour and allegations that the Hamilton Harbour commissioners, who administered the port for the federal government, were involved in corrupt practices. A few concerned and angry city politicians, led by Hamilton controller Herman Turkstra, had campaigned to bring the Mounties into Hamilton. In the context of the times, the fight against political corruption was riding high on the public's agenda, especially because of the high-profile Watergate investigation in the United States, which would lead to the resignation of President Richard Nixon. In Canada, there was a growing appetite for similar investigations, which here fell to the Mounties in their capacity as federal law-enforcement officers and defenders of the greater good.

Stamler, like the Mounties investigating the USARCO case, soon found himself caught up in the murky world of Hamilton politics and business, which was particularly murky in the scrap industry. Modern Hamilton has been built largely on the wealth generated by its two giant steel companies, Stelco Inc. and Dofasco. But it was the scrappers, who gather and supply metals to feed the steel-company blast furnaces, who individually became wealthy and powerful. This scrapocracy, as it were, tended to live – like the Levys from USARCO – in the finest homes in Westdale and the historic western suburban towns of Ancaster and Dundas. Along with the Levy and Lax families, the Goldblatt, Hotz, Posner, Frank, and Waxman families were also among the largest benefactors to the community; they had enormous political and social influence, and controlled, directly and indirectly, most boards and municipal government appointments. Hamilton has been and continues to be treated as their fiefdom.

Meanwhile, Hamilton also was home to at least three Italian organized-crime families, who exerted their influence from the U.S. border to Toronto. The strength of the Mafia testified to the laissez faire attitude of the rest of the city. Sometimes it seemed that just about everyone – including many police officers and politicians – had his or her fingers into just about everything. Hamilton was a you-scratch-my-back-I'll-scratch-your-back city. With all this, many wondered if there was any such thing as a square deal in Hamilton.

Although Stamler's mission in 1973 began with what was going on under the water in the harbour, his investigation soon turned to what was happening on shore, especially with some of the city's numerous scrapyards. A scrapyard is an all-cash business whose inventory is virtually impossible for a non-expert to evaluate. At a glance, few people can discern red brass from copper or even the difference between the various grades of copper. All the copper might look the same to the naked eye, but the price differential between grades may be as much as a dollar a pound – a considerable swing when deals can involve thousands of tons at a time. Stamler realized that the scrapyards were the perfect vehicles for laundering the illegal proceeds of organized crime, which was exactly what was going on in Hamilton.

In Hamilton, Stamler found that the rot ran deep. The Mountie investigator soon gathered enough evidence to show that local, provincial, and federal bureaucrats had been on the take, making decisions and creating unnecessary public work, the intention of which was to benefit unscrupulous businesses. As he followed one lead after another, Stamler realized that there was more work than any one team of investigators could accomplish, so, where appropriate, he spun off some aspects of the Hamilton Harbour case to other investigative agencies, such as Revenue Canada and the Ontario and Quebec provincial police forces.

The Quebec police, in particular, didn't bother following up any of the leads Stamler had provided, but Stamler and the Mounties eventually laid fraud charges and won convictions against a number of people in the Hamilton Harbour case. Their investigation didn't end there, however. The leads generated in Hamilton pointed to crimes elsewhere, and Stamler and his fellow Mounties followed them. This resulted in two other high-profile cases – the Dredging Scandal, which involved a well-established fraud by leading businessmen and their companies, and the Sky Shops case, which involved political corruption and illegal tendering processes at the country's leading airports. In each of those cases, as well, the Mounties were able to convict some of the most powerful businesspeople in the country of defrauding the federal government.[2]

After such obvious successes, the lowly taxpayer might have expected that the government would have encouraged and supported such federal investigations, but that's not what happened in Canada. As we saw earlier in the book, for a variety of political and economic reasons, precisely the opposite has occurred. The promise of federal law enforcement – as exemplified by the Commercial Crime Branch – as a defender of both the public treasury and the greater good, began and, in many respects, ended in the late seventies, although it wasn't immediately apparent.

Even before the Hamilton Harbour case had gone through the courts, a working relationship had developed between the various law-enforcement agencies in Hamilton to deal with organized crime there. In 1977, in the wake of Rod Stamler's Hamilton Harbour investigation, a formal agreement was made, whereby the RCMP, Ontario Provincial Police, and Hamilton–Wentworth Police set up what was known as the Joint Forces Unit. The intention of this collaboration was that the JFU would mount large, complex investigations that overlapped the respective jurisdictions of each police force.

Fifteen years later, in 1992, as the USARCO investigation, which would have been a case made to order for the JFU, given its wide-reaching mandate, was beginning to heat up, the JFU was disbanded for budgetary and political reasons, having seen most of its cases falter and fail, amid finger-pointing between each police force. Some Mounties say that the primary reason the JFU failed was because the Hamilton–Wentworth Regional Police was perceived as not being as co-operative as the other forces might have liked. Others put it more bluntly. As one Mountie said: "Every time we were closing in on somebody, the Hamilton police would find a way to screw things up."

In any event, the break up of the JFU was not inconsistent with the emerging vision of what federal law enforcement should be – which is not very much at all.

The deeper one delves into Hamilton, today, the more it becomes evident that, when a business-minded government talks about the notions of efficiency and competition, it doesn't fully appreciate what it says or does. When government talks about efficiency these days, the only measure seems to be in *perceived* financial savings, not real savings. By the same token, competition is seen only in terms of whether a certain service is provided by either the public or private sector. The entire notion of competition between various arms of the public service is usually discredited as inefficient and, therefore, something to be avoided.

At first blush, such policies make sense, because they appear to address the issue of limited public resources. But at a deeper level, there are serious and often-ignored public-policy implications. When overlapping regulatory and law-enforcement jurisdictions are eliminated in the name of efficiency, the effect is that only one regulator is left to protect a certain sector of society. That's not the way public police should operate. In the United States, for example, a person living in New York City might find that offences such as fraud are investigated by any number of agencies, including the New York city police, the state police, the FBI, the U.S. Postal Inspection Service, and even, if the fraud involves counterfeit money, the Secret Service. In Canada, where the formal law can be grey about issues such as jurisdiction, in practice jurisdictions are being arbitrarily delineated and are totally separate. When jurisdictions are carved out this way, a victim in Toronto, for example, can usually appeal to only one police force. If the Toronto police reject a complaint, there is little likelihood that the Ontario Provincial Police or RCMP will take up the matter, even if it is in the public interest that they investigate.

Governments have sold the public this idea of a guardian monopoly, yet it is just as dangerous, if not more so, as Microsoft having a monopoly on computers and software programs. Monopolies of any kind lead to corruption. That's what happens in small backwoods towns almost anywhere. The police, without scrutiny or competition, can turn into tyrants. There is no reason why it can't happen in cities, provinces, or across an entire country. When a police force has a virtual monopoly over a jurisdiction, favouritism and inconsistent and ineffective enforcement become commonplace.

The situation in Hamilton was aggravated by another "efficiency," which was introduced in the late eighties by the Ontario government.

This involved the scrapping of the Ontario Police Commission, a province-wide board which exercised control over municipal policing, as a check against local corruption. The province also had the right to appoint members to local police commissions, as a second check. With the abolition of the Ontario Police Commission, all control over local policing was delegated to municipal governments as part of the downloading of responsibility and costs to the lowest level of government.

Like the approach taken by the federal government as it became more business-minded, the Ontario government said its intention was to make the local police more responsive and accountable to local citizens. The effect, however, was to bring a local police department more under local political and business control than it otherwise might have been. Ontario set up a citizens' review committee, but it was largely deemed to be ineffective. With the demise of the JFU in Hamilton, other police forces found themselves effectively blocked from conducting serious investigations within Hamilton, because, as a senior Mountie put it to me, "As soon as the Hamilton police found out what we were doing, they would barge in and exercise their own jurisdictional rights. Their attitude was, 'If your case collapses because of what we did, so be it.'"

It should come as no surprise, therefore, that in recent years the Hamilton–Wentworth police force has become almost universally distrusted by other police forces. By the same token, there are indications of corrupt behaviour going largely unchallenged within the Hamilton–Wentworth force, more so than in other Canadian municipal departments. And now there is no Ontario Police Commission to investigate; in Hamilton, like the rest of Canada, downsizing has led to there being no real independent police watchdog or police force dedicated to investigating another police force. By and large, the Hamilton–Wentworth Regional Police, like most other Canadian police forces, are left to investigate and oversee their own affairs, a decidedly scary prospect.

Twenty-five years after Rod Stamler began the 1973 Hamilton Harbour investigation, the situation in Hamilton is not much different from what it was then, when the Mounties marched in and got their men. Today, local citizens and some politicians agree that, outside of the province of Quebec, the Hamilton–Wentworth region is one of the most, if not the most, corrupt municipalities in the country. Ethnic organized crime continues to maintain a strong hold, but the problem goes well beyond that.

In Hamilton, during the nineties, there was such an overwhelming atmosphere of government-business mutual interest and bonhomie that the guardians had gone over to the business side. Even the small band of disheartened Mounties trying to enforce federal laws in the Hamilton area had effectively been rendered neutral.

The obstacle the Mounties faced came, oddly enough, in the form of a civic-minded policy to create jobs in Hamilton. It was called Vision 2020. This long-term plan was a blueprint for Hamilton to become a self-sustaining community by the year 2020 by leading the world in the development and implementation of recycling systems and technologies. The intention was to bring government and business together to solve the city's problem, but the effect was to ensure that business, scrupulous or otherwise, could operate without any political, regulatory, or local media scrutiny. Everyone in the community was enlisted as part of the "team," working hard to improve Hamilton's fortunes. It appeared to be a wonderful marketing success, but it created the opportunity for a major disaster.

In the 1970s Mountie investigators like Rod Stamler might have been able to avert what was about to happen, but in the 1990s, the guardian mentality of the Mounties had been largely compromised.[3]

•   •   •

After the murder of Morris Lax, both the Mounties and Sergeant Dave Broom of the Hamilton police had begun rattling around in Hamilton's skeleton-clogged closets. They found that the tentacles of the USARCO investigation spread far, wide, and deep into Hamilton's business and political scene. The police documented the movement of scrap to Montreal and elsewhere, and were beginning to get excited, but just as they did, problems began to arise.

The Mounties were on a short leash from the federal government, and it was getting shorter every day. Like all the RCMP federal officers, those in Hamilton were beginning to feel the effects of the changes provoked by

"Police-Challenge 2000," which had been introduced in Parliament three years earlier. Throughout this period the RCMP had been reassessing its federal mandate through a process called Federal Law Enforcement Under Review (FLEUR). The effective decriminalization of white-collar crime – fraud committed under the cover of business – was the direction in which the force was heading. The new RCMP view about fraud, as we have already seen in Chapter Eight, was that investigators should target the ill-gotten assets of criminals which might be seized on behalf of the government. At the highest levels of the RCMP there wasn't much of an appetite any more for the force to conduct difficult, time-consuming investigations, which USARCO promised to be. Now the brass wanted guarantees that suspects would be convicted or at least proof that there was enough money lying around that might be seized in order to make the exercise appear worthwhile. In the USARCO case, it was the worst possible scenario. Whatever money there may have been had disappeared, and there were no other tangible assets to the company, only liabilities, and significant ones, at that.

What this meant for the USARCO investigation was that the RCMP turned the investigation over to the Hamilton–Wentworth Regional Police. In the new world of policing in Canada, as envisioned by Pierre Cadieux in "Police-Challenge 2000," local forces were going to have to take up the slack and expand their duties and responsibilities. Without the RCMP doing their job, protecting the greater good, local police don't stand a chance in mounting complex, multi-jurisdictional, or politically sensitive cases.

Sergeant Dave Broom from the Hamilton–Wentworth Regional Police was left to try to mount such an investigation in a hostile environment. His investigation was exposed and vulnerable to political pressure. Broom refuses to talk to the media about what happened in the USARCO and Lax investigations, but many of those interviewed by him were impressed by his determination and professionalism. This much about what Broom managed to find out has been pieced together from police and other sources.

He tracked down some of the missing USARCO copper, and is believed to have stumbled onto the trail of another copper scam. By late 1995,

Broom had recommended to his superiors that there was enough evidence to justify a massive investigation into corruption in Hamilton, which by now had expanded to the activities of other industries and corporations. Broom estimated that such an investigation would cost $5 million, but the senior officers in the force refused to go along with him. They said there was neither money in the budget nor a crying need for such an investigation. And then there was the political pressure that was brought to bear on the department.

As one high-ranking Hamilton police officer put it, "There was a meeting. We were told that the people targeted in these investigations were 'good people,' and that it wouldn't be in the best interests of Hamilton if they were investigated and charged. Hamilton had enough problems, and it didn't need another black eye." This meeting was confirmed by others.

Broom was said to be furious and wanted to continue, but lawyer Herman Turkstra put an end to that. Turkstra used a subpoena to drag Broom into a seemingly unrelated and bizarre civil matter. At the time, Philip Environmental, the company Turkstra was representing, was trying to win regulatory approval for an industrial dump, the Taro East Quarry, on the edge of the Niagara Escarpment above the Hamilton suburb of Stoney Creek. Michael Hilson, a former Philip accountant, had filed an intervention against the proposed landfill with the provincial ministry of environment. Hilson said that, based on his experience, he didn't believe that Philip was an ethical company nor as financially sound as it claimed to be. Philip immediately sought and received an unprecedented, wide-ranging injunction against Hilson and a host of unknown people named John and Jane Doe, preventing anyone from circulating or publishing Hilson's comments. No one, not even the *Hamilton Spectator*, attempted to oppose the injunction (although the injunction was partially overturned in August 1998). Hilson also was sued for $30 million in damages. The grounds for the injunction was an entirely unsubstantiated claim by Philip's lawyers that a group of unknown conspirators were trying to defame Philip and drive down the share price of the company.

Ironically enough, Turkstra, who had been instrumental in bringing then-RCMP inspector Rod Stamler to Hamilton to conduct the Hamilton

Harbour investigation in 1973, turned to Stamler, who was now in private practice, to help him out again. Stamler's role was to identify and ferret out the alleged conspiracy against Philip. Stamler never managed to do so. But one of those who had talked with Hilson was Broom, who was conducting his investigation into the USARCO affair, the Morris Lax murder, and Philip.

While there appeared to be no hard evidence of a conspiracy to hurt Philip, Turkstra used the civil-court discovery process to question nine people, including MPP Toni Skarica and Sergeant Broom, about their respective involvement in the "conspiracy." In the context of the discussion about the government's plan to limit the role of federal law enforcement in Canada, Turkstra's line of questioning of Broom might be both instructive and educational. Remember, *this civil examination was conducted while Broom's criminal investigation was still ongoing*! Not even Broom's superiors tried to protect him from testifying.

Once Turkstra had Broom under oath, he attempted to find out what Broom was doing with regard to Philip, and, it appears, USARCO, because there was some overlap in relationships between parties in both companies. Turkstra wanted to know why Broom was making inquiries in Hamilton, Toronto, and Montreal and whom he was talking to. Turkstra repeatedly asked Broom whether he had the jurisdiction to conduct such an investigation. The clear implication in Turkstra's interrogation was that a local police officer should have been investigating only local matters. Turkstra tried to get Broom to agree with him that anything beyond the boundaries of Hamilton was out of his jurisdiction, and suggested to Broom that he was conducting an investigation only to hurt Philip Environmental. Broom declined to answer any of Turkstra's questions on the grounds that it would compromise the public interest – the police investigation. Turkstra then accused Broom of faking such a privilege: "It's being used to cover the tracks of the defamation that has occurred as a result of the statements made by this witness to people."[4]

Shortly afterwards, the Hamilton–Wentworth Regional Police sent a letter to the Philip company mildly apologizing for Broom's behaviour, although it is clear Broom was at all times carrying out his duties as a peace officer, and had done nothing wrong. Frustrated and disappointed by the unwillingness of the force to back him, Broom was reassigned to other duties with another investigative agency outside Hamilton. He was ordered by his superiors never to discuss the case, which he hasn't. With the transfer of Sergeant Broom, the police investigation into USARCO was now dead and would likely never be revived. By the time the Broom investigation had been shut down, Plastimet was up and running on the old USARCO site on Wellington Street.

There is one other development worth noting. As has often become the case in such matters, the Toronto-Dominion Bank didn't make a criminal complaint, but instead launched a civil suit to recover the outstanding $20 million of the loan it said it was owed, which is still before the courts. At one point the bank had seized the Wellington Street property and blocked both Frank and Monte Levy from entering it, but the bank soon learned how gullible it had been. The land on Wellington Street, though it abutted a low-income residential neighbourhood, was one of the most contaminated pieces of real estate in the world, saturated with everything from heavy metals to battery acids to PCBs to a depth of at least twenty feet. In 1994, the Ministry of Environment and Energy found elevated levels of lead on sixty-seven residential properties near the site.[5] The bank could never sell the USARCO lands without a monumental investment in a cleanup. Backed into a corner and unwilling to lay a criminal complaint, the bank allowed the Levy family to regain control of the property.

Soon, they were overseeing a number of new business ventures. Frank Levy was running Davida Industries Ltd. from the site. Monte Levy and Kirk Kaplansky began doing business under the name of Phoenix International. It ran a brass-smelting operation that would have looked at home anywhere in the Third World. Malcolm Elliott, the accountant for the late Morris Lax, visited the site in 1996. This is what he told me he saw: "Bundles of plastic were piled almost sixty feet high. The plastic was less than a hundred feet from the brass smelter. The chimney for the smelter went out a hole in the roof. When they poured out the brass, it sent sparks everywhere. Few of the workers could speak English. To get through the building, you had to climb over the mountains of plastic. There was no roof to speak of. Puddles of rain water were everywhere, which were used to cool the hot ingots. Get this: the whole operation had been approved by the Environment Ministry, the Labour Ministry, the city, and the fire department. Welcome to deregulation." Two other people confirmed Elliott's observations about what was going on in the building.

The plastic-recovery business on the old USARCO site was being run by Jack Lieberman. Lieberman's previous family business, Hamilton Iron and Metal, had gone bankrupt, and the new owner of that property reported having to dispose of four-thousand tons of waste plastic after he took over the property. Lieberman also had spent time in jail for defrauding the provincial Environment Ministry, a fact which the ministry neither publicized or seemed to care about in granting him a new licence for Plastimet.

In spite of the evident past and current problems, and the fact that the Levys and Liebermans were behind on their municipal taxes, nobody at City Hall or any other level of government questioned what they were doing. Plastimet was seen to be a child of Vision 2020, the grand plan to transform Hamilton. As such, the guardians closed their eyes to what was going on, although the fire department had begun to realize there might be a problem. It had finally ordered a sprinkler system installed at Plastimet – but two days too late.

Malcolm Elliott says the Plastimet fire provided vivid evidence of much that is wrong with Hamilton and a portent for the rest of Canada, as the RCMP retreats from its federal law-enforcement duties. "When it comes to corruption in Hamilton our company is sort of immune, because everyone considers us to be loose cannons, especially because of our relationship with the police after Morris Lax was murdered. But the effects of the corruption can't be ignored. Plastimet was existing in the cracks of the superstructure in Hamilton. Everyone had ripped off everyone else so nobody was going to complain to the police. The police won't take any action until there is a victim, and even then they're not too eager. The fire department's outrage was a joke. They allowed that business to operate. The city let them go even though they were in tax arrears and had a lousy track record of payment. All the regulators were corrupted, morally or otherwise. The Labour Ministry only deals with companies with nine of more employees. So what do these companies do? They set up a bunch of businesses on the same site each with eight employees or less. There might be one hundred people working at a location and the ministry isn't interested in the conditions, but, boy, they're on our backs for the most petty things. The Environment Ministry has become so corrupted it's unbelievable – although the word on the street is that one of their bureaucrats is fair about it: he charges the same price for everything. In the end no one has looked at the recycling business for what it really is: this is an industry that must stockpile thousands of tons of dangerous and volatile materials at a time. You could fill Ivor Wynne Stadium with all the plastic inventory in Hamilton, and there wouldn't be enough room. This is an industry that can kill everyone in this city with one of its errors, and there's absolutely no regulation."

One police officer close to the case put it this way: "Ordinary people have to realize that the Plastimet fire is the real cost of not investigating economic crime or the courts not treating it seriously. How many lives have been irreparably damaged? People should have been put in jail a long time ago. But nobody will ever go to jail for what happened, and there was so much to go to jail for." (In fact, Frank Levy and Jack Lieberman were convicted in June 1998. They each received two years' probation and were ordered to pay $170,000.)

The Plastimet fire occurred in a municipal election year. In the run-up to the November 10, 1997, election, Arthur Kelly, the editor of *Biz*, a magazine about Hamilton-area businesses, vented his disgust with what was happening in the city: "Hamilton is the community of choice of fly-by-night operators, who feel free to violate fire and safety codes, and ignore taxes. Council's cautionary response to each act of wrongdoing makes it a virtual accomplice."[6] In a previous issue, Kelly wrote: "Rumours of corruption and insider trading continually surface, which is why Hamilton is the pariah of southern Ontario. . . . Numerous bureaucrats are on the take, construction is a fixed game, the tendering process is a joke, the local marketplace is subject to manipulation, and . . . the politicians are either too tainted, frightened, or naïve to mount a challenge to the real powers controlling the city."[7]

On July 9, 1997, when Plastimet went up in flames in Hamilton, the thick, black, poisonous smoke served as vivid testimony to the potential dangers facing Canada today. Government at all levels has ceased to think like a guardian, but has become so business-minded as to be guilty of wilful blindness of the consequences of its actions. Meanwhile, so many of the police, Mounties and otherwise, have become confused and disheartened, mainly because their sense of duty has been compromised. The natural instinct of a police officer is to serve the public and enforce the law, but more and more police officers are being chastised, as was Sergeant Dave Broom, for simply trying to follow their instincts and do their duty.

In that context, the Plastimet fire and the situation in Hamilton, today, is the real bottom line. If the Mounties are prevented from fully carrying out their federal law-enforcement duties and responsibilities, then the local police are vulnerable to political influence, with the ultimate result that there is no one left to defend the greater good.

Chapter Fourteen

.... ● ....

THE ROLEX GUARDIANS: TWO-TIER
POLICING, OR IS IT THREE?

SINCE "POLICE-CHALLENGE 2000" was tabled in the House of Commons by Solicitor General Pierre Cadieux in 1990, the federal government has advocated the notion that Canada should move to a two-tier system of policing, an idea the provinces and some municipalities have gone along with. As we've already seen, this new "business model," known as community-based policing, is designed to make policing both more economically efficient and more effective. The concept, however, is hardly new; it is very much a throwback to the way in which policing was delivered in the late nineteenth century. Communities back then essentially policed themselves, calling on the underpaid and sparsely manned public police forces only in the direst situations. In earlier chapters we visited municipalities such as Dauphin, Manitoba, and Burnaby, British Columbia, where the Mounties have formed liaisons with business and where citizens patrol the streets and conduct surveillance on behalf of the police. That's the community policing that is widely marketed by politicians and police forces across the country, and is most visible to Canadians.

Then there's the community-based policing that nobody really talks about and is barely visible, if at all; that is, the change in the way the RCMP investigates white-collar crime – fraud committed under the cover of business.

After "Police-Challenge 2000" a process was set up within the RCMP which became known as FLEUR (Federal Law Enforcement Under Review). The intent of the FLEUR process was to find ways for the RCMP to deliver federal law-enforcement services in a more efficient and effective manner than in the past. Some Mounties thought the solution to the RCMP's problems with federal law enforcement could be solved by an increase in its budget, since, as we saw in Chapter Two, less than one-sixth of the RCMP budget today is devoted to federal law enforcement. But increasing the budget was not an option; the government wanted the RCMP to decrease its budget. The government also wanted the RCMP to comply with the vision set out in "Police-Challenge 2000": that responsibility for some federal policing be pushed down to the local level and that some duties be shared with the private sector, such as forensic accountants and their private investigators. One final aspect of this de-emphasis on pure law enforcement was that the RCMP focus its resources instead on identifying and seizing the assets of major crime groups, which is what Integrated Proceeds of Crime units are doing today. The monies the IPOC units seize are being deposited in general government revenues. For the government and many of the current leaders of the RCMP, all this seems to make good business sense. For critics, it doesn't. In essence what the government has done with the co-operation of the RCMP is effectively to decriminalize white-collar crime and to transform most such crimes into mere financial transactions, whose punishment is measured only in dollars.

Promoters of this two-tier policing – particularly the forensic accountants themselves – believe that this is the way law enforcement in Canada should work. At the same time, critics says, the evidence is already in that there are serious problems with the concept. Since 1990, white-collar crime has become nearly epidemic across the country, to the point where it is becoming as institutionalized as the corruption one might find in a Third World country. In recent years, one spectacular case after another has emerged, including the $1.8-billion Castor Holdings fraud, based in Montreal, the $1.6-billion Bre-X gold-stock scam on the Toronto Stock Exchange, and, the mysterious loss of hundreds of millions of dollars of copper inventory, earlier this year, by Philip Services Corp. (formerly Philip Environmental Inc.) in Hamilton, Ontario, to name just a few.

In light of the staggering size of these individual cases, it should come as no surprise, therefore, that over the past decade the annual cost of fraud to the Canadian economy is estimated to be 1.5 to 6 per cent of the country's $800-billion gross domestic product. That is, between $12 billion and $48 billion a year is being stolen from individuals, corporations, and government.

But in these post-FLEUR days, when an individual or corporate victim turns to the RCMP for help, more often than not the RCMP will actively refer victims to forensic-accounting and private-investigation companies across Canada. The victims are being told to conduct their own investigations, and then, once they are completed, to bring them back to the police, who may or may not then agree to pursue the matter.

As the RCMP (and other Canadian police forces in their wake) rush down this road, there are many unanswered questions, and new ones are raised almost every day. But, I think, the two main questions are these:

- Are victims of white-collar crime and the public getting their respective money's worth from two-tier policing?
- Does two-tier policing serve the public interest at all, or is it just an accounting trick, with rather serious implications for the rule of law in Canada?

Let me attempt to answer these questions by taking you on one final journey – inside forensic accounting and private investigation in Canada. In the opening chapter, we caught a glimpse of this world when we saw a team of forensic accountants and private investigators executing an Anton Piller order – a private search warrant – in Peterborough, Ontario. Now, let's go a little deeper.

In late 1991, former RCMP assistant commissioner Rod Stamler, the central figure in my first book, *Above the Law*, was working in Toronto as a private investigator. Since I was researching white-collar crime, Stamler suggested that I become a private investigator so that I might better understand the subject matter. Over the next three years I largely abandoned journalism and worked on a semi-regular basis for Toronto-based forensic accountants and lawyers. Those were heady days. In the aftermath of "Police-Challenge 2000," forensic accountants were being touted in the media as the new guardians – smarter, quicker, and more effective than the public police.

The forensic-accounting business was "invented" in 1975 by Toronto accountants Robert J. Lindquist and Don Holmes, who wished to create a hybrid discipline which ostensibly combined the principles of accounting, investigation, and expert testimony. As the media-wise Lindquist put it: "An auditor is like a watchdog. But a forensic accountant is like a bloodhound."[1] Lindquist and Holmes started out helping police analyse and articulate complex fraud investigations, making them more presentable for the courts.

It was no accident that the notion of "forensic accounting" was born in Canada; probably no other democratic country in the world needed such professionals more than Canada did in 1975. White-collar crime had been treated as a criminal act in Canada only since 1965, and in the intervening decade the RCMP had realized such successes as the Hamilton Harbour case, one of Stamler's triumphs. But by 1975, as we've seen, the Mounties were struggling to survive. The McDonald and Keable commissions had led to political shackles being placed on the force. Government-mandated affirmative action changed the demographics of the force, which was good, but this was done by largely abandoning the meritocracy, which was not so good; those who got to the top and to key positions were not necessarily the best or most competent. Decentralization of commercial-crime investigation, among other things, had also begun to take its toll.

Businesses, especially multinational corporations, found that their complaints to the RCMP, which ranged from overt criminality to arcane competitive problems, were not being treated promptly or seriously by the federal police. This wasn't all the fault of the police, however. Some businesses had begun to use the police as their corporate gestapo. Time after time, businesses would lay a criminal complaint, allow the police to conduct their investigations, and then, at the courthouse steps, force a financial settlement under threat of continuing with the case. The complaints would be withdrawn, and the police's time and effort would have been wasted. A corporation's short-term and financial interests may have been well served by the process, but the public interest certainly wasn't. Serious crimes were reduced to a series of financial transactions, and no real or effective punitive or deterrent measures were imposed. The record shows that many of these criminals were usually back on the street and soon on to another scam, hardly chastened by their experiences. Meanwhile, the police, who more often than not were treated as mere pawns in the power play, were left holding the bag.

By its self-interested and unethical behaviour, corporate Canada not only created its own problems with policing but also provided the impetus for the undermining of the public police. In Canada a corporation is treated as an individual before the law, but when it misbehaves or abuses the legal process, the tendency of the legal system is to let it off the hook, whereas a "real" individual might be charged with mischief or any number of criminal offences. When it comes to complaints by corporations, therefore, is it any wonder police departments began to back away from investigations, leaving a vacuum to be filled by the public sector.

In the two decades since forensic accounting was first conceived, Don Holmes and Bob Lindquist have gone their separate ways. Holmes has earned a reputation as a solid and well-respected accountant, but Lindquist is also revered in many other quarters – by government bureaucrats, police administrators, and some members of the media – almost as if he were a cult leader. He sets the tone for the industry. Lindquist is considered both a superb investigator and a visionary. When he constructed his forensic-accounting firms, he attempted to break down the traditional barriers within investigative fields. According to his plan, accountants, former police officers, and former investigative journalists were encouraged to work together on cases because each brought unique talents and insights. Accountants had financial expertise, the ex-police knew how to create court-ready cases, and the ex-journalists were often quicker and more astute than the police at unravelling complex, multifaceted cases. Whereas the police did their investigations in an A, B, C, D manner, the journalists often went A, B, M, Z, and then came back to fill in the blanks, a useful talent when a client's meter is ticking. With my background as an investigative journalist, I fit the role.

As a private investigator I travelled across North America and did what traditional private investigators do – surveillance, following suspects, and gathering evidence. I earned my degree in "dumpster diving" and came to know the habits of my targets so well I could often pick out their garbage bags from anyone else's just by taking a whiff of the contents through a hole poked in the plastic. I worked closely with the police in both Canada and the United States, and in a number of cases, which must remain confidential, my investigations resulted in criminal charges being laid and in civil-court victories. But my work wasn't all of the gumshoe variety. Sometimes I was paid to act as an investigative consultant to forensic accountants and lawyers, advising them on possible avenues to explore in an investigation.

In their brief existence, forensic accountants have managed to create their own mythology – they're the white knights of the private sector. But after rubbing shoulders with them for a while, it didn't take long for me to recognize some serious flaws in the beast, not least of which was the pursuit of easy money.

Most of the country's leading forensic-accounting companies are huddled around the intersection of King and Bay streets in Toronto, where a headquarters of a major bank sits on each corner. While senior public police investigators might be reduced to working out of cubby-holes and brown-bagging it for lunch, forensic-accounting practices display their wealth in designer furniture and art-covered walls. It's an expense-account world, where every second is billable. One prominent and leading member of that community stands out in my mind as typical. When given a choice in his company to choose a telephone local, he selected one ending in 2274 – CASH. He knew exactly what the numbers spelled. Every day on his computer he totted up his current billings and compared them on a running basis to the previous year. In an era when many Mounties and other police officers must take second jobs to make a living, the take-home pay of this "investigator" is said to exceed $600,000 per year. Forensic accounting in Canada's largest cities is a world of fine wines, expensive dining, and fabulous jewellery; financial kills are a near-daily occurrence, mainly because there is virtually no regulation of any kind.

These firms like to crow about their successes, such as they are, but you never hear about the downside for society. Most firms won't even look at a case in which the budget is under $30,000, because a decent biller can run up that kind of tab with expenses in about two weeks without even conducting a serious private investigation. Other firms have even higher thresholds. There is no sense of altruism and no *pro bono* work that I could see. No client gets anything for free.

The obscene amounts of money being made aside, one public-policy issue in particular crystallized my thinking on this subject. It seemed to me that the Mulroney government's preoccupation with privacy issues, and especially the creation of a privacy commissioner within the bureaucracy, had a negative effect, which no one in politics or the media seemed interested in addressing.

As the federal police were being downsized and the scope of their jurisdiction narrowed, more of the responsibility for investigation was being thrown onto the backs of the victims and the private sector. This toughening of privacy legislation was making it nearly impossible for both the police and the private sector to conduct reasonable and valid investigations. Take the issue of criminal records. As was pointed out earlier, the concept of formal criminal records was conceived so that ordinary society could keep track of and identify felons. In today's world, the police are withdrawing from traditional areas of enforcement. Criminals can travel physically or through cyberspace far and wide and at will, thereby enhancing their ability to conduct their nefarious activities. The world of financial dealings has become extremely treacherous. Therefore, it seemed to me that, for society to protect itself and thrive, ordinary people must be able to identify criminals easily. But privacy legislation has made that all but impossible. As well, libel laws have been constructed so that, in many instances, other than the contemporaneous publication of a conviction, the media risk a civil suit if they publish a person's criminal record, even if the details of that record are relevant to a story.

I approached Bob Lindquist about the problem. I suggested to him that there was a serious societal issue that no one was addressing, and that someone of his stature and eminence should speak out and add his voice to the debate.

"I couldn't do that," Lindquist said. "We do a lot of business with government. Our company couldn't be seen in any way to be acting as an advocate of any kind. We wouldn't get any business."

As good an investigator as he might well be, the self-professed "bloodhound of the bottom line" turned out to be a "guardian" for whomever paid his fees. That's the nature of business. Business is self-centred and driven by self-interest. It has no mandate or will to defend collective interests – the greater good – no matter what its marketing slogans promise to the contrary. Forensic accounting is no different. As good and honest as he may be at his chosen profession, Lindquist is a hired gun, who does not see his role as defending the public or national interest. That's the role of government.

Yet the forensic-accounting business has it both ways. It pretends to act like a government agency – as an alternative law-enforcement agency – but it is not bound by any of the usual restrictions. Like any accountants, they are a self-regulating profession, answerable only to themselves – not to the public. Private organizations such as the Association of Certified Fraud Examiners have sprung out of nowhere, but these are businesses, with no regulatory authority.[2] By and large, as long as a member's books are in order, and everything appears to line up on the balance sheet, accountants and their private investigators are given the benefit of the doubt by their governing bodies. But that doesn't mean everything is all right. Far from it. The high-handed behaviour of some of his fellow forensic accountants is so flagrant that one of them, Al Langley from Toronto, told me: "I can see serious regulation coming." When? No one seems to know that yet.

• • •

The backbone of any forensic-accounting operation are their "marquee players." These are usually not the accountants. They are people who can

274 • THE LAST GUARDIANS

enter a boardroom and confidently sell a range of services, from corporate security to Anton Piller orders and Mareeva injunctions (which are used to freeze the assets of defendants in civil cases). Bob Lindquist is a marquee player, but few forensic accountants are. They don't have the name and reputation he enjoys. In most Canadian forensic-accounting firms the marquee players are former high-ranking police officers, usually Mounties. For example, former RCMP commissioner Norman Inkster runs KPMG Investigative and Security Inc., even though the day he took the job he conceded at a press conference that he didn't know anything about fraud investigation. "I guess I'll have to learn on the job," he said. Former assistant commissioner Rod Stamler is now with a group of companies which operate in a number of countries under the flag of Forensic Investigative Associates Inc. FIA is the prime investigation company for Price Waterhouse, where Bob Lindquist runs the forensic practice. Former RCMP deputy commissioner Henry Jensen has a hand in running a similar operation at Deloitte, Touche. And the list goes on.

Ranked beneath these former police executives are dozens of other former police officers, usually Mounties, in their forties and early fifties, who handle the day-to-day investigations. Ex-Mounties, as we saw in Chapter Eight, also have a stranglehold on security jobs within Canada's banks and financial institutions. Every one of these ex-Mounties left the force on partial pensions, which they began to collect as soon as they left the public service. Along with the forensic accountants, many start their new careers at a salary in the $100,000 to $125,000 range. "We have fourteen former commercial-crime officers," says Inkster, who points to an advertisement headed, "Where Are They Now?" advertising the firm's ex-police officers, a group which also includes a former Metro Toronto Police officer and a former member of the Montreal Urban Community Police service.[3]

All the police officers had been schooled and trained by the taxpayers, and now, at the peak of their powers and abilities, they are plucked away. Some, such as former RCMP staff sergeant John Beer, were in the middle of important and highly controversial cases when they left. Beer, along with Corporal Glen Harloff, had investigated and laid charges against former NHL union boss Alan Eagleson. Both left the force before the case went to court, though Eagleson was convicted. Harloff joined Price Waterhouse, after having served twenty-one years in the Mounties.

The ex-police officers have their own mystique, which is used to lure potential clients. They are seen to be crack investigators, although that's not necessarily the case. Over the past decade, with the demands of government imperatives beating down on them and business-minded attitudes infecting the police, many police investigators seem to have become confused about how to conduct investigations. More than one company has learned that lesson. "I don't hire ex-police officers as investigators any more," says Kevin Bousquet of the Corpa Group, a Mississauga-based private-investigation firm. "They're not creative enough and they don't work hard enough. Too many of them have a civil-service mentality."

Bousquet's view of the talents and abilities of ex-police officers is instructive, and fast becoming accepted in private-investigation circles. As we've already seen, the vast majority of the highest-paying jobs in private investigation go to ex-Mounties who served in federal law-enforcement duties. One reason for this is that ex-Mounties tend to hire other ex-Mounties, partly out of loyalty and partly out of their belief that they are not only the best-trained investigators, but are also the best investigators. Mounties, even after they've left the force, still carry with them the mystique that "they always get their man."

In the private sector, however, as Bousquet points out, ex-Mounties don't always get their man – far from it. More often than not these days, even the ex-Mounties themselves are surprised to learn that they don't have the investigative skills and abilities they thought they had as police officers. The reason that so many of these police officers fail in the private sector is apparent: as the nature of policing has changed to meet political, economic, and social imperatives, the police themselves have been changed, and not necessarily for the better. Instead of making cases, the police have been instructed to look for alternative solutions to problems. By taking this approach, an investigator has a tendency to build files rather than conduct a focused investigation bent on gaining a conviction in court. While such an approach might save court expenses, the net impact of this kind of thinking is that individual investigators begin to lose their instinct and intuition; they cease to be law-enforcement officers in the purest sense. Because they are not required to be on the edge, they tend not to be as sharp as detectives once were. During this same period, detective work in the RCMP has become very much a nine-to-five job, when it should be anything but.

Kerry Eaton, himself an ex-municipal police officer, echoes Bousquet's sentiments. Eaton, who supervises investigations for Adjusters Canada in Guelph, Ontario, says that, contrary to what the public may think, many police officers from all forces these days have a rather limited understanding of how to conduct a difficult investigation on their own. "Ex-police officers come through the door and expect that we should give them a job because they were police officers. In the main we've been very disappointed by our experiences. The majority of them aren't sophisticated enough and don't really know how to investigate."

What we have is a generation of police officers who, after being pummelled by political, social, and economic imperatives, have lost much of their investigative instinct.

As true as that all might be, however, none of it really matters in the afterlife of a Mountie. Forensic-accounting firms don't really want ex-police officers all that much for their investigative skills, but rather for their sales potential. When a forensic accountant is trying to land a lucrative investigation, the sales pitch to a client usually goes smoother and tends to be more successful with former high-ranking Mounties sitting at the table helping to make the pitch. Once the contract is signed, the billing starts. Like the accountants themselves, the services of the ex-police officers are billed out at between $275 and $400 an hour. It's virtually impossible for a client to see one of these people alone. They often travel in twos, threes, or even large packs, driving the cost of investigations up to enormous levels.

But there is a much darker side to all this. The attractiveness of ex-police officers as investigators for forensic accountants is predicated on their having a special knowledge and background. What that amounts to is their inside knowledge of public policing, as well as their connection to the ex-police network that operates around the world. The ex-police network controls the financial and security industry and, to tap into the otherwise highly secure information within those industries, one must be an ex-police officer. In the United States, for example, a network of ex-police officers has built its own criminal-intelligence database.

As we have seen, the RCMP's Integrated Proceeds of Crime units rely heavily on the ex-police network operating within financial institutions to get information about suspicious transactions. This is all done under a formal agreement with the Canadian Bankers Association. For forensic accountants, whose primary work is white-collar crime, having access to this network is critical to their success.

This potentially pernicious network exists and is seen to be a necessity because of the unwillingness or inability of the federal government over the years to maintain and properly finance both a federal police force and a justice system capable of dealing with economic crime. In the name of business-like efficiency, a system of investigation and justice is being set up parallel to the rule of law in the country.

An individual police officer is bound by the law, regulations, and his or her oath. In the private-investigation system there are easily flouted rules and little accountability. The ex-police officers are just that – ex-police officers. They hold out the promise of guardians, but are not the guardians themselves. This perversion of intention strikes hard at the sensibilities of some dedicated police officers, who left public policing to enter the world of forensic accounting and private investigation armed only with their ideals. The moral relativism they encounter exacts a heavy price. "Throughout your entire career you are trained to serve the public. The public comes first. Doing the right thing is what policing is all about," says one former Mountie, who asked for anonymity. "Then, when you go into the private sector, you find the rules are changed. You're not there to do the right thing, you're there to do what the client wants you to do. It's really difficult to adjust your thinking. Some guys just can't do it."

The true role of the ex-police officer as an investigator hit home during one of my own private investigations in the early nineties. Working for Rod Stamler, I had been building a case against a particularly despicable fraud artist. There was absolutely no question about this man's guilt. I had gathered more than enough evidence in Ontario, Quebec, the United States, and the Caribbean. I could even connect him to traditional organized-crime leaders. As I was closing in on him, the man called Stamler's office one evening and left a message on his voice mail. It seems that he wanted to hire Stamler to conduct a counter-investigation, not realizing that Stamler was behind the first investigation.

Clients on the edge of criminal or civil law, or sometimes those who are clearly over the line, often enjoy the benefit of using their ill-gotten gains to defend themselves, and, despite their protests to the contrary, forensic accountants and ex-police officers are not all that shy about taking this money. The intrinsic value of ex-police officers in such cases is not so much as investigators, but as lobbyists. In these situations – which, with the dramatic increase in white-collar crime are prevalent – forensic accountants are hired to come up with plausible scenarios to explain a defendant's behaviour. The ex-police officers, on the other hand, are often employed to use their influence to act as a suspect's or defendant's agent, schmoozing with police investigators, negotiating with Crown attorneys, or fending off civil litigants and the media. "It's not moral relativism, we're not advocating their positions," Stamler once said to me when I asked him about a similar situation. "We're no different than defence lawyers. Everyone has a right to defend themselves."

At the same time, in the forensic-accounting investigative atmosphere, ex-police officers are usually treated only as the sizzle. It is not uncommon at some firms for the accountants to lead the investigation, because they consider themselves to be "the professionals." As former Metro police sergeant Dick Dewhirst, whom we met in Chapter One, put it, "These accountants have such an inflated sense of their own importance that it's scary. All they are is a bunch of B.Comms who started calling themselves professionals fifteen years ago. They don't have much real education, but they look down at police officers as if they are knuckle-draggers – or at anyone, for that matter, who's not like them."

The accountants' way of conducting an investigation often runs counter to good investigative technique. "The accountants come in and, if there are twenty-eight areas that might need investigation, they attack all twenty-eight and eat up 90 per cent of the budget," said one prominent investigator still working in the field. "The way it should work is that the investigators come in and quickly assess the situation and target the five or six most likely areas of wrongdoing. *Then* the accountants should be called in. But that would cut into the ability of accountants to bill their clients through the roof. It's an inefficient and ridiculous system where nobody seems to care about the client's needs or money."

More often than not, when they are involved in cases, ex-police officers find themselves in tricky waters. After leaving public policing, they now suddenly come to think of themselves as entrepreneurs – more so than as investigators. What they all soon learn is that private investigation usually requires risk-taking, which for most police officers in antithetical to their own nature and training; police are averse to taking risks. The pressures on both forensic accountants and their ex-police private investigators are enormous. While their clients might be paying their exorbitant fees for an investigation, the clients also demand results for their money. To get these results, forensic accountants and their investigators often must get close to the line in terms of the law, especially with regard to privacy legislation. Therefore, in conducting investigations, they often take extraordinary measures to cover their own tracks.

For example, there is the problem presented by what is known as "A" and "B" information. "A" information is anything that can be gained on the public record. Forensic-accounting firms and their investigative arms have little difficulty gathering "A" information. The problem is, anyone can do that. Clients want more than what's stashed away in some computer database or readily available from a government office. They want the real dirt, the inside stuff, bank-account information, telephone records, credit-agency reports, credit-card use, and, in rare circumstances, wiretapping. But no group of professional accountants or ex-police officers wants to get caught with *real dirt* – "B" information – under their fingernails. No lawyer conducting a case wants to be told directly about the "B" information, because it can never be entered on the record. But most lawyers expect their investigators to get such information and use it to their advantage.

What many forensic-accounting companies have done is set up arm's-length – or ostensibly arm's-length – relationships with investigative firms. This gives the accountants and their clients plausible deniability and insulates them against allegations of wrongdoing. Meanwhile, the investigative firm might subcontract out parts of the investigation to the ends of the earth. The "B" information specialists are loosely regulated, if at all. All the information gathered might be collected in, say, Toronto, and the investigative report written there. But the report and the account will be sent from some protected offshore locale, where a single secretary operates a telephone, a fax machine, and a computer. It is a nearly impossible trail for anyone to follow.

Then there is the use of pretexts to get information. Some are relatively harmless: people calling up and pretending to be telemarketers trying to enlist a new credit-card user, for example, when they're really private detectives looking for personal financial information. But in recent years in Canada, the pretexts have included people who are really private investigators posing as journalists. For example, in Toronto, a company operated for years as a "freelance press agency." It was nothing more than an investigative front, being manned for the benefit of ex-police officers working at a reputable firm in the financial district.

The great irony here is that many businesses are largely devoid of any sense of ethics or integrity. What matters is the bottom line. Yet governments, in their wisdom, are ceding large areas of policing jurisdiction, which are entirely dependent upon ethics and integrity to such businesses. No matter how much one tries to dress it up, in their private-sector "police work," forensic accountants and their ex-police investigators – no matter how many bars they might have worn on their shoulders when they were guardians – are still doing an undeniably dirty job. Neither of them owes their first allegiance to either the public or national interest. Their entire business is played out on the edges of the rule of law.

It's an irony not lost on former commissioner Norman Inkster, who, you will remember, set in motion the plan to move the RCMP's federal services out of Toronto. A few years later, he left the force and joined KPMG. There he was given the task of setting up a private investigative force in Toronto, which would try to fill the gap left by the Mounties. Inkster began writing reports for government (and, most recently, the RCMP), in which he suggested that forensic-accounting firms should and would be conducting more economic-crime investigations in the future. "If one were a conspiracy theorist, you might think Inky pulled a fast one," joked RCMP Inspector Gary Nichols.

Today, in his thirty-fourth-floor office at Commerce Court, Inkster doesn't seem all that comfortable with what is happening in the world of federal policing and private economic-crime investigation. If a police officer who goes into private practice thinks he's there to defend the public, businesses soon teach him otherwise. The ex-police officer soon learns that business is anything but honourable and that rules are made to be broken. For example, Inkster says, one of the things he finds frustrating is the way business will deal with wrongdoing and criminality in their own operations. "We'll do a lot of work, and catch a thief," Inkster says, recalling one case, "but instead of going to the police, the company will often quietly fire the thief, and then give him a glowing recommendation for his next job!"

Honesty and integrity seem to be such rare commodities in the business world that KPMG has spotted a business opportunity. It has started an Ethics and Integrity Practice. The principal in charge is Michael C. Deck, an ordained Anglican priest, who went back to school in the late eighties and earned his M.B.A. For $350 or so an hour, Deck will visit companies and give their leaders ethical and spiritual advice. He says his practice is beginning to thrive.

Every fraud survey KPMG has conducted in recent years indicates that the public, by an overwhelming majority, believes that the police are under-resourced, but government has remained intransigent. The public police are being downsized. What Inkster has seen first-hand is that the less police are able to do, the greater is the attraction of serious economic crime, and that concerns him. "Every time the RCMP's budget is cut back our business booms," says Inkster, but he doesn't think that's the way it should be. "My candid opinion is that, even though we are the consequences of the downsizing of the police, our position is that police departments ought to have all the resources they need to carry out these investigations. There should be no need for corporate Canada to turn to the private sector to assist them. I know that would put me out of job if that were to happen, but that's what I think is right."

Although he won't articulate it, what may well be bothering Inkster is the realization that the growth of forensic accountancy and private investigation is a tacit admission of the breakdown of the rule of law in Canada. In our enlightened world penal terms for financial crimes are deemed barbaric. White-collar criminals are not considered by the justice system to be dangerous to society, despite the abundance of evidence to the contrary. The effect on these criminals is much like the effect of the very public campaign against high-speed chases: if drivers with something to hide suspect the police won't chase them, they are more likely to try to get away. In financial crimes, the criminals realize that, in the unlikely event they get caught, they will be able to use some of their ill-gotten gains to defend themselves, perhaps to hire forensic accountants and investigators. The rest of the money can be tucked away offshore for their personal use once the flap is over a few months or a few years down the road. Finally, with restrictions on the ability of Canadians to check a person's criminal record, the criminals can be back on the street and "legitimate" in no time to commit yet another series of crimes – as history has shown is the case of many white-collar criminals.

In this milieu, the Rolex guardians of the private sector give the appearance of being law enforcers, when really they are not much more than glorified debt collectors and public-relations consultants. That being the case, their business, in and of itself, presents a serious public-policy dilemma. The question no one has bothered to ask is, whose interests are *not* being served by the forensic-accounting business? The answer is simple: the ordinary consumer, the taxpayer, the unfortunate, and the poor. In fact, they are the real victims of this two-tier policing system.

The prime clients of forensic accountants are large corporations and wealthy individuals, who usually hide behind corporate entities. They hire forensic accountants and their investigators when they feel they've been victimized by a fraud. The resulting investigations often turn into veritable public catfights.

When I interviewed him in spring 1997, RCMP Commissioner Philip Murray lamented the inevitability of two-tier policing and investigations in Canada – the public police doing what they can, with some of the cases being delegated to the private sector. With the concurrence of government, the private sector is trying to gobble up many of the duties and responsibilities of the public police, particularly the areas in which they might make a profit by charging for services.

While forensic accountants are being encouraged to hive off white-collar and corporate investigations, private security companies are trying to usurp the role of the public police in patrolling inner cities, and even towns. In the fall of 1997, for example, Intelligarde International, a Toronto security firm, was allowed to bid on second-tier non-emergency services in the new city of Quinte West in Southeastern Ontario. Their competitors were the Trenton City Police, which won the bid, and the Ontario Provincial Police. A number of companies are attempting to win the right to conduct basic investigations for the police "to free up more resources for serious crime," as the popular sales pitch goes. But the public police and the public should have learned from their experiences by now that already-implemented civilianization and privatization programs have failed to deliver on their promises. Nonetheless, as the private sector moves in, public police budgets have been slashed. In the confusion caused by new systems management, the public police are caught in a death spiral, doing less with less.

The very phrase "two-tier" justice still implies that all Canadians would still have access to justice, either through public or private means, and that the rule of law will not be affected. Commissioner Murray says that it would be "unfortunate" if people were treated unequally, but he feels that he has no weapons with which to fight back against the wishes of the government. In his view the RCMP – and the public police, in general – should be empowered to enforce all laws in Canada.

But no one has addressed the true fallacy of two-tier policing: such a system is a veritable impossibility. In the real world there can be no such thing as two-tier policing. A country either has one-tier policing – where everyone is equal under the law – or *three-tier* policing. The third tier comprises what we might call "the victim class." These are the people who have little or no recourse to justice. Their cases aren't big enough or interesting enough for the public police, or too big and complicated for them. Meanwhile, these same people can't afford to hire forensic accountants or mount their own private prosecutions. Those in the victim class come from all walks of life. They are the firefighters and residents who were made sick by the Plastimet fire in Hamilton. They include the small-business owners and investors who have lost everything to one fraud or another.

But the victim class stretches beyond white-collar crime and other frauds. There are those living in isolated communities across the country who are paying for twenty-four-hour policing, but who find they must fend for themselves from 2:00 a.m. until the sun comes up in the morning. They are the victims of crime that are arbitrarily considered too small for the police to investigate – thefts from vehicles, mischief, and minor assaults, for example. They are the family in Burnaby whose house was destroyed by teenage invaders. They are the inner-city residents who must pay twice for their policing: once through their taxes for the public police and a second time through their rent for private security because the public police are no longer all that interested in basic police work.

The privatization of public policing functions invites the public to accept as something good and normal an insidious and corrupting element, which by its very presence bastardizes the intent of the law. The virtual decriminalization of fraud undermines the concept of the rule of law, particularly with respect to the idea of equality before the law, which is fundamental for the continuing health of our social and political structure. This second tier of policing is focused almost entirely on commerce and money. Its intent is to reduce criminal cases to mere debt collection and a series of financial transactions.

When large public companies become victims of crime today, they are encouraged to call in forensic accountants and private investigators rather than the police. In these cases, the results of the investigation are rarely made known to shareholders or the public. In essence, such investigations are often used to protect the interests of managers who have failed adequately to protect the consumers' or shareholders' interests. What seems to be lost in the equation is that, when companies don't lay charges, a double standard is automatically created. A corporation is an entity much like a social order, composed of relationships that are based on standards of behaviour and trust.

If a corporation abrogates its responsibilities under the rule of law, it in turn abrogates the civil rights of its own constituents. When corporations cynically use the justice system as their enforcers, or when companies don't lay charges after they have been victimized by criminals, their actions tend to confound and confuse – legislators, the legal system, and the police. When a corporation chooses out of self-interest to conceal its victimization, it in turn undermines the rule of law. Their real victims are left unseen and perhaps uninformed. The destructive potential of this lack of knowledge may have a profound impact on shareholders, small investors, consumers, and suppliers to the company. By refusing to deal with criminals in an open way, corporations abrogate the trust they share between themselves, the shareholders, and the wider community.

The true victims of such unprosecuted fraud are those at the end of the line, usually at the bottom reaches of the economic ladder. The cost of the corporate losses and investigations are passed on to them in higher prices or higher taxes. That is the perverse engine driving the exorbitant fees being charged by forensic accountants and private investigators – every dime being paid to them is a tax write-off against a corporation's earnings.

In the opening pages of this book, one of the questions I asked was: Is there too much government in business or too much business in government? My answer should, by now, be obvious, as should the ramifications for law enforcement, and specifically for the RCMP. As I stated earlier, for a government or any of its institutions to operate like a business, they must perform like a business in reverse. Production is defined by the services that can be cut, profit by the money saved from those reductions. The victim class is the personification of the "profit" government is making on the legal system. These people are "cost centres" which have been eliminated, made to disappear beneath the bottom line. As the government forces the RCMP to cut back on its federal law-enforcement function, it is hiding the true costs of private policing with accounting tricks. That is the way modern Canada is being run. Public-policy decisions are not being reflected in the so-called bottom line, and maybe that's what bothers Norman Inkster so much about his own business and about his former calling as commissioner of the RCMP.

Conclusion

.... ● ....

THE RCMP – THE LAST GUARDIANS

THE ROYAL CANADIAN Mounted Police celebrated its one hundred and twenty-fifth anniversary in 1998. At a time when the RCMP was clearly in a state of crisis, Commissioner Philip Murray devoted much of his attention to the ceremonies, going as far as promoting a drill sergeant from Regina to an officer's position in Ottawa to oversee the planning of events across the country. Throughout the year, proud Mounties in felt hats, red serge, and Strathcona riding boots could be found on parade in every corner of the country. The Mounties were making a statement that they are Canada's police force, but the fact that they felt compelled to do so by making such a big splash out of a largely phony event shows how desperate the force really is about its own future.

In the hundreds of interviews I've conducted, on my visits with the force across Canada and in newspapers, magazines, and books, I've found dozens of suggestions for how the RCMP might be improved.

Some believe the force has become too politicized because the RCMP commissioner is considered to be a deputy solicitor general. But the politicization goes far beyond any bureaucratic title the commissioner might have. The present RCMP has become politicized not by direct political control, but by the manner in which the government has controlled police operations through budgetary restrictions in some areas, such as federal law enforcement, or demands for income in others, such as contract policing.

Former assistant commissioner Michel Thivierge, among many, believes that the force has become too big and too diverse, making it virtually impossible to manage or to enforce the law as well as it should. A Mountie can be anything from a patrolman in Nova Scotia to an organized-crime specialist in Toronto, from an equitation instructor in Regina to a forensic analyst in Ottawa – but government restrictions on hiring, salaries, and promotion practices treat them all the same, a cause for low morale and a brain drain out of the force. No matter how well-intentioned the RCMP's leaders might be, it is virtually impossible for the right people to be promoted to the right jobs for their respective talents and abilities. "The promotion system is harming the ability of the RCMP to be an effective law-enforcement agency," says Thivierge, who speaks for many others who believe that the RCMP must find a way to accommodate an elite within the force. "In my view there should be a separate federal law-enforcement unit, which exists outside the normal salary and promotion structure within the force," Thivierge says. "As it stands, everyone is equal, no matter what they do or where they are stationed. It doesn't make sense, and the only way each might be able to win a promotion is by moving into fields where they are not expert. That only serves to harm the force."

Some inside the force, such as Assistant Commissioner John L'Abbé, see the future of the RCMP as a national police force, staffed by elite members of all other police forces. "Only then would the RCMP be a truly national police force," L'Abbé says.

That immediately raises the question at the heart of the issue: Should the RCMP be primarily a national police force or a federal one? That is, should the main function of the RCMP be a service that provides policing across the country or should it be more focused on federal law enforcement? Only after one can answer that question will it be possible to find realistic solutions to the RCMP's problems. However, the search for that answer won't be easy or palatable for many Canadian leaders, as the route will inevitably lead them to challenge fundamental assumptions about the nature of Canada itself. Foremost among these are the abiding myths about the origins of the RCMP, its history, its successes and failures, its strengths and weaknesses.

I've attempted to address some of the assumptions and debunk some of the myths in order to show how the RCMP came to be in the state it is in today. The Mounties started out as a small and temporary federal para-military force in 1873, whose purpose was to assert Canada's sovereignty in the North-West and protect the native population and settlers. We saw how Ontario and Quebec – primarily Quebec – have resisted the notion of a federal police force such as the RCMP growing to its full potential. In the 1896 federal election campaign, Wilfrid Laurier floated the notion of disbanding the Mounties, an idea that resurfaced during the First World War, but both times problems which had to be dealt with immediately gave the Mounties a reprieve. Almost from the day it was conceived, therefore, the RCMP has evolved in a way that can best be described as a reaction to the provincialism of Quebec and Ontario.

By the sixties, this reality was enhanced by the 257 recommendations made in 1963 by the Glassco Commission into the Organization of Government. Among the key recommendations were that Quebec – and French Canada in general – be given a larger presence and say in the federal government, that Ottawa should devolve some of its powers to the provinces, and that government should operate more like a business. Throughout the next thirty years, the governments of prime ministers Pierre Trudeau, Brian Mulroney, and Jean Chrétien championed the Glassco recommendations. This concluded in 1990, with "Police-Challenge 2000," which attempted to put the thinking first articulated in Canada by the Glassco Commission into practice. "Police-Challenge 2000" set the tone for the approach government is taking towards policing today: that federal law enforcement be de-emphasized in favour of local policing and that private enterprise be called on to perform more law-enforcement functions at all levels. Whether or not all this reform is good for Canada might be just a matter for enlightened debate, if it were not for one other thing, which has always been overlooked.

The foundation for the reform of the RCMP, *particularly as a federal law-enforcement agency*, is based on one of the largest and most outrageous frauds ever perpetrated on the Canadian people. That was the Commission of Inquiry Concerning Certain Activities of the Royal Canadian Mounted Police, or the McDonald Commission, which made its report in 1981.

Most Canadians recall the McDonald Commission as being called to investigate wrongdoing by the RCMP's counter-intelligence wing, the Security Service, which was investigating suspected terrorist organizations in Quebec in the sixties. The lasting impression of the RCMP created by the commission – an impression which continues to be perpetuated by the media – is that the RCMP was out of control and needed to be reigned in by government.

In fact, what McDonald found – and this bears repeating – is that the Security Service at all times was properly motivated and acting in the best interests of Canada, but that the laws at the time with regard to counter-intelligence activities were inadequate. It further bears repeating that, at the time of the incidents in Quebec, RCMP members who were attached to the Security Service were not considered peace officers and did not have the powers of arrest or search and seizure. The McDonald Commission recommended that the Security Service become an agency separate from the RCMP, and in 1984 it emerged as the civilianized Canadian Security Intelligence Service. This has always been seen as the major accomplishment of the McDonald Commission, which may or may not have been a good thing, depending upon one's point of view.

But the real effect of the McDonald Commission was that it knocked the RCMP off the course on which it was headed in the early seventies: that is, enhancing its capabilities as a federal law-enforcement agency. After McDonald, the RCMP found that it was not only under political control, but also that this control was being exercised largely by or at the direction of Quebec politicians and bureaucrats in Ottawa. Armed with the McDonald Commission recommendations, such as they were, these political and bureaucratic leaders implemented, in an incremental fashion, policies that have served to dismantle the RCMP as a federal institution.

All this should be disturbing to most Canadians, but perhaps the most disturbing thing of all – and something that continues to be overlooked – is the origin of the McDonald Commission itself.

As I pointed out in Chapter Four, the McDonald Commission was called only after the persistent and rather thin complaints of two former Quebec-based Security Service agents, Donald McCleery and Gilles Brunet. In 1991 Brunet was revealed by the CBC show *the fifth estate* to have been a Soviet spy. This was confirmed earlier this year by former Security Service agent Peter Marwitz, who conducted an extensive investigation and concluded that Brunet, after joining the RCMP in 1968, was paid at least $700,000 by the Soviet Union.

In the aftermath of the McDonald Commission, the RCMP has consistently been treated as a problematic institution by the federal government. While Ottawa says it has simply been trying to be fiscally responsible, almost every move it makes seems intended to destabilize and demoralize the proud and loyal members of the RCMP. They know that, to be effective law-enforcement officers, they must be independent of government, but almost to a man or woman these days, Mounties feel they have become subject to political control. The rule of law has been subverted by the rule of politics.

Is it any wonder, then, that as one travels across the country it doesn't take long before the average, polite, eager-to-please Mountie breaks down and vents his or her frustration. As I write, many scenes play out in my head. In Ottawa, all I can remember are the happy and smiling faces at headquarters – on Mounties who think everything is all right. But on the road, it was different, much different.

Across Canada the RCMP seems to be in a state of total confusion, performing so many different roles and carrying out so many duties that it is sometimes impossible for individual members to know who they are and what they are supposed to be doing. For example, in Ontario detachments, such as Bowmanville, Milton, and Hamilton, individual federal investigators told me about how helpless they feel about not only their own fate, but that of Canada. "How can we be the country's top police force and not have an office in Toronto?" is an oft-asked question.

At Depot in Regina, I recall two series of interviews. It was like being in a confessional, as one Mountie after another came into the room, bared his or her soul, then left. Many of them said they would talk to me only if

I told the real story, and after I assured them that was my intention, they would open up. None of them ever got angry – at least they didn't show it – but in all of them one could feel both their immense pride in being a Mountie and their pain over what was happening to the force. They desperately want to be the best, and they are absolutely committed to serving Canada, but almost every man and woman in red serge feels that they are being blocked from being all that they could be – handcuffed, as it were.

That is my investigation. In essence, what I found was that the RCMP has organized itself in such a way that it is not serving the public interest as well as it should. It's one of Jane Jacobs's monstrous hybrids, too large and cumbersome, with so many conflicting and overlapping duties and responsibilities that it is impossible for it to have a grand vision of any kind. The RCMP's primary function in Canada should be the enforcement of federal laws and the defence of the greater good, but it devotes less than one-sixth of its budget to that important mandate, and even that is in decline.

Therefore, these are my conclusions and recommendations:

1) A full public inquiry should be held at the earliest opportunity to review and examine the expectations of Canadians for the RCMP, its mandate as a federal institution, and its structure. This inquiry should review and examine decisions and policies which have shaped the RCMP, as well as the efficacy of the planned direction of the force. A key area for review must be the rationale for and feasibility of the federal government providing, outside Ontario and Quebec, a 30 per cent subsidy to provincial governments who use RCMP contract services and a 10 per cent subsidy to municipalities for those that use RCMP services. As well, such an inquiry might examine:

   i) the relationship between government and the police;

   ii) the feasibility of dividing the RCMP into three different institutions: a federal law-enforcement agency; a national police service to provide laboratory, communication, forensic, and national police-training capabilities, among other things; and a contract policing division;

iii) the feasibility and efficacy of setting up a serious-fraud office within the RCMP, as part of a larger program involving the training of prosecutors and judges to deal with such crimes in an expeditious fashion;

iv) the feasibility and efficacy of setting up competing full-fledged federal law-enforcement agencies in the areas of revenue, immigration, customs and excise, and finance or treasury;

v) the feasibility and efficacy of reuniting CSIS with the RCMP's federal law-enforcement agency, so that both agencies might work better together in the public interest.

vi) The regulation of forensic accountants and their private investigators.

2) There should be a thorough federal review of the issues of privacy and secrecy in Canada. For years, various observers, including the country's privacy commissioner, have complained about government secretiveness, but the issue goes well beyond what the government does not want to reveal about its operations. For Canadians to be able to protect their own interests, there must be better and cheaper access to government information. By the same token, in criminal investigations, Canadian police should have access to income-tax information, as is the case in the United States. The public must have easier access to criminal-record information.

In closing, let me add that the Royal Canadian Mounted Police is recognized around the world as being a symbol of Canada. Probably no police force anywhere enjoys a greater local, national, or international reputation than the Mounties. But to view Canada through the eyes of the Royal Canadian Mounted Police is to see a country in extreme distress, a country where pragmatism and cynicism have reigned for so long at the highest levels that it's difficult to tell any more where the truth lies.

The Canada that I believe in is one, great unified country, but the grand plan – as reflected in the continuing decentralization of the RCMP, for example – seems to be for a collection of regions or modern-day duchies with few, if any, common standards or goals and no real checks and balances. In this faux federalism, as it were, Canadians have been manipulated and deceived into believing that the government is their enemy, and that the institutions of government are largely a waste and a danger to our freedom and standard of living. Through a preoccupation with economic issues, ordinary citizens have been led to a place of fear and emotional destabilization where they can be made to accept almost anything. They have been gradually encouraged to give their power over to those who purport to have ready-made economic solutions to every problem.

But in a democracy such as ours, the government is only the enemy if it is controlled by self-interested parties, and not by the people. The challenge facing Canada, therefore, is not to get rid of the government and replace it with corporations; the challenge is to fix government, cut through the welter of rhetoric and marketing, and get to the truth.

If Canada is to survive intact it must have strong federal public institutions which are driven, not by commercial interest, but rather by the disinterest of a true guardian. That is and must continue to be the role of the RCMP in Canada. But, as we have seen, the RCMP is under seige, and must be saved. Without the RCMP, Canada as an independent, unified nation is at risk, because there are no other protectors of the greater good. For Canadians, today, the Mounties are the last guardians.

NOTES

CHAPTER ONE: INTRODUCING ANTON PILLER

1. [1976] Ch. 55 (C.A.). The only earlier reported case was *E.M.I. Ltd. v. Pandit,*
    [1975] 1 W.L.R. 302 (Ch.)
2. See, e.g., *Thermax Ltd. v. Schott Industrial Glass Ltd.,* [1981.] F.S.R. 289 (H.C.J.),
    at p. 291, per Browne-Wilkinson, J.; *E.M.I. Ltd. v. Pandit,* per Templeman,
    J.; *Yousif v. Salama,* [1980] 1 W.L.R. 1540 (C.A.), per Donaldson, L. J.
3. Robert J. Sharpe, B.A., LL.B., D.Phil., *Injunctions and Specific Performance*
    (Toronto: Canada Law Book, 1983).
4. Shortly after the raid, both Dewhirst and Boucher left Lindquist, Avey.
    Dewhirst went to work for an insurance company, while Boucher joined
    another private investigation firm, Intelysis, Strategic Global Research &
    Analysis.
5. In my previous book, *Above the Law* (Toronto: McClelland & Stewart,
    1994) I referred to Norman Inkster as the eighteenth commissioner, but
    was later reminded by members within the force that he was only the sev-
    enteenth. Lt. Col. W. Osborne Smith was in charge between Sept. 25, 1873
    and Oct. 17, 1873, at the time the force was being assembled. Smith was
    deputy adjutant general of the militia and officer commanding the
    Winnipeg Military District. He lobbied to lead the force but was rejected
    by Prime Minister John A. Macdonald, and subsequently was never con-
    sidered by the RCMP to have served as commissioner. The first official
    commissioner was G. A. French, who led the force from Oct. 18, 1873, to
    July 21, 1876. French had served with the Royal Artillery, and when
    appointed was inspector of artillery and commandant of the Canadian
    School of Gunnery.
6. See Paul Palango, "Why the Mounties Can't Get Their Man," *Maclean's,*
    July 28, 1997.

7. Various reports, including, 1997 Fraud Survey Report by KPMG Investigation and Security Inc., and reports by the Association of Certified Fraud Examiners of Austin, Texas.
8. David K. Foot with Daniel Stoffman, *Boom, Bust & Echo* (Toronto: Macfarlane, Walter & Ross, 1996).

CHAPTER TWO: THE LEGACY OF NORMAN INKSTER

1. Carolyn Abraham and Doug Fischer, "How RCMP hid probe into Airbus," Montreal *Gazette*, December 8, 1995.
2. From a conversation with the author, May 1994.

CHAPTER THREE: THE GLASSCO COMMISSION

1. On April 22, 1975, Bryce was appointed to head a royal commission into corporate concentration in Canada. His report was ignored by the Trudeau government.
2. George P. Grant, *Lament for a Nation: The Defeat of Canadian Nationalism* (Toronto: McClelland & Stewart, 1965), 13.
3. David Hume, *Theory of Politics*, edited by Frederick Watkins, (Nelson, 1951), 81.
4. Quoted in Rick Chodos, Rae Murphy, and Eric Hamovitch, *The Unmaking of Canada: The Hidden Theme in Canadian History since 1945* (Toronto: Lorimer, 1991), 11.
5. Jane Jacobs, *Systems of Survival: A Dialogue on the Moral Foundations of Commerce and Politics* (New York: Random House, Vintage, 1992, 1994).
6. That might not have been their only pay. In one of the many scandals of the day, the Affair of the Six, Guy Marcoux, a prominent Quebec doctor, alleged in a pamphlet that the six Créditistes had been paid by the Liberals in a secret conspiracy. Marcoux alleged that a meeting had taken place, which was attended by a number of key Liberals as well as by unsavoury characters including John C. Doyle, a controversial Newfoundland financier who was later charged over defrauding shareholders of Canadian Javelin of tens of millions of dollars. According to Marcoux, another at the meeting was a Quebec loanshark named Moise Darabaner, who would later emerge as the central figure in the Lime Pit Murders, a lynchpin in the development of the RCMP's Commercial Crime Branch. The allegations by Marcoux were denied and ultimately unprovable, and his complaint faded away.
7. Jacobs, *Systems of Survival*, 215.
8. Saul, *The Unconscious Civilization*, 86-7.

CHAPTER FOUR: QUEBEC VERSUS THE MOUNTIES

1. The Mounties' work on a whisky-smuggling case caught the eye of John J. Healy, editor of the *Fort Benton* (Montana) *Record*, who wrote on April 13, 1877: "Horses were sacrificed for the arrest, but the M.P.s are worse than bloodhounds when they scent the track of a smuggler, and they fetch their men every time."

2. John S. Moir and D. M. L. Farr, *The Canadian Experience* (Toronto: McGraw-Hill Ryerson, 1969), 305.

3. Editor William Thorsell, whose pro-American leanings are well-known, has written a number of diatribes over the years, including this, in an editorial, published September 3, 1997, on the death of Ottawa mandarin Robert Bryce: "Postwar centralization of Canadian federalism . . . helped to alienate Quebec and stoke nationalism. Ottawa's mandarins disdained the provinces as obstacles to rational economic management. Former Quebec premier Maurice Duplessis saw that this struck at the heart of the role of the provinces under the 1867 Constitution."

4. Blair Neatby, quoted in J. M. S. Careless and R. Craig Brown, eds., *The Canadians, 1867-1967* (Toronto: Macmillan of Canada, 1968), 159.

5. The Ontario Provincial Police became a permanent force of salaried police constables on Oct. 13, 1909, although it had been a volunteer force since Sept. 17, 1792, and partly paid since 1875. The Quebec Provincial Police had a similar lineage beginning in 1870. Officers became fully paid in 1922 and the name was changed to the Sûreté du Québec on June 21, 1968.

6. The area then was known as the North-West Territories.

7. *Hansard*, House of Commons, March 9, 1920, 243. Gouin's argument is one that other provincial governments adopted in 1979 in a celebrated case known as *Regina v. Hauser*. The provinces tried to argue that because they had been granted *primary* responsibility for enforcing criminal law, this amounted to *exclusive* responsibility. The implication, therefore, was that if the courts agreed with that argument, that meant *any act* on the part of the federal government or Parliament to deal with law enforcement, in whole or in part, would not be within federal constitutional competence. While the court rejected the argument, the implication was clear – the provinces have long campaigned to strip the federal government of most of its legal authority.

8. What people tend to forget is that the American Central Intelligence Agency is responsible for international espionage and not domestic security.

9. Peter C. Newman, *The Canadian Establishment* (Toronto: McClelland & Stewart, 1975), 97.

10. As quoted in Pierre Elliott Trudeau, *Against the Current: Selected Writings, 1939-1996* (Toronto: McClelland & Stewart, 1996), 249.

11. Peter Stursberg, *Lester Pearson and the Dream of Canadian Unity* (Toronto: Doubleday, 1978), 440.

12. Ibid.

13. Ibid., 312-329.

14. In *Above the Law*, virtually every chapter in one way or another touches on suspected or actual criminal behaviour in Quebec. This wasn't deliberate. My intention was to write a book about the development and success of the Commercial Crime Branch. The overwhelming Quebec factor in the story never really occurred to me until I was well into the advanced planning stages of the book.

15. Much of the previous few paragraphs is taken verbatim from "Handcuffing the Horsemen," Chapter 12 in *Above the Law*. I felt I couldn't phrase it any better the second time around.

CHAPTER FIVE: THE TRUDEAU EFFECT

1. With the exception of the short-lived government of Joe Clark from May 1979 to February 1980.

2. Raymond Breton, an associate of Trudeau's at *Cité Libre*, quoted in Kenneth McRoberts, *Misconceiving Canada: The Struggle for National Unity* (Toronto: Oxford University Press, 1997), 124.

3. House of Commons debates, October 8, 1971.

4. McRoberts, *Misconceiving Canada*, 48.

5. Pierre Elliott Trudeau, *Federalism and the French Canadians* (Toronto: Macmillan, 1968), 55-6.

6. George Radwanski, *Trudeau* (Toronto: Macmillan of Canada, 1978), 110.

7. Ron Graham, *One-Eyed Kings: Promise and Illusion in Canadian Politics* (Toronto: Collins, 1986), 55-6.

8. Pierre Elliott Trudeau, *Memoirs* (Toronto: McClelland & Stewart, 1993), 138-43.

9. Quoted in McRoberts, *Misconceiving Canada*, 10.

10. In 1996, I interviewed Lalonde about the Lalonde Doctrine for an article in *The Tobacco File*, a newsletter I created and edited for two years. Lalonde said he was proud that his "doctrine" had resulted in positive public policies such as seatbelt legislation, but he worried that it might not be as useful in such controversial areas as epidemiology. "So many factors enter into the equation," Lalonde said. "Epidemiology takes a decade or two or three to see trends. If governments were to ban smoking tomorrow, we wouldn't see a

decrease in lung cancer." Even though I am a non-smoker, I took on the project because of my concern about the efficacy of what government was doing in the name of the Lalonde Doctrine and the long-term ramifications for Canadian society.

11. Michael Mandel, *The Charter of Rights and the Legalization of Politics in Canada* (Toronto: Thompson Educational Publishing, 1994), 42.

CHAPTER SIX: A TALE OF TWO FORCES

1. Abraham and Fischer, "How RCMP hid probe into Airbus."

2. As this book was being written in May 1998, the Schreiber case was still being pursued. On May 29, 1998, the Supreme Court of Canada overturned two earlier decisions by a Quebec judge and a Federal Court judge, both of whom had ruled that Schreiber's Charter rights had been violated when RCMP investigators sought access to his private Swiss bank account.

3. Prost's letter was quoted in "Mulroney to sue Ottawa over 'false' bribe claim," *Toronto Star*, November 19, 1995, 1, and in "Money key to lawsuit's settlement," *Globe and Mail*, January 11, 1997, 1.

4. History is replete with Quebec MPs of all stripes attempting to subvert the RCMP's work in their home province. A good example occurred in September 1997, when Conservative MP André Bachand announced in the House of Commons that the RCMP was investigating Liberal fundraisers in Quebec over alleged influence peddling. He said that the bagman Pierre Corbeil was allegedly seeking donations in return for government favours. The Liberal Party's Quebec wing promptly issued a statement saying that Human Resources Minister Pierre Pettigrew had been told about the allegations on March 6, 1997, and immediately reported them to the RCMP, which was given a free hand to conduct its investigation. Corbeil was charged in October 1997 with four counts of influence peddling.

   Bachand's action in announcing the investigation in the House could be seen as a matter of political partisanship. But the Mounties saw it otherwise. History had taught them that somehow, someway, their targets always found a way to disrupt, destabilize, or dismantle their investigations in Quebec. In this case, the link was rather clear: Pierre Corbeil may have been a Liberal, but his brother, Jean, had been a cabinet minister in the Mulroney government. As I said, nothing came easy for the RCMP in Quebec.

5. Rochon quoted in Tu Thanh Ha, "Judge's decision on financial data favours Mulroney," *Globe and Mail*, May 1, 1996, 5.

6. *Casey Hill v. The Church of Scientology and Morris Manning*, Supreme Court of Canada, file no. 24216, July 20, 1995. The court awarded $300,000 in

general damages against the defendants, $500,000 in aggravated damages, and $800,000 in punitive damages against the Church of Scientology.

7. John Ralston Saul, *Voltaire's Bastards: The Dictatorship of Reason in the West* (Toronto: Viking, 1992), 135.

CHAPTER SEVEN: POLICE LTD.

1. According to Cadieux, Normandeau worked "in collaboration with Mr. Barry Leighton and the personnel of the Police and Security Branch of the Ministry." See Preface, "Police-Challenge 2000: A Vision of the Future of Policing in Canada" (Ottawa: Office of the Solicitor General, October 1990).

2. As a prize for his co-operation, the government recommended that Norman Inkster be made head of Interpol, a largely honorary post he held until he left the force in 1994.

3. From an interview with the author, 1997.

4. S. T. Wood was commissioner from March 6, 1938, to April 30, 1951. Prior to the formation of the modern RCMP in 1920, Aylesworth Perry began serving Aug. 1, 1900, and continued to March 31, 1923.

5. Provincial governments regularly revisit the issue. In 1997, the government of Newfoundland, considered replacing the Mounties with the Newfoundland Constabulary, but dropped the plan after a favourable deal was negotiated.

6. Individual municipalities negotiate contracts with the federal solicitor general for RCMP services, except in British Columbia. There, a general policing agreement exists between the province and Canada for the provision of municipal police services to specific municipalities.

7. Tim Harpur, "Cuts pushing top scientists to leave Canada," *Toronto Star*, October 5, 1997, 1.

8. Kim Pemberton, "Vancouver's new chief to run the police like a business," *Vancouver Sun*, June 25, 1997, B1.

9. "Police 'Outgunned' by White Collar Criminals," *Toronto Star*, Aug. 26, 1997, 10.

10. Funicelli is a constable in Vancouver. An estimated three thousand Mounties belong to members' associations across the country, which are not officially recognized by the force. Since the early seventies the Mounties have had a divisional-representative system within the force to deal with internal employee matters. In a 1997 ruling, a Quebec judge referred to the div-rep system, as it is known, as nothing more than "a company union."

11. Steven R. Covey, *The Seven Habits of Highly Effective People: Powerful Lessons in Personal Change*, New York: Fireside, a division of Simon & Schuster, 1989.

12. Ibid., 46, 262.

13. Those who endorsed Covey's ideas include the following: John Pepper, the president of Procter and Gamble; William Rolfe Kerr, Utah's commissioner of higher education; Tom Peters, author of *In Search of Excellence*; Rosabeth Moss Kanter, editor of the *Harvard Business Review*; Senator Jake Garn, the first senator in space; *Dun's Business Month*, Ariel Bybee, mezzo-soprano of the Metropolitan Opera; Richard M. DeVos, president of Amway; Ken Blanchard, author of *The One-Minute Manager*; Edward A. Brennan, chairman, president, and CEO of Sears, Roebuck and Co.; *Fortune Magazine*; Senator Orrin G. Hatch; Nolan Archibald, president and CEO, Black and Decker; James C. Fletcher, Director, NASA; Charles Garfield, author of *Peak Performers*; *Business Week*; Robert G. Allen, author of *Creating Wealth and Nothing Down*; F. G. "Buck" Rodgers, author of the *IBM Way*, Fran Tarkenton, NFL Hall of Fame quarterback; Anthony Robbins, author of *Unlimited Power*; *USA Today*; Marie Osmond; Roger Staubach, NFL Hall of Fame quarterback; W. Clement Stone, founder of *Success Magazine*; Gregory J. Newell, U.S. Ambassador to Sweden; M. Scott Peck, author of *The Road Less Travelled*; and Norman Vincent Peale, author of *The Power of Positive Thinking*.

14. From an interview conducted with the author, May 1997.

15. Seymour Melman, *Profits Without Production* (New York: Knopf, 1993), 51-3.

16. Gabriel quoted in Saul, *Voltaire's Bastards*, 225.

17. Traute Rafalski quoted in Saul, *The Unconscious Civilization*, 87. The actual, now-third-hand, citation is: "Social Planning and Corporatism: Modernization Tendencies in Italian Fascism," *International Journal of Political Science*, spring 1988, 18(1). The quotation was taken from Paolo Ungari, *Alfredo Rocco e l'ideologia giuridica del fascismo* (Brescia, 1963).

CHAPTER EIGHT: TAX COLLECTORS WITH AN ATTITUDE AND A GUN

1. Fully described in *Maclean's*, July 28, 1997, the Central Communication Intercept System involves the use of "jukeboxes," each of which can handle one hundred telephone lines simultaneously and which can be expanded to 640 lines. Conversations are recorded on an optical disc and monitored at all times by human attendants. The jukeboxes are located in twenty-seven locations across Canada.

2. Don Dutton, "Lax Canadian laws attract crime money," *Toronto Star*, October 20, 1985, F1.

3. "RCMP to pursue profits from drugs in a new tack against illegal trade," *Globe and Mail*, March 17, 1992, 3.

4. "RCMP launches high-finance units to nab rich criminals," *The Journal*, published by the Addiction Research Foundation, Toronto, March 1, 1982, 1.

5. National Crime Authority, Annual Report, published by the Commonwealth of Australia, 1994.

6. John Braithwaite, *Crime, Inequality and Public Policy* (London: Routledge and Keegan Paul, 1979), and Harry J. Glasbeek, "Why Corporate Deviance Is Not Treated as a Crime: The Need to Make 'Profits' a Dirty Word." *Osgoode Hall Law Journal*, 22: 393, each quoted in Mandel, *The Charter of Rights*.

7. Mandel, *The Charter of Rights*, 234.

8. A good overview and introduction can be found in Linda McQuaig, *Behind Closed Doors: How the Rich Won Control of Canada's Tax System* (Toronto: Viking, 1987). See also such news stories on tax concessions as "Political pressure influenced loans," *Globe and Mail*, June 20, 1998.

9. Terrence Wills and Linda Diebel, "Beatty to probe charges banks funnel drug cash," Montreal *Gazette*, October 23, 1995, 1.

10. Mandel, *The Charter of Rights*, 233.

11. David Bercuson and Barry Cooper, "Canada has outgrown its road system," *Globe and Mail*, September 6, 1997, D2.

CHAPTER NINE: REGINA

1. The following summary of decisions affecting the rights of accused was published in the *Globe and Mail*, August 9, 1997:

   Regina v. Lavallee, 1987: Law of self-defence broadened to permit battered women who see no way out to strike back even when not in immediate danger. Vote: 7–0.

   R. v. Smith, 1987: Seven-year minimum sentence for importing narcotics struck down as "cruel and unusual punishment." Vote: 5–1.

   R. v. Vaillancourt, 1987: Law of constructive murder rendering a person guilty of murder in any accidental killing committed during a serious crime such as robbery struck down as unconstitutional. Vote: 7–1.

   R. v. Askov, 1990: Unreasonable delay in criminal trials may result in charge being dismissed. Vote: 9–0.

   R. v. Hébert, 1990: Confessions are inadmissible in court when undercover police officers induce them from accused people who have already refused to be questioned. Vote: 9–0.

   R. v. Stinchcombe, 1991: Prosecutors' obligation to disclose their case is widened to include nearly everything in their files, particularly if it might help the defence in serious criminal cases. Vote: 7–0.

R. v. Bain, 1992: Crown's power to disqualify four jurors for each one disqualified by defence scrapped as a rights violation. Vote: 4–3.

R. v. Finta, 1994: Accused war criminals may be found guilty only where they are shown to have possessed a high degree of moral blameworthiness. Vote: 4–3.

R. v. Daviault, 1994: Accused may use drunkenness as defence in sexual assault or other crimes if in state akin to automatism or insanity. Vote: 6–3.

R. v. O'Connor, 1995: Medical records of sex-assault complainants must be handed over to lawyers for the accused if they establish that records are "likely to have relevance." Vote: 5–4.

R. v. Stillman, 1997: DNA evidence seized by police in unauthorized invasion of a suspect's bodily integrity will not be admissible in court. Vote: 6–3.

CHAPTER TEN: NIGHT PATROL IN DUCK BAY

1. Robert Knuckle, *In the Line of Duty: The Honour Roll of the 73 RCMP since 1873* (Burnstown, Ontario: General Store Publishing House, 1994). Constable Beyak was working volunteer overtime when officers at the scene of a fatal accident called for assistance. Rushing late to the scene, Beyak found herself stuck behind a slow-moving transport that was throwing blinding snow up on her windshield. Beyak attempted to get around the truck. She instantly smashed into a car being driven by the coroner who was returning from the accident scene. The ambulance following behind him crashed into the other two vehicles. Coroner Everett Klein and Beyak were killed instantly. Beyak was the one hundred and eighty-seventh Mountie killed in the line of duty.

2. This card was later amended to include the following instruction at the bottom: "(Arresting Officer: Insert information on local availability of legal aid duty counsel or 'on call' legal aid duty counsel, and/or telephone book as required)."

CHAPTER ELEVEN: COMMUNITY-BASED POLICING

1. Lilles wrote: "One half of these custodial dispositions were for property offences, and only 17 per cent were a result of convictions for violence." Between 1986-87 and 1992-93, there was a 41 per cent increase in the number of cases receiving custody as the most serious disposition and a 25 per cent increase in the number of youth remanded in custody pending

trial. This extremely high rate of incarceration is due to the fact that your court judges in Canada order 31 per cent of the youth they sentence into custody. . . . It is difficult to understand why our criminal-justice system is singling out youth for disproportionately harsh treatment, and why our society supports these efforts so strongly. Is it because we are afraid of young people? In fact, it makes more sense to think of young people as victims."

2. Malcolm K. Sparrow, Mark H. Moore, and David M. Kennedy, *Beyond 911: A New Era for Policing* (New York: Basic Books, a division of HarperCollins, 1990), 10.

3. Quoted in William T. McGrath and Michael P. Mitchell, eds., *The Police Function in Canada* (Toronto: Methuen, 1981).

4. One of the new bibles of this movement is a 1993 book by David Osborne and Ted Gaebler, *Reinventing Government: How the Entrepreneurial Spirit Is Transforming the Public Sector*. Osborne and Gaebler argue that there is a need for private-sector involvement in government to mitigate the financial pressures being felt by government today: "Most people have been taught that the public and private sector occupy distinct worlds; that government should not interfere with business, and that business should have no truck with government. This was a central tenet of the bureaucratic model. But as we have seen, governments today – under intense pressure to solve problems without spending new money – look for the best method they can find, regardless of which sector it involves."

5. Cadieux, "Police-Challenge 2000," 16.

6. Sparrow *et al.*, 109-10.

CHAPTER THIRTEEN: HAMILTON

1. In interviews with the author.

2. For a complete look at these three cases, see Palango, *Above the Law*.

3. On April 16, 1996, Philip Services launched an $11-million lawsuit against me, the day before I was to give a speech to the Hamilton Women's Canadian Club, entitled, "Are public and private institutions serving the region of Hamilton–Wentworth as well as they might?" Philip claimed that I had libelled the company while conducting research for the CBC program *the fifth estate*. The show was first broadcast on March 26, 1996. In return, I launched a separate action against Philip and some of its officers, directors, and agents, including its lawyer, Herman Turkstra, claiming, among other things, that they were using "libel chill" to prevent me from carrying out my duties as a professional journalist. At the time of this writing, the cases are before the courts.

4. From an examination in aid of a motion, *Philip Environmental Inc. v. Michael R. Hilson, John Doe, Jane Doe and other persons unknown*, conducted November 27, 1997, file no. 10986/95, Mark J. Nimigan, official examiner.

5. Adrian Humphreys, "A legacy of problems: USARCO property had a long history of troubles. So why was it still open, neighbours and officials are wondering," *Hamilton Spectator*, July 19, 1997, 11.

6. "The Great Crusade: Hamilton residents marshal force to win back their city," *Biz*, winter 1997. The magazine cover headline read, "Days of Thunder: Hamilton's leadership crisis must be addressed at the ballot box."

7. Arthur Kelly, "This Hallowed Ground: A well of tears in a city of promise," *Biz*, summer 1997. The cover headline read, "We Shall Overcome: The battle to save Hamilton."

CHAPTER FOURTEEN: THE ROLEX GUARDIANS

1. Quoted in "The Bloodhounds of the Bottom Line," published by KPMG Peat Marwick Thorne, 1990. This glossy corporate book presented 101 sketches of actual fraud investigations in various sectors of society. Shortly after the book came out, Lindquist left KPMG to form his own company, Lindquist Avey Macdonald Baskerville Inc. In the mid-nineties, he was forced out of that company and moved to Price Waterhouse. His former partners continued using his name after he left.

2. Established in 1988, the Association of Certified Fraud Examiners, based in Austin, Texas, had fifteen thousand members, divided into chapters, across North America. The organization provides useful training courses for fraud detection, but there is no question that it is a business. It had an estimated market value of $30 million, not bad for a nine-year-old organization. Both my wife and I are CFEs.

3. Leo Campbell served 28 years in Toronto and Kevin McGarr 26 years in Montreal. The Mounties included the following: Inkster (37 years a Mountie), Philip Banks (25), Earl Basse (25), John Beer (29), Bill Cotter (20), John Hess (28), Chris Mathers (20), Doug Nash (25), Steven Neville (27), Ross Oake (22), Don Svendson (26), and Brian Tario (27).

SELECTED BIBLIOGRAPHY

Boulton, James J. *Uniforms of the Canadian Mounted Police.* North Battleford, Saskatchewan: Turner-Warwick Publications Inc., 1990.

Cadieux, Pierre. "Police-Challenge 2000: A Vision of the Future of Policing in Canada." Ottawa: Office of the Solicitor General, October 1990.

Canada. *A Geographical Overview of Crime and the Administration of Criminal Justice in Canada.* Ottawa: Statistics Canada, 1996.

Careless, J. M. S., and Craig R. Brown, eds. *The Canadians, 1867-1967.* Toronto: Macmillan of Canada, 1967.

Chodos, Rick, Rae Murphy, and Eric Hamovitch. *The Unmaking of Canada: The Hidden Theme in Canadian History since 1945.* Toronto: Lorimer, 1991.

Damasio, Antonio R. *Descarte's Error: Emotion, Reason and the Human Brain.* New York: Avon Books, 1994.

Drache, Daniel, and Duncan Cameron. *The* Other *Macdonald Report,* Toronto: Lorimer, 1985.

Francis, Daniel, *National Dreams: Myth, Memory and Canadian History.* Vancouver: Arsenal Pulp Press, 1997.

Freeman, Bill, and Marsha Hewitt. *Their Town: The Mafia, the Media and the Party Machine.* Toronto: Lorimer, 1979.

Friedland, Martin L. *A Place Apart: Judicial Independence and Accountability in Canada.* Canadian Judicial Council, May 1995.

Glassco, J. Grant, Robert Watson Sellar, and F. Eugene Therrien. *Royal Commission on Government Organization.* Ottawa, 1962-63.

Graham, Ron. *One-Eyed Kings: Promise and Illusion in Canadian Politics.* Toronto: Collins, 1986.

Grant, George P. *Lament for a Nation: The Defeat of Canadian Nationalism.* Toronto: McClelland & Stewart, 1965.

Jacobs, Jane. *Systems of Survival: A Dialogue on the Moral Foundations of Commerce and Politics.* New York: Random House, Vintage, 1992, 1994.

Kelling, George L., and Catherine M. Coles, *Fixing Broken Windows: Restoring Order and Reducing Crime in Our Communities*, New York: Martin Kessler Books, The Free Press, 1996.

Knuckle, Robert. *In the Line of Duty*. Burnstown, Ontario: General Store Publishing House, 1994.

Lambert, Allen Thomas, Robert Deprés, John Edwin Hodgetts, and Oliver Gerald Stoner. *Royal Commission on Financial Management and Accountability*, Final Report. Ottawa: Minister of Supply and Services, 1979.

LaSelva, Samuel V. *The Moral Foundations of Canadian Nationalism: Paradoxes, Achievements and Tragedies of Nationhood*. Montreal and Kingston: McGill–Queen's University Press, 1996.

Macleod, R. C., and Schneiderman, David. *Police Powers in Canada: The Evolution and Practice of Authority*, Toronto: University of Toronto Press, 1994.

Mandel, Michael. *The Charter of Rights and the Legalization of Politics in Canada*. Thomson Educational Publishing, 1995.

Martin, The Honourable G. Arthur. *Report of the Attorney General's Advisory Committee on Charge Screening, Disclosure and Resolution Discussions*. Toronto: Queen's Printer for Ontario, 1993.

McBride, Stephen, and John Shields. *Dismantling a Nation: The Transition to Corporate Rule in Canada*, second edition. Halifax: Fernwood Publishing, 1997.

McDonald, Mr. Justice Dennis C., D. S. Rickerd, and Guy Gilbert. *Commission of Inquiry Concerning Certain Activities of the Royal Canadian Mounted Police*. Ottawa: Minister of Supply and Services, 1981.

McQuaig, Linda. *Behind Closed Doors: How the Rich Won Control of Canada's Tax System*. Toronto: Viking, 1987.

McRoberts, Kenneth, *Misconceiving Canada: The Struggle for National Unity*. Toronto: Oxford University Press, 1997.

Meekison, J. Peter, *Canadian Federalism: Myth or Reality*, second edition. Toronto: Methuen, 1971.

Melman, Seymour, *Profits Without Production*. New York: Knopf, 1983.

Moir, John S. and D. M. L. Farr. *The Canadian Experience*. Toronto: McGraw-Hill Ryerson, 1969.

Moore, Barrington, Jr. *Social Origins of Dictatorship and Democracy*. Boston: Beacon Press, 1966.

Moore, Christopher. *1867: How the Fathers Made a Deal*. Toronto: McClelland & Stewart, 1997.

Morton, Desmond. *A Short History of Canada*, second revised edition. Toronto: McClelland & Stewart, 1994.

Newman, Peter C. *The Canadian Establishment*. Toronto: McClelland & Stewart, 1975.

O'Donovan, Joan E. *George Grant and the Twilight of Justice*. Toronto: University of Toronto Press, 1984.

Osborne, David, and Ted Gaebler. *Reinventing Government*. New York: Addison-Wesley, 1992.

Palango, Paul. *Above the Law: The Crooks, The Politicians, The Mounties, and Rod Stamler*. Toronto: McClelland & Stewart, 1994.

Radwanski, George. *Trudeau*. Toronto: Macmillan of Canada, 1978.

Saul, John Ralston. *The Unconscious Civilization*, Concord, Ontario: House of Anansi Press, 1995.

———. *Voltaire's Bastards, The Dictatorship of Reason in the West*, Toronto: Viking, 1992.

Silver, Isidore, ed., Edwin Schur, general ed. *The Crime-Control Establishment*. Englewood Cliffs, N.J.: Prentice-Hall, 1974.

Skelton, Oscar Douglas, *Life and Letters of Sir Wilfrid Laurier*, vol. 2, 1896-1919. Toronto: Carleton Library, McClelland & Stewart, 1965.

Skolnick, Jerome H., and James J. Fyfe. *Above the Law: Police and the Excessive Use of Force*. Toronto: The Free Press, Maxwell Macmillan Canada, 1993.

Soros, George, "The Capitalist Threat," *Atlantic Monthly*, February 1997.

Sparrow, Malcolm K., Mark H. Moore, and David M. Kennedy. *Beyond 911: A New Era of Policing*. New York: Basic Books, a division of HarperCollins, 1990.

Stansfield, Ronald T. *Issues in Policing: A Canadian Perspective*. Toronto: Thomson Educational Publishing, 1996.

Stursberg, Peter. *Lester Pearson and the Dream of Canadian Unity*. Toronto: Doubleday, 1978.

Tanghe, Raymond. *Laurier: Architect of Canadian Unity*. Montreal: Harvest House, 1966.

Trudeau, Pierre Elliott. *Against the Current: Selected Writings, 1939-1996*. Toronto: McClelland & Stewart, 1996.

———. *Federalism and the French Canadians*. Toronto: Macmillan of Canada, 1968.

———. *Memoirs*. Toronto: McClelland & Stewart, 1993.

INDEX

Thivierge, Michel, 184, 189, 232; business methods used in RCMP,
145-46, 148; community-based
policing, 228; defederalization of
RCMP, 122-24; RCMP promotion
policies, 187, 287-88; RCMP relations with Quebec, 101, 115-17
Thom, Grant, 185-86
Thorsell, William, 107
Toronto-Dominion Bank, 251, 262
Trillin, Calvin, 2
Trowell, Reg, 138
Trudeau, Pierre, 44, 247; approach to
federalism, 77-90, 92-97, 99-100,
229; business methods applied to
government, 202, 289; decentralization of government functions,
53, 201; defence of RCMP, 17, 78-79,
93-94; October Crisis, 71-72
Truman, Harry, 45
Tupper, Charles, 59
Turkstra, Herman, 253, 260-61
Turner, John, 50, 65

U.S. Postal Inspection Service, 1

Unemployment Insurance, 172
United Steel and Refining
Corporation (USARCO), 249-52,
255, 258-62

Venner, Thomas, 133
Vickery, Jim, 26
victims of crime, 137, 284-86
von Hayek, Friedrich, 46

Wallach, Tom, 192
War Measures Act, 71, 88
Watergate, 253
Waxman family, 253
Weber, Max, 144
Western Frontier Constabulary, 56
Westman, Jim, 235
white-collar crime. See economic
crime
Wilks, Dave, 213-14
Williams, Howard, 13
Willms, Paul, 236
Wilson, Don, 133
Wilson, James Q., 214-15
Winnipeg General Strike, 62